THE BONUS FAMILY HANDBOOK

THE BONUS FAMILY HANDBOOK

The Definitive Guide to Co-Parenting and Creating Stronger Families

JANN BLACKSTONE, PsD

ROWMAN & LITTLEFIELD
Lanham • Boulder • New York • London

Published by Rowman & Littlefield
An imprint of The Rowman & Littlefield Publishing Group, Inc.
4501 Forbes Boulevard, Suite 200, Lanham, Maryland 20706
www.rowman.com
86-90 Paul Street, London EC2A 4NE, United Kingdom
Copyright © 2024 by Jeanette Blackstone

British Library Cataloguing in Publication Information Available

Library of Congress Cataloging-in-Publication Data
Names: Blackstone, Jann, author.
Title: The bonus family handbook : the definitive guide to co-parenting and creating stronger families / Jann Blackstone.
Description: Lanham : Rowman & Littlefield, 2024. | Includes bibliographical references and index. | Summary: "The Bonus Family Handbook introduces readers to a completely new approach to co-parenting and blending families. It teaches even the most contentious parents and bonus parents how to work together in the name of their children, reinforcing collaborative co-parenting to help form a supportive, loving family"—Provided by publisher.
Identifiers: LCCN 2024011779 (print) | LCCN 2024011780 (ebook) | ISBN 9781538179086 (cloth) | ISBN 9781538179093 (epub) Subjects: LCSH: Stepfamilies. | Parenting, Part-time.
Classification: LCC HQ759.92 .B5428 2024 (print) | LCC HQ759.92 (ebook) | DDC 306.874/7—dc23/eng/20240325
LC record available at https://lccn.loc.gov/2024011779
LC ebook record available at https://lccn.loc.gov/2024011780

♾️™ The paper used in this publication meets the minimum requirements of American National Standard for Information Sciences—Permanence of Paper for Printed Library Materials, ANSI/NISO Z39.48-1992.

Contents

Contents

Acknowledgments

Any book written is never written only by the author, but by a team. My team is quite extensive, but this is the time I would like to thank all the people who supported this effort.

First, I would like to thank my family. Writing a book is a very solitary existence, and it always takes longer than you think it will. My family made quite a few sacrifices as I worked to finish this project, but the end result is exactly what I envisioned. It is the culmination of my life's work and I am so grateful for your support. Thank you to my daughter Anee, her husband Brian, and my grandson Easton, for their understanding when I said, "I can't, I have to finish my book." Thank you to my daughter Harleigh, for her insight and spot-on suggestions. Thank you to my cousins Debby and her husband Mike, who regretfully is no longer with us, for their support, friendship, and understanding while allowing me to write uninterrupted instead of feeding the horses like I was supposed to. Finally, thank you to my own bonus family: my co-parent Larry, my counterpartner Sharyl, and my two bonus kids Melanie and Steven for the years of cooperation, love, and support. We have grown and learned together that communication, acceptance, respect, and empathy (CARE) is the answer to successfully making a blended family bonus. A special acknowledgment to Jennfer Bain, my daughter Anee's bonus mom. Her presence and desire to positively contribute even after my daughter's father passed has brought the bonus concept full circle. You have all been my teachers, in good times and bad. Bonus Families would not be the movement it is without all of your contributions.

Second, to my friends. Thank you, Mary Holden and Dan Neuharth, PhD, for your proposal editing expertise. And Steve Clair, retired family law attorney, for your sense of humor and technical support. You are the best.

I'd also like to thank my editor at Rowman & Littlefield, Christen Karniski, for her patience, understanding, and intuitive ability to organize my ramblings into a cohesive read. To Joanna Wattenberg, sincere appreciation for your understanding when it took me so long to reply to very important emails. And finally to Catherine Herman for her excellent ideas, ongoing patience, and inherent creativity.

Thank you to my clients who keep me honest and current and all my followers on social media who sincerely try to put all the tools I have included in this book into practice.

Thank you to Jill Martin for her support and helping to spread the word, even during an extremely trying time in her life. You are an example for us all.

Finally, thank you to my agent, Clair Gerus, for her constant support, enthusiasm, and understanding the importance of writing a book like *The Bonus Families Handbook*.

I am so grateful to have you all in my life. I can't thank you enough.

Foreword

David L. Hill

Whenever our now-grown kids hit a relationship rough patch, I tell them the story of the day their mother moved out of the house. I explain how I wandered the brick and plaster shell that had incubated our lives together as a family, and I realized their mother was not all that was missing. It was also bereft of toothpaste, laundry detergent, and paper towels. I wasn't going to get very far without a trip to Target . . . our Target, the one where we pushed kids around in red grocery carts and stopped for giant pretzels and slushies on a good day.

Walking in the sliding glass door with its red frame, I was overcome by grief. Here I was, not with three children hanging from the cart and begging for Matchbox cars and Barbie clothes, but as that saddest of creatures, a single dad, alone, short on paper towels. I choked back tears, pulled out a cart, and took a right turn around the $1 bin on my way to toiletries. I looked at my feet and literally counted the tiles as I marched: one, two, three. . . .

Not only had my whole identity—father of a nuclear family, husband to a beautiful and accomplished wife—driven away in a panel truck, but our kids were now, like both of us before them, children of divorce, destined for all the trauma and angst that label entailed. How could I, we, have let this happen to them? Would they ever be okay? Would we?

Fast forward to this Easter weekend: mimosas and deviled eggs on the porch, ceiling fan looping overhead. Two of our adult children are deep in conversation with their mom while I catch up with my former father-in-law and his wife. I only hear random phrases from the animated conversation my wife and my ex-wife are sharing, something about dogs, cats, travel, work, the kids who are away at college. The sun is shining, the garden is flowering, and the sounds of laughter blend with barking dogs, clinking glasses, and a distant ice cream truck chiming its way through the neighborhood. Our 19- and 24-year-old kids dash out the door to see if they can catch that truck in time to snag a SpongeBob popsicle. We are a long way from that day in Target.

Separation and divorce represent a type of ending, sure. A family we hoped to create with another person no longer has that shape. We will grieve. We will mourn. We will cycle through Elizabeth Kubler-Ross's stages of grief—denial, anger, bargaining, depression, and acceptance—in no particular order and sometimes all at once. Relationships end, and when they do, it sucks.

But when you have kids, it's not really an ending. You and another human being, someone you presumably felt intimate with at some point, share these children. For your kids, it is just a change, a new chapter in a long story that has barely begun, a winding pathway to something new. As hard as it is to believe when you're counting your paces to the toothpaste aisle, it's also a beginning for you. This is a story you and your co-parent will write together, with input from other authors you may not yet know. Coming chapters will be happy, sad, adventurous, scary, comforting, hopeful. You don't get to choose all the characters and plot points, but you still craft this narrative.

Jann Blackstone knows these stories inside and out. As a co-parent, a bonus parent, and child custody and divorce mediator, she has both lived her own story and helped countless others write and edit theirs. One thing is true: You and your co-parent love and value your children. Starting with this fundamental foundation, you can now make choices about how to engage with each other and how to add new people to your family, people who will offer their own strengths and perspectives to enrich your children's lives. It may seem impossible right now, but I promise you can do it. So, take a deep breath, count your footsteps if you must, and let this book help guide you to write your own bonus family story, as complicated, rich, and fascinating as the children you all love.

David L. Hill, MD, FAAP

Divorced dad, bonus dad, pediatrician, host of *Pediatrics on Call* podcast, and award-winning author of countless parenting books including *Dad to Dad: Parenting Like a Pro*, *Caring for Your Baby and Young Child*, *Baby's First Year Milestones*, and *Co-Parenting Through Separation and Divorce* (coauthored with Dr. Jann Blackstone).

INTRODUCTION

I understand firsthand how difficult a breakup can be. You're coping with the pain of the breakup while trying to look like you have it together for the kids. You never know if you are doing things right. Then you meet someone new and it's great, but they have kids, and you have kids, and that puts a new spin on things. Plus, everyone has former partners and extended family. The frustration of dealing with a former partner whom you can't seem to get through to can be overwhelming. Not to mention the sleepless nights worrying that your child isn't safe at the other home.

The Bonus Family Handbook is my way of taking you by the hand and gently walking you through building a new working relationship with your child's other parent, whom we now refer to as your co-parent. It then guides you through integrating someone new and eventually combining your families. At first, this may sound like the same approach families have been using for years, but it's not. It's a new approach, offering co-parents, their new partners, and family members a way to successfully work together. I call this type of family a "bonus family." Not a stepfamily, where everyone is at odds and merely trying to survive. Or, even the more politically correct "blended family." A bonus family is beyond blended, a family for today, using communication, acceptance, respect, and empathy (CARE) as tools to address the real issues families just like yours face every day.

My personal introduction to co-parenting was not from co-parenting with my daughter's father. We didn't co-parent. I thought we did, but we really didn't for years after our divorce. We rarely spoke. We rarely compared notes. He didn't even know we had joint custody of our daughter. He visited her religiously every other weekend. He paid child support on time every month. I remember asking him when she was a teenager why he never asked for extra time or took her on vacation. "You had sole custody!" he said. "You would have just said, 'No!'" I remember feeling incredibly sad by his words.

By then, I had learned so much about co-parenting that I had to own that I had contributed to his misunderstanding. Of course, I wouldn't have said no, but why didn't he know that? I had gone back to school. I had authored books and appeared as an expert on TV and radio. More than that, I had worked with families like ours for years, and here, my own ex-husband had no idea we legally had joint custody of our daughter.

It was not until I said, "What are you talking about? Of course, we have joint custody," that I realized how bad our communication had been. I had sole physical custody, which meant she lived with me as her home base and went to school from my home, but he always had joint custody and equal say in her welfare. I don't think he understood the difference. Since we spoke so rarely, it was never clarified.

Our communication improved when our daughter became a teenager. My attitude had changed because of what I learned over the years. I saw firsthand how important it was to reach out to a co-parent in the name of your child. I secretly vowed to fix what I could with the little time we had before she became an adult. "Right" or "wrong" became just words. The welfare of our child became the driving force.

I don't want to give the impression that we fought or that we were always at odds. Quite the opposite. We just didn't talk or compare notes, which I have learned is almost as bad.

Fast forward to my bonus family life. While all this was happening on one side, on the other side I was co-parenting with my husband and his ex-wife. Although they had been separated for 2 years and finally divorced, they could barely speak to each other when I moved in.

I've told the story many times of how my husband handed me the phone when his ex-wife, Sharyl, called because he couldn't stand to talk to her. I had never really talked to her, and here I was trying to explain to her why her ex-husband couldn't stand the sound of her voice. She never understood why his reaction was so extreme, and truth be told, neither did I. She never seemed that "bad" to me. Although we had our "ex-wife/now-wife" issues in the beginning, our outlook on parenting was very much the same, and the animosity melted away in time. Good thing, since her kids lived with me every other week.

During that fated conversation, what struck me was her true confusion about why her ex-husband disliked her to such a degree. The first thing she asked when I initially said, "Hello," was, "Jann, why does he hate me so much?"

That got me. Until that point, I was convinced I would be strong, direct, aloof, sort of a bitch back if I ever spoke to her. But her sincerity stopped me in my tracks, and so my energy automatically matched hers. I think that surprised her—me, as well, if I am to be honest. The next time she called, she asked for me and that started an unusual collaboration that eventually became a true friendship.

What ultimately brought us all to our senses was that we realized the mutual impact we had on each other's children. By then, it was "yours, mine, and ours" kids all watching how the parent figures were trying to navigate the back-and-forth. I say "parent figures" because even though my biological kids didn't live with Sharyl, they were witnesses to her life. Her decisions for her children affected my children. The kids were being raised as siblings. Her rules often overlapped ours. The kids even compartmentalized our relationship. She was Sharyl, Melanie and Steven's mom. She had her responsibilities. My husband and I were "the parents" with our responsibilities. I didn't realize this until I overheard our kids talking about what "the parents" said, and it hit me that in their minds, we each had specific roles, but they saw all three of us as a team. There's the village it takes, right there.

One night my bonus family—my husband, yours, mine, and our kids—were planning a family vacation. We knew we wanted to go to the beach somewhere but couldn't decide between Mexico or Hawaii. We were going for a week and had settled on spring break when the "ours" child, who was by now 6 years old, popped up, "Hey, wait a minute! Can Sharyl get off work?" She just took it for granted that her sibling's mother would be going with us. We all laughed a little. "No, honey," I said. "Sharyl will stay home at her house. This vacation is just for our immediate family." She seemed to understand the distinction, but her first thought was to include Sharyl.

That was when it became obvious that the kids saw us as a family. They inherently understood where the line was drawn, two separate homes, who was biologically related to whom, but they knew we were in this together.

The one true benefit to forming a working relationship with my husband's ex-wife was that as we got along better, so did she and my husband. We mimic what surrounds us. Now that Sharyl and I were collaborating, not fighting, it just seemed out of place for her and Larry to be at odds. This made me realize how much I had contributed to the poor communication with my own daughter's father. I was so wrapped up in doing it right on the bonus family side that I didn't realize how I had dropped the ball on the other side. To create a real bonus family, *everyone* must be in sync. All the parent figures must use the best interest of all the children as the reason they bend over backward to keep communication open.

For this reason, I decided the first chapter of this book should be on co-parenting. This may feel a little like backtracking. After all, this is a book about combining families. Shouldn't we already be experts on co-parenting at this point? That would be nice, but it isn't always true. There are all sorts of things that play into learning to cooperatively co-parent. Therefore, the reason we start with co-parenting is that learning how to successfully problem solve with a co-parent sets the stage for cooperative problem solving with a new partner and combining families. The principles are the same. A cooperative mindset is contagious.

I am proud to say that Bonus Families as a nonprofit organization has been in existence now for over 25 years. I built the first website myself in 1999 and had no idea what power the internet had to spread the word. I had used the word "bonus" in lieu of "step" since writing for *Working Mother* magazine in 1994, but the internet was now worldwide. I began getting emails from parents all over the world, particularly from the Scandinavian countries where the collaborative concept was wholeheartedly embraced. A few years later, a good friend's sister lived in Sweden, and I met her at a party while she was visiting the United States. She explained that in Sweden, using the word "bonus" as a prefix to the word "parent" or "child" depicted respect. I got so excited! That is exactly what I wanted. I wanted the bonus distinction to automatically let others know this was not just a stepparent or a stepchild but a loved, respected member of my family. Australia and New Zealand also came on board very quickly. So did Canada and the UK. When I started getting emails from countries like Greece and Madagascar, I realized how much everyone all over the world was looking for direction. The family unit was changing, and the old-school approach just wasn't working.

Originally, I met clients in a chatroom I had incorporated into the Bonus Families website. Nothing like now, when I work mostly via Zoom. I never saw them face to face, but the emails of gratitude were just the same. So many parents hated to be at odds. They were done fighting. "What do we do?" became the universal question. "Put the children first" is still my universal answer. When you truly do that, decisions are easy. Making decisions based on your self-interests only complicates problem solving. It changes nothing.

My bonus family life became all-consuming, and I went back to school over the years to gain the necessary degrees to work as a child custody recommending counselor for a superior court in California. There, I met some pretty contentious clients, but working with them was by far the best education I could ever ask for. It allowed me to work with parents from all walks of life, economic status, cultures, religions, and ethnicities. Now retired from the court system, I continue to work with Bonus Families, the nonprofit, and have a private practice where I work exclusively with parents trying to improve their co-parenting skills.

From working with families for so many years, I know that most of us just try to do the best we can. I will share my stories as well as those of others with whom I have worked (names and genders have been changed to protect identities) in an attempt to offer guidance and arm you with the best problem solving tools I know. As Maya Angelou, the American poet, memoirist, and civil rights activist wisely said, "When you know better, you do better." *The Bonus Family Handbook* will be a source of knowing better and, as a result, doing better when co-parenting, meeting someone new, and raising children together after a breakup. It is my sincere hope that *The Bonus Family Handbook* will successfully guide you through possibly the toughest thing you've ever done—creating a loving, working, bonus family.

But there's more. A very important component to becoming a bonus family is following something I call "good ex-etiquette" or "good behavior after divorce or separation." Originally, ex-etiquette was a department on the first Bonus Families website. Currently, the department features at least 200 articles answering questions posed by readers and is still the most-read department on www .bonusfamilies.com. Ex-etiquette is also the title of the syndicated column I write for Tribune Content, and the Ten Rules of Good

Ex-Etiquette has guided many exes and their families to more positive, loving relationships.

CARE is a tool I refer to in this book. It is an abbreviated version of the Ten Rules of Good Ex-Etiquette. It is an acronym for Communication, Acceptance, Respect, Empathy and is designed to be a simpler and more direct guide to help co-parents and extended family problem solve when forming their bonus family.

Better explained, when asked, most co-parents say they must improve their Communication, so I will offer different tools to do just that. The next component in CARE is A for Acceptance. Acceptance is possibly the most important component to gaining bonus status. People are different, with different histories and things to make them tick. Being accepting of those differences is a key component to gaining bonus status. Next, Respect for their history and Empathy for their situation will bring it full circle. That's CARE. Using CARE allows us to problem solve together on every level for every problem and you will see how I incorporate the strategy in each chapter.

HOW TO USE THIS BOOK

Of course, I would love you to read this book from beginning to end, but grasping the important concepts for better co-parenting and working toward bonus status when combining families is far more important. With that in mind, there is an extensive index at the back of the book that allows you to look up words and concepts and go directly to what you need to know.

As you read through this book you may also see some catch-words that I have developed that will make grasping the concepts a little easier. Besides "bonus" in lieu of "step" in relationship to family members, I also use the term "counterpartner" to refer to the relationship between your new partner's co-parent and your co-parent's new partner. Basically, I am talking about moms and bonus moms or dads and bonus dads, or not to be gender specific, someone from your child's other home that performs many of the same duties you do for the children. It's confusing to write "your new partner's co-parent or "your co-parent's new partner" each time a reference must be made, and I wanted a word to describe the relationship that was sensitive to both parties. The word "counterpartner" is based on the root word "counterpart," meaning "a person holding a position or performing a function that corresponds to that of another person or thing in another place." Attaching the word "partner" hopefully implies a collaborative spirit.

Two more words I use interchangeably are "divorce" and "breakup." The percentage of married to unmarried parents is about equal these days in the United States. Add to that the number of people with children pairing up for a second or subsequent time, married or not, that means more people are living in bonus families than in conventional married two-parent homes. So, I use the words divorce and breakup interchangeably to cover everyone's lifestyle. The principles of sharing custody and creating your bonus family are the same if you were married or not married when you had children.

I also use the words "wife," "husband," "spouse," "other parent," and "partner"—all meaning the other person in your current relationship. And I use "co-parent" and "ex" to refer to a partner in a past relationship. Quite frankly, other than referencing my column, Ex-Etiquette, I rarely use the word "ex" unless it is to explicitly differentiate between the positive co-parent mindset and the negative ex mindset. "Ex" is simply an outdated reference when it comes to co-parenting.

Finally, I have tried to keep this book free of gender bias. Sometimes I arbitrarily use the word "he," sometimes "she," sometimes "they," "them," or "their." Please know that this book is designed for *anyone* looking for help while co-parenting and constructing a family after a breakup.

I'd like to close with a message for all who use this book: My life's work continues to be helping parents put aside their hurt, anger, and revenge for the sake of the children they share. The more parents I work with, the more I see they just don't realize the impact they all have on each other's lives and on each other's children's lives. Let's change that. Let's be a model of love and acceptance for our children, demonstrating firsthand how CARE (Communication, Acceptance, Respect, Empathy) can enrich their relationships. If we can do that, we will have all reached bonus status.

The Story Behind *Bonus*

As Melanie ran from one side of the basketball court to the other, her mother, Sharyl, and I sat in the bleachers searching for a new term for "stepmother." I was married to Melanie's dad, and since stepmothers were assumed to be wicked and mean, Melanie had confided that her friends automatically thought she hated me, and that was not true. Joking, we tried all sorts of alternatives, but everything we thought of seemed either inappropriate or insulting to either Sharyl or me.

"Blended" was the politically correct word at the time, but while you could be a blended family, you couldn't be a blended mom or blended dad. We continued our joking, complete with my monologue on the new whitening and brightening version of Mom—the "bonus" version. When *bonus* was used in that fashion, I knew it was the right word. "Bonus" did not insult Sharyl and it acknowledged my contributions. "Bonus" was beyond blended. It was the perfect word to describe the new collaborative approach to combining families that we had eased into—and it was working!

When I went home and looked up the word "bonus" in the dictionary, I was further convinced it was the right word. The dictionary explained, "A *bonus* is a gift to reward performance—something extra or additional, an asset given freely." From that day forward I was their "bonus mom." They were my "bonus kids," and we were a "bonus family." No more negative connotations. "Bonus" was our word of choice. This was 1993!

I remember the first time I heard a celebrity refer to herself as a "bonus mom." It was somewhere around 2000. By this time, I was working as the director of Bonus Families, the nonprofit organization I started in 1999. Gazing at my latest issue of *People* magazine, I was stunned to see the headline screaming, "Jada Pinkett Smith is a 'BONUS MOM!'" In just 6 years, the concept had gone mainstream! I got so excited I sent her a Bonus Mom T-shirt!

Not long after, I heard Trisha Yearwood use the term in an interview. She openly acknowledged her place as a third voice for the kids she loves—supporting their mom and dad, Garth Brooks, in their co-parenting. That was exactly right. A bonus mom or bonus dad supports the parents' rules, looks for ways to promote cooperation, and is a loving third voice.

The bonus concept continued to grow over the next 10 years. Then, in 2012, I attended a women's conference in Northern California. Wynonna was the keynote speaker. A part of her talk was dedicated to explaining why she called her stepkids her "bonus kids," why she was their "bonus mom," and why her husband was her kids' "bonus dad." She explained the bonus concept perfectly.

At the end of the speech, Wynonna's support staff announced that she would entertain questions from five people from the audience and asked the people to come to the front who wanted to talk to her. I hesitated but decided I would brave it and walked up to the front of the auditorium. I was last, of course, and when it was my turn, I explained I had coined the term "bonus."

She didn't believe me. Into the microphone very loudly, she said, "Nuh-uh!" The entire room erupted into laughter. She continued to joke for a second, but when she could see I wasn't kidding, she looked at me and said, "You mean like bonus mom, bonus dad, bonus families? Seriously?"

"Yep," I said. And the room was silent. Then, all of a sudden, she boomed, "Well, you go, girl!" Applause built slowly until the whole room was cheering.

Exactly what I had wanted all those years had happened! "Bonus" had become an accepted alternative to the word "step." But it was more than that. This was proof that "bonus" was now recognized as a movement, a community, and a mindset based on love and acceptance. People were finally accepting that "Bonus is beyond blended" and realizing that CARE (Communication, Acceptance, Respect, and Empathy) was the answer to creating a strong family after a breakup and starting over.

Over the years I have heard many celebrities use the term "bonus." From the already-mentioned Jada Pinkett Smith to LeAnn Rimes to Gwyneth Paltrow to Princess Beatrice to Gisele Bündchen to Dakota Johnson to social media personality Tabitha Brown. Even Vice President Harris has described her family as a "bonus family." More and more are using love and acceptance as their guide and jumping on the bonus bandwagon.

* * *

Since I coined the term "bonus" so many years ago, here are four frequent questions I am asked:

Isn't "bonus family" just a play on words?

No. It's a new word and a new concept. Culturally, racially, and sexually, people identify with labels to describe themselves. In the past, when people combined families, they used to be called a "stepfamily," but that was dependent on being married and had negative connotations. Thanks to the Grimms' fairy tales, stepmothers are viewed as evil and wicked. It is time to scrap the old concept of "step" and offer a new and improved model of a combined family based on love, empathy, and respect for each family member's individuality and history.

What constitutes a bonus family?

The words "bonus family" began as another word for "step-family," but since so many couples live together and do not marry, a bonus family is not dependent on the parents being married to each other. Nor must the parents identify as straight. The unit includes two adults, at least one with children, who combine their families to become one family. An adoptive family is not a bonus family. An adoptive parent is not a bonus parent. Once a parent adopts a child, legally, he or she is the child's parent.

Think of "bonus family" as being the ultimate goal, something to which you aspire. It's a completely new unit based on a desire to accept and understand all the members of your family.

A bonus family embraces a loving, cooperative, inclusive spirit, but it is not communal living. It's a cooperative approach to merging families. Each family is autonomous and can be separately referred to as a bonus family. Bonus is a state of mind.

Why call these children bonus daughter, bonus son, or bonus child?

The meaning of "red-headed stepchild" is clear enough; it is used to describe a person who is neglected, mistreated, unwanted, or second best. Being called a "bonus child," on the other hand, reinforces a child's sense of individuality and boosts feelings of self-worth.

What about "blended?" Isn't that an appropriate label when two families "blend" together to become one family?

When you blend things together, you lose the individual ingredients. Flour and eggs don't care, but people do. It matters to a child if he or she used to have a room of his or her own but now must share a room. It matters that the child is half of their other parent. It matters that they had to leave their friends or their baseball team because their mother and father are no longer together. If there was trauma in their past, that needs to be considered as well. As in anything, combining components can make the final product stronger or compromise its strength. Making it a point to respect each family member's history and individuality makes each one feel as if they matter, and because they matter as individuals, they are more willing to accept family membership. Bonus family membership.

The bonus family philosophy takes a cooperative rather than combative approach to sharing children's time and forming a family with a new partner. It suggests that all four parents (when both biological parents find someone new) band together in the name of their children to co-create a new relationship after the breakups. This new model is based on the parents' relationship as co-parents, not as battling exes. It offers all the children their collective adult best. As a result, the children can grow up in a calm, loving environment, not one ruled by an old-school breakup philosophy based on anger, hurt, selfishness, competition, and insecurity.

Many say this is impossible—there's too much animosity from the past when parents break up. It's not impossible. I lived it firsthand. It was not easy, but it was certainly not impossible. And over the years, I have guided thousands of families to effectively become bonus. Use this book as your guide toward bonus status. Use your heart to stay there.

PART I

SETTING THE STAGE TO BECOME BONUS

CHAPTER 1

Co-Parenting With CARE

LET'S SAY YOU AND YOUR FAMILY ARE TAKING A CRUISE. YOU ARE on one end of the ship and your partner is on the other. Your three children are in the middle, playing a game to keep themselves entertained. All of a sudden, the sun disappears and it starts to storm. As the wind and rain pound the ship, it springs a leak near your partner's end and the ship starts to fill with water. As the ship lists to one side, the kids tumble toward your partner's end of the ship. The water is coming in fast and furious and the kids are struggling to keep their heads above water.

Let's stop the story for a minute. In the midst of all this chaos someone hands you a message that says you and your partner are no longer together. Do you say, "Cool! Since we are no longer together, that hole is your problem. It's on your side!" Or, with your co-parent's help, do you start to bail to save your kids?

The second solution is the bonus family concept in a nutshell. It's not rocket science, but it is a different approach to an age-old problem—a collaborative effort while co-parenting, with the end result being healthy, more emotionally stable children after a breakup—and healthier parents, as well.

Some think it is ridiculous to believe that parents who could not get along when they were together can put aside their differences now that they are no longer a couple. Then there are those parents who were never a couple at all but still must co-parent once they have a child. Everyone's new co-parenting mantra? "In the best interest of our children."

My ex and I dated in high school and broke up three times between our sophomore and senior years. Each time we ignored each other, so I thought when we split this time we would never speak again. We got on each other's nerves so much that I celebrated with old friends the day my divorce was final. At our son's little league game, I tried to sit as far from her as I could, but when I realized he couldn't find me in the crowd, I moved closer [with] each inning. That hit home (no pun intended). This breakup would be different. My ex was no longer just a girl I dated in high school but the mother of my child, and it was obvious that [our] child loved us both.
   – SAMUEL, CO-PARENTING WITH JANET AND FATHER TO
AUSTIN, AGE 6

Although child custody laws have not changed in almost 40 years, the family structure, attitude, and approach to breaking up and starting over certainly have. Custody laws require parents to share their children's time, spending half, or at least a percentage of their time, with each parent. That means many of our children today have two homes, and therefore, allegiances are checked each time those children go back and forth. It can be difficult for children to relax in either environment, anticipating the time they must leave one home and go to the other. Yet parents continue to approach their life after a breakup using the same approach to co-parenting as they did when joint custody was first introduced in the early '80s—when few really knew the impact that living in two homes might have on children. Parents just retire to their corners, thinking they are now autonomous entities.

Nothing could be further from the truth. You are in this together, and if you think you aren't, you're fooling yourself.

Why is successful co-parenting so important?

If you have a parenting plan in place that requires your children to go back and forth between homes, then some sort of co-parenting is required. Most parents believe that their children are resilient and will easily cope with the trials of their parents' breakup. But research shows that our children's physical, mental, and emotional well-being are affected when witnessing ongoing conflict. If the conflict continues after the breakup, that's even worse. There may be no visible scars, but our children are permanently affected all the same.

LAYING THE GROUNDWORK: PUT THE CHILDREN FIRST

We've heard this for years, but what exactly does "put the children first" really mean to you and your co-parent? It means that you must have enough respect for your children to put their needs before yours. Forget about "the principle of the thing" when disagreeing with your co-parent and make your mutual love for the children the principal thing. From this day forward make all your decisions based on what is best for them, no matter if you must be uncomfortable, admit you are wrong, swallow your pride, move, do without, or go slower in a new relationship than you would like. Your children did not ask for their family to be disrupted. They did not agree to your separation or divorce. If you have made the decision to change their life, they should legitimately be your first priority. Putting the children first is at the root of cooperative co-parenting and forming a living, breathing bonus family, and I will refer to the premise of "put the children first" throughout this book.

Now, you may be thinking something like, *My child is so young. He doesn't understand what's going on.*

This is one of the biggest co-parenting misconceptions co-parents can have. Young children may not understand intellectually, but they certainly can feel stressed when there is parental conflict. Haven't you walked into a room where people have been arguing and you want to ask, "What's going on?" You *feel* the tension, yet no one is speaking. Just like adults, children feel when there's friction in the air. However, depending on their age, they may have trouble expressing what they are feeling. So, what we see is that they are fussy, disorderly, don't sleep well, or don't eat well. They may wet the bed after being dry for months or years. As they get older, they may have trouble concentrating or staying organized. Constant unease and inability to find comfort in their surroundings change who they are. It is unfortunate, but eventually, they will view stressful conflict as normal and seek it out in their own relationships as they get older, not because they like it, but because it feels familiar.

Oh, don't be so dramatic! We all feel stressed. They'll get over it, you might say.

I liken stress to how X-rays affect the human body. X-rays are cumulative. One doesn't bother you, but X-rays over a period of time have been proven to possibly cause cancer. Stress is no different. Too much over a period of time impacts your physical, psychological, and emotional health. Studies show that children as young as infants can feel and may be influenced by the tension and hostility of parental fighting.[1] Children internalizing stress as early as infancy has been identified as contributing to problems with adjustment.[2] And finally, to drive the point home, studies also show that children exposed at an early age to trauma, including domestic violence, have a smaller hippocampus—the brain area related to learning and memory formation. Therefore, it is very possible that children's behavior problems and inability to cope with stressful situations could originate from their reaction to their parents' unrestrained fighting and arguing.

The example we set as parents sets the stage for our children's futures. They watch everything we do. If parents argue, their children learn to problem solve by arguing. If parents work together to find solutions, their children learn to do the same. It doesn't matter if parents live together or live apart. Parents are their children's primary role models. If parents think out of the box and problem solve creatively, their children will learn to problem solve creatively as well.

Therefore, it is imperative not to simply co-parent but to co-parent *well*. Our children are watching, and how their parents interact with one another determines their quality of life.

SETTING THE STAGE TO CO-PARENT *WELL*

Co-parenting in its true sense is more than just raising your kids with your ex after a breakup. It's changing your directive from fighting with an enemy to collaborating with an ally, all in real-time. The past cannot be changed. The future can, and it is up to you.

This Is a New Day: From Ex to Co-Parent

Countless co-parents inherently know their communication style is not working, but they do not know what to do about it. Their co-parenting relationship is just an irritating extension of their life when they were together. As a result, they expect the worst and keep track of each other's mistakes. No change is ever made. They see each other as exes first and co-parents second, if at all.

But you aren't co-parents second. If a co-parenting relationship is to flourish, the ex-relationship must be left in the past. You must openly respect your co-parent as your child's mother or father. Your common ground is not your ex-relationship or all the years you spent together. Your common ground is your child. It's up to both of you to take back your power as individuals, not governed by all the terrible things you both did in the past but governed by what you want to be RIGHT NOW. You must create a new and completely different relationship with one another. To do that, there must be a mental shift prior to any interaction *and* a personal commitment to establishing a new cooperative co-partnership.

And this is how you do it . . .

First Things First: The Correct Mindset

If you have ever read any of the books I have written or have gone to any of the Bonus Families Workshops, you know that I believe the proper mindset sets the stage for your life. I have seen first-hand that you act in conjunction with your thoughts. How you think sets the stage for how you act. If you hold a grudge and are resentful before you talk to someone, your interaction will not be productive. While you are telling the story, you are remembering everything they did to you, everything that has happened, and you simply can't put it away in order to problem solve. It all starts with the proper mindset. You must enter into your co-parenting relationship with an open mind and a collaborative spirit.

Allow Your Co-Parent to Change

> *But you have no idea what they did to me . . .*

Unfortunately, breakups bring out the worst in people, and your co-parent may have been terrible in the past. But if you poll friends and family, most will see a completely different person than you see. Because they are loved, their friends and family allow them to change and improve with time. They forgive their past mistakes and trust them to do better now that they know better. Exes don't. Because they are hurt, they will remind you years later of all your mistakes. During mediation I hear countless reasons why "10 years ago, you _____ (fill in the blank)." Evidently, in retaliation, that justifies one's poor behavior *now*.

But there's another way to look at it. That means in the time since your breakup, you have both had time to grow, to become better individuals, and to learn that nothing is more import-ant than the children you brought into this world. It's time to acknowledge the possibility that your co-parent could have pos-sibly grown into a better person, just as they must allow you to do the same. I know I am not the same person I was a few years ago, nor is my child's father. I would never want someone to hold me to the mistakes I made in the past. "When you know better, you do better." Grant your children's other parent the same grace.

Leave the Past in the Past

Let's talk about what the past really is—a point of reference. You know who you were, and you know who your ex was, and you know your history as an unsuccessful couple. You can depend on those memories, even though they may not be good ones, and you can easily identify because you were there.

Or can you? A recent study done at Northwestern University is one of the first to document that every time you remember an event from the past, your brain networks change in ways that can alter the later recall of the event.[3] That means the next time you remember, you might recall not the original event, but instead, you recall events in line with how you retold the story most recently. Each time you tell the story, the memory becomes more or less intense, depending on your point of reference at the time of telling. It's not uncommon to embellish the worst. It makes a better story, and you are the star of the show. You don't even know you are doing it.

> *After my divorce from my daughter's father, my daughter and I moved in with my parents for a while. I was a working mom and needed help. My mom was always there. One evening, I was once again agonizing over something that had happened. I will never forget what she said to me. "Jannie, when you throw out the garbage you don't go back outside, open the can and examine what you threw out. You throw it out, close the can, and walk away. It's time to close the can and walk away . . . "*

You see, we assign an emotion to each memory we have, from eating a dinner we love to how we feel after the death of a loved one, from being betrayed by our ex to how we felt the first time our baby smiled at us. These memories, with their assigned emotions, color how we think and feel each time we remember that memory. So, each time we think of the betrayal, we remember how we felt, and we are right back in the past even if whatever we are remembering happened years ago. That means you are living in the past, a place you do not remember accurately and cannot change.

But I've heard past behavior is the best gauge of future behavior. . . . There is, of course, some truth to that—if you make no changes, the past will predict the future. However, your memories do not have to control how you act now. Re-create a new relationship, not with your ex, but with your co-parent, using your children's welfare as the basis for your future interaction. Retell THAT story. You no longer have to sit in the failure of your past ex-relationship, dependent on reconstructing all the bad memories to justify a position. Instead, compare notes with your co-parent about your great kids. Unite in helping your children deal with their struggles. *You do not have to be a couple to love your kids together.* You can create the exact relationship you would like to have now, acting exactly how you would like to act toward each other as you support one another co-parenting your children.

Understanding How Preconceived Notions Affect How You Act

What you think about prior to your interaction predicts how easily you cooperate when problem solving. It's more than negative mindset, negative outcome; positive mindset, positive outcome. It's that your children are watching and everything you do registers.

Now, you may be thinking, *But I can't. I get anxiety just thinking about talking to my ex.* Parents who share custody and expect their children to go back and forth between their homes do not have the luxury of saying, "I can't." The degree to which you co-parent is up to you, but "I can't," which implies that you've tried and will no longer try anymore, isn't fair to your children, particularly if every few days they are required by law to switch houses. Each time they leave one home and go to the other they are asked to check their allegiance. Whether your choice is to speak to your co-parent every day or only occasionally, you still have a responsibility to your children to put them first and work together in their name.

Thoughts Become Action

I often use analogies to explain how a negative outlook based on past experiences colors your opinion of your next interaction—and what you can do to create a more positive approach.

Let's say you love the ocean. You have a favorite beach you visit quite a few times a year. Rain or shine, it doesn't matter; you love this beach. It makes no difference that you must climb 100 steps down a mountain to the sand. You love to walk along the edge drinking your morning coffee, toes in the sand. You let the waves barely touch your feet because your favorite beach is known to have a dangerous undertow and you might get pulled under.

One day, as you walk along the water's edge, an unexpected wave knocks you to the ground and you are caught by the undertow about which you were warned. Struggling to breathe, as it pulls you out to sea, you scratch your shoulder on a reef that could not be seen simply walking near the water's edge. Panicking, you wrestle the waves, turning over and over until you realize the waves have dropped you back on the sand. You are fine but shaken and bleeding from hitting the reef. With each crash of a wave, the saltwater burns your scratches and you have to sit on the sand to catch your breath before braving the 100 steps back up the mountain.

Based on the harrowing experience just described, your attitude about spending time at the beach could certainly shift from your favorite place to your most avoided, and the thought of going back to your favorite beach after you almost drowned could fill you with anticipation. The ocean has now become a trigger. Each time you think of your favorite beach, you remember what happened, and your heart starts to pound. Everything from smelling the ocean air to hearing the waves hit the sand fuels your anxiety. Just thinking about your next visit makes you feel out of control, so you stay a good distance from the water's edge, even though walking near it used to give you so much pleasure.

I've just described a reaction to trauma often referred to as PTSD, or post-traumatic stress disorder. Most think of PTSD as a response to the trauma of war. However, it can also be in response to any trauma, from a car accident to almost drowning at your favorite beach. Think of the ocean, you start to sweat. The same thing happens when thinking about interacting with an ex who has caused you pain in the past. Remembering whatever negative memory you attach to the experience frames your next interaction and can make it impossible to have even the simplest conversation. So, you lash out before they do. You want to control the process because if you don't, you might get pulled under. Meanwhile, your children are going back and forth between your homes and watching the entire show. No wonder our children often dig in their heels and say, "I don't want to go." It's the only way they can stop being in the middle of their combative parents.

"It's Not Me, It's Him . . ."

This is about the time I hear, "It's not me, it's him" or "I don't do that, but she does." From being perpetually late when exchanging the children to bad-mouthing the other parent when the kids are present, rarely can we see our own contribution to a problem. Most of the time we think, "It's clearly their fault."

But, when co-parents get caught up in an "it's not me, it's you" tit-for-tat war, blaming each other for each dilemma, they are giving up their power to fix the problem. Since it was all the other person's fault, they were the cause, there's nothing you can do. You are the victim. As the victim, you can convince yourself that things just happen to you and are out of your control. Victim mentality can be very seductive. It takes all the pressure off. But it also prevents either of you from moving forward. You will always be the victim. They will always be to blame.

See the best in my ex? You mean the person who cheated on me and then tried to convince me it was my fault? You want me to create a positive co-parenting atmosphere with someone like that?

What you describe is hurtful, and it is understandable if you want to hold a grudge. But you have to ask yourself how perpetuating that grudge will affect your life now and in the future and how it will affect your children. Hopefully, they do not know the specifics surrounding the breakup. Even if they do, I've never worked with a child who really cares which parent is right and which is wrong. They acknowledge the hurt, but most still harbor a wish that their parents will reconcile at some point. That means, even if you are completely disgusted with your ex, your children are not. They do not hurt in the same way you do. How you act toward their other parent while your children are growing up, no matter if you were ever in a relationship with their parent or not, will affect them for the rest of their life.

Therefore, a cordial relationship where you can problem solve in the best interest of your children is always the best course of action. And, for the record, in most states, adultery does not play a role in deciding the custody of children. If there is a parenting plan in place that requires you to share your children's time, the court expects you to put your issues aside and parent your children regardless of what happened.

Some may ask, *But isn't disagreeing normal? Doesn't everyone fight a little, particularly those who are no longer a couple?* Absolutely, we all disagree from time to time. Disagreeing isn't the issue. It's *how* we disagree that's in question and for how long. The type of arguing that is detrimental to our children and our ability to properly co-parent is when the insults fly and threats are made; when co-parents lose their temper, scream, yell, dismiss each other, or are condescending and bad-mouth each other in front of the kids.

Find Your Mutual Interest

All successful relationships are built on some sort of mutual interest. You both like to play pickleball. You both like to work out or go to the gym. You like the same music, or you both love bird watching, or you have the same political or religious beliefs. However, most estranged parents are stuck in their old relationship and think now that they have broken up, they have nothing more in common. They mentally rehash what happened in the past and sit in their anger and resentment. Unless estranged parents can identify and accept that they do have a common interest—*their children*—they will not be able to problem solve or even feel it necessary to come to an agreement about anything.

When you accept that there is no one except your child's other parent who loves your child as much as you do, you now have a reason to work together. Accepting that fact puts co-parents on an equal playing field. They are no longer two autonomous single parents raising their children on their own but allies "in the best interest of their children," equally responsible for giving their children the best life possible, whether they live together or apart.

USING CARE WILL MAKE THE DIFFERENCE

I talked about CARE in the introduction of this book. CARE is an acronym for the attitude and mindset necessary to improve your ability to problem solve during a conflict. It can be a conflict with anyone. Of course, most of my clients are co-parents, but CARE works with best friends, crotchety bosses, contrary children, as well as an ex with whom you no longer feel you have anything in common. When you are having a disagreement, think CARE:

Communication

Acceptance

Respect

Empathy

Let's examine the components of CARE one by one and analyze how adopting this mindset will help to problem solve effectively.

C is for Communication

I have worked with thousands of couples over the years, and I fine-tune my approach to each couple. To get to know them, I start with a conversation about the issues they feel they need to improve. Everyone, and I mean everyone, starts with, "We need to improve our communication. We can't talk to each other."

Say that in court and the order will become "communicate only in writing." This is done to verify who is the instigator of the disagreements. "Texting okay" is often added to the stipulation.

The Impact of Texting on Co-Parenting Communication

Texting is convenient, but it is not a communication tool. It's a notification tool. It's something you use to tell your co-parent you will be 15 minutes late or that Johnny's dentist appointment is now on Tuesday. You cannot discuss your children's welfare via text, but for many, it's become the path of least resistance. Don't really want to talk to your co-parent? Text them. However, if you don't agree or feel attacked through text, it's easy to get into text wars—lots of words and angry emojis that go on for days and serve no purpose but to verify two people's inability to put their own issues aside in the name of their children.

Ironically, estranged parents are often ordered to only communicate by text. They are told to use a co-parenting app to record everything that is said so that their insults are admissible in court. If you must record your poor choices on an app to submit to the courts as proof of your inability to communicate with your co-parent, you need this book more than ever.

The following modes of communication are based on *talking* and *listening* to your co-parent. You cannot truly co-parent by only texting.

Active Listening

Active listening is a communication tool that will help your co-parent grasp that you understand their point of view. You ask open-ended questions and responses to prompt your co-parent to tell you more. The more you know, the more likely you are to understand, thereby allowing you to negotiate rather than the discussion spiraling out of control.

Active listening involves both verbal and nonverbal cues. Some useful nonverbal cues are tone of voice, eye contact, and body language. It could be as simple as leaning toward the person speaking to let them know you are truly listening. Eye contact when speaking or listening communicates that you are focused on the conversation.

Since much of your communication with a co-parent may be done via telephone, verbal skills are also important. Listen, then summarize what you have heard and repeat it back. If you are correct in your understanding, you validate your co-parent's feelings. If your assumptions are wrong, this will give your co-parent a chance to correct you and clarify how they feel and what they are trying to say.

I often use active listening in child custody mediation to help disgruntled co-parents understand each other's perspective. When there is a pause in the conversation, I might say something like, "So what you are telling me is that your co-parent is undermining your visits with the children by not helping them to prepare for their time with you?" The angry co-parent might clarify by saying, "Exactly. The kids are never ready when I arrive, and they resent having to hurry and never really settle in when we are together."

Or, they might say, "No, it's not that she doesn't help them prepare. They are always ready to go when I arrive to pick them up. It's what she says while they are preparing. I overhear it. Like when she says, 'I'm going to be so lonely in this big house while you're gone.' That makes the kids feel awful about leaving, and they never seem to settle in."

Curiosity

The best tool to improve your active listening chops? Curiosity. Regard it as your secret weapon. Being curious means going into an interaction with no ulterior motive other than having something to learn. When you stay curious about what someone might be feeling, trying to understand their motivation, you are less likely to take things personally because you're listening to their explanation.

Phrases that will aid you in listening more actively are:

- "Really? I'm curious why you feel that way." (This prompts someone to explain their point of view.)
- "Hmmm . . . that's interesting." (This acknowledges that you were listening without judgment.)
- "Tell me more . . ." (Prompts the other person to volunteer more information.)
- "So, what you are saying is . . ." (Asks them to validate that they were heard correctly.)
- "I see" (or even "And?" or "Uh huh.") (Prompts them to further explain.)
- "What does that mean to you?" or "What does that look like?" (Asks them to explain exactly what something means to them.)

All of these phrases encourage the other party to not only talk but explain what they are thinking and feeling. When they are allowed to explain, they will feel heard and hopefully feel validated in their position. That will set the stage for easier give-and-take. Again, it's important to note that feeling heard is a stepping-stone toward agreement, but it's not a guarantee that you are on the same page. It is the beginning of better communication—a step in the right direction.

Trust and Transparency

When working with estranged parents and listening to their complaints, it has become obvious to me that the main problem most co-parents face is they just don't trust each other. Since trust is essential to any working relationship, especially a co-parenting relationship, rebuilding trust is crucial to the ability to comfortably interact and problem solve together.

Building trust begins with small gestures. Little things like saying "Your mother and I" or "Your father and I" to the children when talking about decisions you and your co-parent have made. Learning that you can depend on your co-parent by both of you doing what you say and saying what you will do.

Adding transparency to your interaction also helps to build trust, but most co-parents find true transparent communication difficult. They tend to shy away from the truth when it is not favorable and makes them look bad. Most know when their co-parent is not being completely honest, and this makes them feel like there is a hidden agenda, like when someone hedges on what might have happened in an explanation or leaves things out (lying by omission). Both behaviors do not build trust in your co-parent.

Here's an example that illustrates how quickly trust can erode between co-parents:

> *We agreed on something. Last time, it was when Noah's father would call him when he was with me. He said 5 o'clock was good. We were home to talk at 5:00. He called at 6:00. So, next time we*

changed it to 6:00. He didn't call until 7:00. He doesn't see the big deal, but I can't trust anything he says.

Examples like this are why your co-parent may already think of you as someone who says one thing and does another. Honest, transparent communication improves your credibility, which eventually leads to trust. If you say you will call at 5:00, call at 5:00. If you can't, let your co-parent know why. This is a perfect time when texting works well. "Something came up and I can't call at 5:00 p.m. tonight. I'll call tomorrow at 5:00 p.m." The sooner you can offer the heads-up, the better, especially if you know they are making special concessions to receive the call.

More Ways to Build Trust: Ask Their Opinion

An easy way to build a rapport with someone is to ask their opinion. It makes them feel respected and reinforces trust. Many don't care what their co-parent thinks, and that's a mistake. Your co-parent's opinion is just as valid as yours. An angry or distrustful co-parent will automatically say, "No!" when a change is requested, just so they don't have to deal with you. And that's learned behavior. Some co-parents are so used to saying *no* to one another that *yes* isn't even in their vocabulary.

Getting Past "No!"

Here's a situation where the co-parents disagree. Asking for their opinion opens the door to a discussion and possibly *Yes*—not just *No!*

> *I need your help with figuring this out. I know Noah is only 10, but now that he's in sports it's difficult to get a hold of him. I go to the school to pick him up, practice runs long, and I can't find him. It may help if he has his own phone. What do you think?*

This co-parent opened the discussion with an important request. "I need your help to figure this out." He then closed the request with something even more important—"What do you think?"

Asking someone's opinion sets the stage for a positive discussion. There isn't an instant *no* when you are asking someone how they feel about something. These co-parents now have the opportunity to share their opinions rather than insult each other. They can negotiate, compromise, and hopefully decide together in the best interest of their child.

A word to the wise: Parents often disagree about the age a child should get a cell phone. In the situation above, the reason to say no must be more than "No. He's only 10." Since the original co-parent gave a reason why he felt a telephone may be a solution, a response to that reasoning is necessary if both co-parents are to feel heard. That means it would be helpful to explain why being "only 10" makes a difference to you. Is it because he may lose the phone? You can get insurance for loss or theft. Is it out of concern he may see things he shouldn't on the internet? You can add parental controls. The more honest and transparent you both are when problem solving, the more likely you will be able to find solutions together.

Tact and Timing

Everyone has a personal agenda and wants to plead their case directly. Tact (how you say something) and timing (when you say something) have a lot to do with how cooperative your co-parent will be.

If you must make a request, consider what was said prior. Was there tension in the room? Are they tired and crabby? Are *you* tired and crabby? Before you speak, read the room. That's using tact and timing.

I just finished a session where the father wanted more time with his son. He and his co-parent have a volatile history, but they have been working together and have made great strides during previous sessions. At the beginning of this session, the mother announced she was exhausted and overwhelmed with the responsibilities of her job, being the primary caregiver to four children, two of whom have special needs, and she just got back from a holiday vacation to Disneyland. Just talking about it made her a little weepy. The father did not read the room. He immediately started in with his requests, and that was not the time to discuss something as emotional as changing the parenting plan. He didn't care. His agenda prevailed and he aggressively took his stance. The conversation did not go well. He forgot about the importance of tact and timing.

A is for Acceptance

There are two sides to acceptance: offering acceptance and feeling accepted—heads and tails of the same coin. For this discussion, however, acceptance is simply acknowledging your co-parent's history and frame of reference as valid and accepting them for who they are.

I was married very young. At first, life was wonderful, but as time went on, we grew to be like oil and water. Our views on everything were completely different. I would read self-help books and offer him passages for change. He ignored me. He didn't want to change and thought my attitude was one-sided. But I knew I was right, and that just fueled our disagreements. We eventually divorced.

About 4 years later, I met someone new and we married. We had three children, and again, life was wonderful for a while, but things slowly began to get difficult. The same things were happening, and I honestly believed if he would just change, we would be fine. Our arguing became a problem, but I didn't want to get a divorce this time. I had children and decided if I wanted to stay married, I would have to be the one to change. I would have to accept my husband for who he was and learn to appreciate his opinions as his, even if they were different than mine. Change was not an option. Acceptance was.

My children are now all teenagers, two in college, and every so often, each child will complain that they just can't get along with their father. I have told them many times they can't change him. "That's just your dad," I tell them, and if they want a relationship with him, they must accept him for who he is. It's funny, but he says the same thing about the kids, and I tell him the same thing.

          – ERICA, MARRIED MOTHER WITH
          TWO COLLEGE-AGED CHILDREN

Although this isn't a story of co-parenting, it explains the attitude of acceptance that is needed to successfully co-parent. Countless co-parents say they can't get along. They disagree and continually try to change each other. But when you truly *accept* someone for who they are and work within those parameters, you let go of your desire to change them. Right or wrong is no longer the all-important consideration. Finding a solution to whatever problem you face becomes the primary concern, especially if it concerns a child you both love.

R is for Respect

Treating your co-parent with respect means regarding them as your equal and offering them the same consideration you would like in a given situation.

I stopped referring to my son's father as "my ex," and you know who brought it to my attention? My son. I could see it in his expression when I talked about "my ex." He would squish up his face like he smelled something bad. I realized it was the word "ex" he didn't like, and when I asked him about it, he told me it made him feel bad. "I don't know," he shrugged. "But, ex, Mom?" So, I started referring to his dad as "my co-parent" or "my son's dad." Surprisingly enough, with that little bit of added respect, my attitude changed.

          – LISA, MOTHER TO NATE, AGE 12

E is for Empathy

Understanding why the E in CARE stands for empathy is simple. Empathy closes the gap of misunderstanding by suggesting you consider how you might feel if put in the same position.

Another way to say it? *Put yourself in their shoes.*

> *My ex-husband and I share custody of the kids. I always made the doctor and dentist appointments when we were together and so I took it for granted that would continue when we were divorced. I never told him when they were going to the dentist. I figured it wasn't his business. I was their mother. Then one day I found out that our youngest had to have a tooth pulled and his dad took care of it. I was furious. I mean irate. How presumptuous to take my child to the dentist without my knowing! I had to stand back and really take a look at my attitude. I realized that must have been exactly how their father felt when I didn't consult him about appointments. Even when the appointment was made on his father's time, I resented not being informed. So, from that minute on, I never took the children to another appointment without keeping their dad in the loop. It was his right as their dad to know, just as it was my right as their mother. That shift has made a significant impact on how we communicate now.*
>
> – Claudia, 35, mother to Jolee, age 4, and Billy, age 7

Now and then I get an angry comment from someone saying that the CARE approach is impractical. "Real divorced people don't get along," one reader wrote. "And being nice and acting like you 'care' won't help. I have no control over my ex-husband."

The truth is, we can't control anyone. You can try, but most will resent it. I have found that people get along when they want to. They forgive and move on. If they are stuck in their anger and revenge, that's when they harbor all the resentments and the children become pawns in the ex-chess match. However, if you approach each other with CARE, which means honest **C**ommunication, **A**cceptance, **R**espect, and **E**mpathy in the name of your children, the tables eventually turn. I've seen it thousands of times. And, I have to say it, it's not difficult to disagree with your ex. To learn to work together in the name of your children, that's an accomplishment and something to be proud of.

Putting It All Together: Problem Solving With Your Co-Parent

I understand how using the CARE mindset will be helpful when problem solving, but walk me through the steps to truly problem solve with someone I must get along with, but we clash every time we speak . . .

Approach It Like a Business Meeting
When in business, you try to stay away from emotional outbursts because when you are emotional, you don't think things through before you speak and it's easy to alienate those you are trying to persuade. Unlike dealing with an estranged co-parent, you don't just call up a co-worker and drop a bomb in their lap. Depending on the established company protocol, you make an appointment and prepare a presentation. You have a plan.

Have a Plan in Place BEFORE There Is a Problem!
A key element to being successful is being prepared and having a productive way to address problems should they arise.

For example, back to a business model. All companies, big or small, have a plan in place to file grievances. This plan is mentioned when you are hired. If it's a small company, you are usually instructed to go to the owner of the company for help. On a larger scale, you might approach HR, file a grievance, and then go through the established protocol to solve the problem, but the key here is there is a plan in place to manage a grievance before there is ever a grievance filed.

I can't tell you in how many co-parenting sessions I have asked parents, "What do you do when you don't agree?" and they look at me like I'm crazy. There is no plan. They problem solve now exactly the way they did when they were together, and we all know how effective that was. Usually, they argue or give each other ultimatums until one gives up, or they are both exhausted and do what they want to do. But that approach breeds contempt and does not lay the groundwork for problem solving together in the future.

Co-parents must anticipate problems and have a go-to plan in place to manage grievances before there are grievances. Then, it's not the end of the world if there is a problem. They know exactly how to handle it, remembering to incorporate the CARE mindset in their approach.

This Is How You Call the Meeting . . .

Notice that it takes a business meeting approach:

1. Make a formal appointment. *How about Sunday afternoon around 3:00 p.m.?*

2. Pick a neutral place, never at either of your homes where it can be perceived as your personal territory. That gives you the home advantage, and it will feel as if you control the meeting. Meet at a restaurant, coffee shop, a place where there are lots of people. People tend to hold their temper in public places.

3. No alcohol or other mind-altering substances while at the meeting and don't have a drink before you go "just to relax." You may not be too drunk to drive, but even one drink may change your attitude and make you less willing to compromise—or more willing to compromise than you might be if you had stayed sober.

4. Be prepared. Have a solution ready and make suggestions that will really solve the problem. Not just "I want suggestions." Demonstrate that you have truly considered what is best for your child. Then ask your co-parent their opinion. Listen and honestly consider their ideas. Ask yourselves, "Is this solution child-focused?"

5. Tackle one subject at a time. If you are trying to decide who will pay for soccer or cheerleading extras, do not bring up missed visitation or child support. Concentrate on one thing at a time. Next meeting, next problem.

6. Bring a picture of the child and put it right in the middle of the table so that both of you can see it. Each time you feel like you are going to lose your temper or go off-topic, look at the picture. That will remind you why you are there.

7. Write your agreement down, both sign and date it, and make two copies. Or take a picture of the written agreement with your phone so that each has a copy. Sound like overkill? It's not. Warring parents often get angry and change their minds or deny the agreement was ever made. Taking the time to write it down assigns importance to the agreement and is a mutual acknowledgment that you both have discussed and agreed upon a course of action. Now, you have truly put your child first.

8. Do not let your emotions get the best of you. I refer you again to #6.

Come to the Table With a Solution

I tell the following story at every seminar I teach because the lesson learned is so important to successful negotiation.

I've had two careers. Years ago, prior to becoming a child custody mediator and working in the court system, I was a sales representative for a marketing firm. I had a problem in my territory that became so severe I felt compelled to reach out to the vice president of sales for direction. He accepted the meeting, and when I walked into his office, he could tell I was upset. I explained the problem, and he agreed something had to be done. What he told me next is something that I have used as a guide in every co-parenting mediation I have performed.

"You know your territory better than anyone. You know what needs to be done to fix the problem. Next time you have a problem, come to me with a solution as well. Then we have a place to start to negotiate. We can compare points of view and compromise, if necessary, to get to the desired result."

When you bring a problem to your co-parent, bring a suggested solution as well.

How to Conduct the Meeting

You've called the meeting, but how do you approach a problem without the conversation spinning out of control? Below is a very simple model that, if followed, will ensure co-parents stay focused on finding a solution.

Bonus Family Problem Solving Model

Step 1: Identify the problem

Step 2: Suggest a *child-focused* solution

Step 3: Negotiate

Step 4: Compromise

Plus, remembering to use CARE will ensure a positive final outcome.

Example:

Elena and Frank have a 12-year-old son, Antonio. His class is going to science camp and Elena is afraid it is too expensive for him to attend, but if he does not go, he will not pass science.

Plus, all his friends are going and that's all the kids can talk about. Money is tight and Elena would like to ask Frank for help, but Elena and Frank cannot talk to each other without it turning into an argument. Elena's hours have recently been reduced. Frank has recently been laid off but he has an interview soon.

Let's compare approaches:

Approach 1:

Elena: Antonio wants to go to science camp with his class. It's in a month and they need a deposit NOW!

Frank: Hey! You know I was just laid off. I pay child support. Use that.

Elena: You lost another job? How many does that make? Child support is for food, Frank! Everything is not my responsibility! This is extra!

Frank: They can't flunk him if he doesn't go. The answer is "no"!

Elena: You are such a flake, Frank. You can't keep a job and your kid needs to go to science camp!

Approach 2: Bonus Family Problem Solving Model Using CARE

Elena: Antonio wants to go to science camp with his class. It is in a month, and they need a deposit by next Friday.

Frank: You know I was just laid off. I pay child support. Use that.

Elena: I can only imagine how concerned you are about money, Frank, but you always land on your feet. My hours were cut, as well.

Frank: Really? I didn't know. I do have an interview next week and I should be making quite a bit more money than this last job.

Frank paused here and thought for a moment. Elena did her best to wait for his reply.

Frank: Do you think there are scholarships available for people out of work?

Elena: I'm not sure, but that's a good idea. I can certainly ask. If they do, let's try to go with that, but if there are no scholarships, would you split the cost with me?

Frank: I can afford half. But please check the scholarship angle first and if the answer is no, would it be possible to give it to you next week when I get my unemployment check?

Elena: Of course. Thank you for your help, Frank.

It is understood that Approach 2 was more effective because Elena followed the Bonus Family Problem Solving Model to a T, all the while using CARE in her approach.

Step 1: Identify the problem (Antonio wants to go to science camp).

Step 2: Suggest a child-focused solution (split the cost).

Step 3: Negotiate (Frank suggested inquiring about a scholarship program. Elena thought that was a good idea and consented to check into it. Elena also suggested splitting the cost).

Step 4: Compromise (agreed to wait for an answer about the availability of a scholarship and agreed to split the cost. A further compromise was allowing Frank a little extra time to pay his half if needed.)

A vital part of this negotiation is that Elena approached Frank with CARE.

Communication: She explained her thoughts carefully without losing her temper. She was direct in her requests and listened to Frank's responses before replying.

Acceptance: She accepted the situation and did not belittle Frank about his job loss.

Respect: "You always land on your feet" was a direct way of letting Frank know that she respected him and had confidence in his abilities.

Empathy: She put herself in Frank's shoes. "I can only imagine. . . ." She acknowledged that she knows he is trying hard to find another job. She offered a solution that appealed to Frank's better nature and led to a compromise.

Language to Avoid During a Discussion: "Never," "Always," and "Liar"

One of the components of effective communication—the C in the CARE acronym—is word choice.

Three words that will ensure your negotiation will go off track when discussions get heated are "never," "always," and calling someone a "liar." When these words are used in a conversation, it's easy to go off-subject and find yourself arguing about what was said, not looking for solutions.

For example, let's look at a conversation using words like "always" and "never." We will again use the Elena/Frank scenario to prove this point.

Elena: Antonio would like to go to science camp.

Frank: He doesn't have to go. You act like this is life and death.

Now consider the next sentence and think about how you feel when it is said.

Elena: You *always* say something like that!

Imagine how you would feel when you heard that response.
Would you be ready to agree or disagree? Most likely, your
response will be, "I do not!" So, Frank's response is then . . .

Frank: I do not!

And, Elena, responding to Frank's response, says . . .

Elena: Yes, you do! You *never* want to help, and Antonio is
the one who suffers.

Elena has now hit below the belt. Because she didn't get what
she wanted, she used Antonio as a way to hurt his father. But the
biggest problem here is that both Elena and Frank have lost sight
of the original issue—help with funding science camp—and they
are now arguing about how they argue, what was said, and who is
wrong. Lost in a sea of "you always" and "you never," no one even
remembers what the original disagreement was about.

"Liar" or "You're Lying!"

In the movie *Something's Gotta Give*, Jack Nicholson's character
says, "I have never lied to you. I have always told you some version of the truth." Diane Keaton's character responds, "There are
no versions of the truth, okay?" There may not be "versions of the
truth," but one's perspective certainly affects what is regarded as
truth. And when co-parents don't agree, one often accuses the
other of lying. This rarely ends well.

It's All About Perspective

This is a really important point for all co-parents to consider. A
different perspective of what is being reported does not mean you
are lying.

Envision you are playing tennis, and the ball falls near the
line. From where you stand, the ball looks in, and you start to celebrate, but from where the referee is standing, the ball is out and
that's how he calls it. End of celebration. Are you lying? Is the ref
lying? The call was determined by where someone was standing

when the ball hit the ground. Their perspective is simply different than yours.

Let's take this one step further. Your co-parent tells a story, explaining each step as they saw it. At the end of the story, you exclaim very loudly, "What? That is not the way it happened! You are lying!"

Are they, or is it a different perspective?

Telling your co-parent they are lying or calling them a liar will not get you the results you want. They will automatically feel as if they must defend themselves from what they feel are your false accusations. The discussion then accelerates into an argument, not about the subject you want to discuss, but of an accounting of what was said as the argument progressed. You can't problem solve when you are more concerned about defending your position than looking for solutions.

Seeing a situation differently does not necessarily mean your co-parent is lying. Two eyewitnesses to an accident standing in two different places have been known to report two different things. That means even eyewitness accounts may not be accurate. Plus, recent studies prove that our memory is quite creative. Most embellish each time the memory is retold. They add or subtract information that will enhance the story—ultimately, the memory changes with the retelling.

Finally, it's important to remember that this will not be your last conversation with your co-parent. Stay away from inflammatory statements that will prevent either of you from being open to discussing something down the road. "That's not how I remember it," or even something more direct like "I don't think that is the truth," is easier to hear than "You are such a liar!" If you feel your co-parent is not being truthful, try to explain your point of view without attacking theirs.

Clarifying the Truth

My child would never lie to me. Parents do not like my reply when they say that to me because I tell them a truth they do not want to hear: "If your child hasn't lied to you, he's the only child who hasn't lied to his parents in the entire world since the beginning of time."

They continue with their explanation. "I have a very good relationship with my child, and they just wouldn't lie to me. There is no reason to."

"So, you think their other parent really fed their child peanut butter when they know they are allergic?"

"Well, no. But that's what Brucey said. He came home with hives all over his tummy. When I asked him what happened, he said, 'Daddy fed me peanut butter.'"

"And you called CPS. What do you think really happened?" I asked.

The father chimed in. "He snuck peanut butter from the pantry, Delia. He's 5 years old."

"Why would he lie to me?" asked Mom.

"Because he is afraid he will get in trouble," I answered. "And so he blamed it on his father, and you believed him."

"Next time," I explained to them, "make sure you call the other parent for clarification before you blame them for a mishap." Children simply process information differently and may pass on things that are completely incorrect. They take a little of this truth and a little of that and make up a story that sounds plausible. A doubting co-parent takes the information and runs with it without clarifying if the story is true. This just perpetuates resentment and distrust between co-parents.

There is also another more effective approach to clarifying the truth when incorrect information is passed between homes.

Using I Messages

A better response? Explain how you are *feeling* in the first person without blaming how you are feeling on the person to whom you are talking. This is called using "I messages."

So, rather than Elena saying, "You *always* say that!" she begins the sentence with "I feel." It's important to note, however, that if you follow "I feel" with words like "that," "like," or "as if," you are expressing your opinion or what *you* believe, but most of all, you are blaming the other person for how you feel. Do that and you will ignite yet another argument.

For example, Elena might say, "Frank, I feel like you don't appreciate anything I do." (Blaming Frank for how she feels.)

Using an I message, she would say, "Frank, I feel unappreciated when my efforts go unnoticed." (An expression of a feeling and explaining why without referencing Frank.)

Frank will then respond to *that* and not become defensive because he was blamed for not appreciating her efforts.

There are phrases we commonly use that mimic "you always" or "you never," and you will get the same negative responses. Reactions like "You do that a lot, you know?" mimics "you always." Be on the lookout whenever you start a sentence with "You" as it will most likely be an accusation or blame and it won't be received well.

"Would" and "Could"

I try to communicate. I really try, but no matter what I say, my co-parent doesn't understand, and it turns into a huge fight.

There may be a good reason. Another word choice that also complicates communication is "would" and "could." Choosing one or the other makes or breaks a negotiation. The definition of "would" is a polite request. "Could," by contrast, indicates a possibility.

If your co-parent says, "I have to work late, *could* you please pick up Michael after school?" they are asking for help, but the way they are asking implies, "Is it possible for you to pick up Michael?" That request will be met with a discussion of whether or not it is possible. "Well, I have to pick up the dry cleaning and I just got a call that my glasses are ready to be picked up at Walmart . . . " Your co-parent may eventually get to yes, but not until he or she has made it clear to you that you are putting them out. After listening and getting aggravated, a common response is then, "Don't worry about it. I will figure it out." But you are resentful because you made yourself vulnerable, asked for help, and just got excuses.

All that simply because of the word you chose to initiate your request.

On the other hand, if your co-parent says, "I have to work late; *would* you please pick up Michael after school?" they are asking for help. By using the word "would," they are making a polite request. You subconsciously hear, "Please help me," and your answer will more likely be, "Of course," rather than offer excuses.

Words That Help Clarify the Truth
Let me give you a little background to the following story so you can see how easily the solution can be applied.

Jeremy's parents had a rocky relationship and an even rockier breakup. Jeremy is a 4-year-old and goes back and forth between his divorced parents' homes. Once Jeremy's dad moved out, he moved on quickly. He met Nancy and they had an instant connection. It is my experience that most estranged couples try it one more time after a separation, and that's exactly what Jeremy's mother tried to do, but Jeremy's father was in love with Nancy and had no interest in trying it again. When Jeremy asked his mother why Mommy and Daddy no longer lived together, Jeremy's mother angrily screamed, "Because of Nancy!" In her mind, if there were no Nancy, she would have already been back with

Jeremy's father. Of course, Nancy had nothing to do with the split, but that's how Jeremy's mother felt. When Jeremy returned to his father's home, he walked in and announced, "Mommy said you don't love us anymore. She said you aren't married anymore because of Nancy! I hate Nancy!"

Jeremy's mother's bad-mouthing had taken on a life of its own. It affected Jeremy's relationship with his father and with Nancy, all based on a significant untruth.

My favorite response when faced with something like this is to use the word "mistaken" in your explanation. Responding with the word "mistaken" clarifies the truth without blame or fault.

For example, first state that the person passing on the information is mistaken: "Jeremy, your mommy is mistaken."

Then state whatever is true: "I lived here in this new house all by myself for 4 months. Then I met Nancy. Nancy had nothing to do with Mommy and I breaking up. I love you very much, Jeremy, and so does Mommy."

Giving Up Your Parental Power

Guilt propels many divorced parents and because they don't want to be at the root of any decisions that have hurt their children, they may blame others for decisions that upset the child.

For instance, let's say the parenting plan says that the child is with parent A on Monday and Tuesday but must return to Parent B on Wednesday. However, the child tells Parent A he does not want to return to Parent B's home. Because Parent A does not want to fight with the child or be responsible for hurting the child any further, they say, "You have to go back, or your mother (or father) will take me back to court." Or "I'm sorry, honey, but the judge says you have to go back."

Basically, both comments give up parental power and make someone else responsible for your child's dilemma. Children look up to their parents as the ultimate authority. They want to depend on their parents to take care of them and make the right decisions for them. Blaming their other parent or telling your child that it was someone else's decision undermines your own parental authority. It says, "I have no control and cannot protect you." Your children will begin to question your reasoning and flounder just as you are floundering by not standing strong.

You can use CARE with not only your co-parent but your child, as well.

Communication: Let your child know where you stand using active listening, curiosity, tact, and timing, and building trust by remaining transparent. "Honey, I'm curious why you feel that way. This is your time with your father/mother. Is there a reason I should know why you don't want to go?"

Acceptance: Accept that your child is a child and is capable of twisting the truth, perhaps on purpose, but more likely because they do not understand the situation or the consequence of their actions. Young children simply cannot process complicated emotional occurrences and may not pass on information accurately.

Respect: Respect your child enough to be honest with them. However, weigh how much information is needed to both soothe and keep your child informed. In the case above, the correct response would be, "This is your time with your mother/father. She/he loves you." Now you have respected both your child and your co-parent.

Empathy: Before deciding pro or con, put yourself in your child's shoes and approach the concern from what you see as their point of view. What will truly make an impact? Arbitrary discipline or discussion with the appropriate follow-up? It's all about approach and if you CARE.

How Friendly Is Too Friendly?

Not everyone can take constant interaction with a co-parent. Merely staying cordial enough to answer a question promptly may be all that is needed. You do not have to be buddies. In fact, being buddies can work against you.

The breakup has [been] hard on the kids, so her mother and I thought continuing to spend time as a family might help. We meet each Saturday or Sunday for pizza or a movie in the hopes it might make the transition easier. Yesterday, my 10-year-old asked when her mom and I were getting back together. We are careful not to be too friendly, so I don't know what gave my daughter that impression. She got terribly upset when I told her I didn't think it was ever going to happen.

— FEDERICO, 44, FATHER TO JENNY, AGE 10

It's quite common for parents to start spending time as a family as an attempt to make the transition easier on their children. However, prior to a breakup, parents are often estranged. They have evolved into rarely spending time together as a family. They may try, but it is often racked with tension, and slowly, the time as a family diminishes to spending time separately with the kids. Then the parents break up, and suddenly their goal becomes spending time together as a family? If a regularly scheduled pizza night is added after a breakup, the family is now spending more time together after the breakup than they did when the parents lived together. It is no wonder their children see reconciliation as a possibility. One can only imagine how confusing it might be if parents are friendly immediately after a breakup after years of being angry with each other.

Right after our breakup my ex and I could see our son was having trouble with the transition, so we decided to spend a day together at the zoo, just like we used to. I was holding hands with my son. As we reached the monkey hill he very matter-of-factly said, "Daddy, hold Mommy's hand, too." I didn't know what to do, so I held Mommy's hand. We both felt extremely uncomfortable.

— JOHN, 37, FATHER TO MICHA, AGE 4

"Just like we used to" implies nothing has changed. But something has changed in a big way! Mom and Dad don't live together anymore. It helps children to know that their parents don't hate each other, but open displays of affection aren't necessary to prove this. Too much time together or joking or even a casual hug that lasts a little too long at a child exchange can prove to be counter-productive, giving children false hope of reconciliation. The goal is to offer a comfortable interaction when the kids are around so that they feel safe and secure in their parents' presence. It doesn't matter how old your kids are. All children, no matter their age, need dependable interaction from their parents.

The key word here is "dependable." Breaking up is chaotic. It adds uncertainty to everyone's lives. Children need to be able to trust their parents' actions. They need to be able to relax with the feeling that their parents run the show and will make good decisions for them. If spending time together as a family after a breakup is in the cards, allow it to evolve naturally once the dust has settled—and even then, be careful not to send mixed messages. The task before us as co-parents is to find that happy medium where all can be respected, and we can comfortably co-exist . . . using CARE as our co-parenting mantra.

LIFE AFTER YOUR BREAKUP

Now it's time to import what you've learned in this chapter into creating your life after your breakup. Hopefully, the groundwork has been laid to work together as a team in the name of your children. We will continue the journey in the next chapter by discussing meeting a new partner and then moving through the process of moving in together and ultimately combining your families. However, there are a few more steps before we get to actually living as a bonus family. Dating is next . . .

Bonus Dating and Integrating Someone New

ALTHOUGH IT SOUNDS A LITTLE ABSURD, ONE OF THE FIRST HUR-
dles co-parents must face together is that of dating other people
after the breakup. The difference with the bonus family approach
to dating and combining families is that dating, like everything
else, is based on collaboration and cooperation where co-parents come to agreement about their approach to dating after the
breakup.

The primary hurdle in the bonus family approach to dating
is accepting that your co-parent is not your enemy but an ally.
You both have an investment in creating a happy life now that
you have decided to split—but more importantly, a happy life for
your children. This is a tough one when you are angry, resentful,
or hurt—collaboration and cooperation are not on your radar,
particularly when it comes to meeting someone new.

DATING, BONUS STYLE

Most of the advice available on dating after a breakup starts
with meeting someone new about whom you are serious. Then
introducing the children is discussed and it progresses from that
point. But that's starting the process in the middle. It's likely that
you will date a few people before you get a sense of who you are

now that you are single, and who will best complement you and your children in the future. Dating, bonus style, asks you to have a clear intention for how you will get to meeting your new serious someone—in full communication with your child's other parent. It is an organized approach with a new attitude, rooted in transparency and honesty. You are no longer a couple, but you still have children to raise and there should be no secrets that will impact those children.

You must remember, this will be the children's first glimpse of their parents as single people. They have already watched you fight. They were there for the breakup. How you and your co-parent approach the transition to dating and settling down with someone new will impact your children for the rest of their lives.

HELPING YOUR CHILDREN THROUGH YOUR TRANSITION TO DATING

Parents harbor a lot of guilt about their breakup. Intellectually, they know what the breakup has done to their children, and they try in every way possible to beat the odds and have their kids rise unscathed from the chaos. Most parents have good intentions, but when called out, particularly by their children, they tend to respond defensively. So, when a child confides their anger or disappointment to their parent, the parent often attempts to defend themselves by saying, "Come on! It didn't happen that way!" or "Be serious. It wasn't that bad." And that response does not offer credibility to anything the child said. Without knowing it, the parent diminished the child's feelings and point of view. If that happens enough, the child will stop talking. They don't feel heard. *Nothing I say matters, anyway.* Without knowing it, the parent has squashed any chance to help their child because they were too busy defending themselves.

C is for Communication

For example:

Child: "I don't feel like I'm your daughter when you are with Julia [new partner]. You get to live with her kids."

Father: "That's not true! I'm always fighting for more time with you."

The child starts to cry.

Father: "I'll just take you home. Is that what you want?"

Now the child is sobbing. She doesn't want to go "home." She wanted her dad to hear that she didn't feel loved. But, instead, he's taking her back to her mother's which just reinforces the fact that she feels like an outsider when she is with him.

This exchange is not exclusive to dating dads and daughters. A parent must read between the lines when a child offers this sort of information. What the father meant, of course, is that he loves his daughter. The "that's not true" was from his perspective and was supposed to put her at ease. But what she heard was, *what you are saying* is not true. So, it diminished some very important feelings. Truly, all the child wanted to hear from her father was reassurance that she was special to him and that he loved her. He responded by defending his actions instead of responding to her needs.

The father's answer also bad-mouthed Mom without his knowing it. It implied that he has to fight her for more time with his daughter. She was the bad guy, not him. Now the daughter has even more on her plate when all she was telling Dad was that she felt overlooked when his new girlfriend and children were around.

A simple, "I love you very much, Ava. I always will. I have been looking forward to this time with you" would have eased the child's insecurity and allowed more opportunities for clarification in the future.

It doesn't matter if it didn't happen the way the child described. It doesn't matter if whatever they describe was not your intent. What you are trying to do is create an environment where your child feels comfortable talking and expressing how they feel. If you argue with them about their feelings, they will stop talking—and it will be because you did not listen.

A Is for Acceptance and R Is for Respect

Bill and Marcy have been dating for 5 months and recently decided to exclusively date. Bill has three boys, ages 6, 9, and 11. Marcy also has boys ages 9 and 11. The fact that they both had children almost the exact same age was not a concern when they first met. They were both so excited to meet someone to whom they were attracted. The end of their marriages was vastly different. Bill's wife had passed due to breast cancer and Marcy's husband had been unfaithful. The kids knew everything about everything, but they did not approach the end of their parent's marriage in the same way. Bill's oldest son struggled with his coping skills and would often have emotional tantrums. Marcy's 11-year-old was happy-go-lucky for the most part. There were times when he was sad about the breakup, but he still spent time with his father. Bill and Marcy often found themselves comparing the boys, with Marcy losing patience with Bill's oldest son's sometimes sullen demeanor. It got to the point that she didn't want to be around him and started to decline invitations to go places with the boys.

We all have different backgrounds and histories. Accepting that and respecting what each has gone through prior to your meeting will allow you to be sensitive to the differences. I'm not saying to sit in the past or coddle children. I've already made it clear how I believe dwelling in the past will affect your relationships in the present. But don't compare children, either. Don't expect them to react the same, look the same, get the same grades, or dress the same. Accept them for who they are. Respect them as individuals with their own successes and failures. See them as individuals, not cookie-cutter copies of what you believe all children should act like, and your relationship with them will flourish.

Compare, and you will find yourself in Marcy's position, contributing to an even bigger problem than ever anticipated.

For instance, if Bill's oldest son were developing an attachment to Marcy, her pulling away at this point in his dealing with his mother's death could really set him back. If she is committed to Bill, a better tactic would be to learn as much as she could about helping a child deal with the death of a parent—even before she met the kids. Since Marcy's children were aware of their father's infidelity, Bill might learn as much as he can about reinforcing loving trust and predictability.

"All this after dating only 5 months?" you might ask. "They aren't even sure if this is something they truly want to explore."

Our children's lives do not stop while we adults try to figure it all out. That means sometimes we will have to take it slower than we would like or be less spontaneous than we would like. That's just the way it is, in the best interest of our children.

E is for Empathy

In Harper Lee's *To Kill a Mockingbird*, Atticus Finch says the iconic line, "You never really understand a person until you consider things from his point of view . . . until you climb into his skin and walk around in it." Here, Atticus is explaining that empathy is the key to understanding others. Empathy asks us to "walk a mile in their shoes." So, now let's look at the breakup from your child's point of view. E is for Empathy.

One of their parents has most likely moved out of the family home. The child may have moved with them. That means your child could have a new room or have to go to another school. They may have to make new friends. If you have stayed in your "old" home and they stayed with you, rooms will look different. Pictures will be gone. The dog may be gone. Although you know intellectually that your life will change and probably want it to be so, your kids have no idea what to expect. They yearn for stability and pray things will soon return to the way they were. But everything is different. This separation has turned their life upside down—and it was their parents' choice, not theirs.

As a result, just about every child I have worked with, short of a child who has suffered severe neglect or abuse, has confided that they hope someday their parents will get back together. Doesn't matter their age, I've heard it from 3-year-olds to 43-year-olds, it's always in the back of their mind. Most, in some way or another, blame themselves for the breakup. "If I was a better kid, they wouldn't have fought so much—and then they would still be together." So, no matter how unhappy you were in your prior relationship, no matter what a poor choice you think your co-parent was for a partner, your children love their mommy *and* daddy and will still hold out for the fact that one or both parents will see the error of their ways, reconcile, and everything will be okay. Actually, better than okay. It will be time for celebration.

What can you do?

Parents worry about their children, and if they can afford it, many want to send them to therapy as soon as possible. But sometimes those facing a breakup—particularly children—need some time for the emotional dust to settle. Even though a therapist may be able to offer counsel, don't be surprised if your children cannot formulate how they feel for a while. Like everything else, they will look to their parents for direction. With that in mind, here's a suggestion I've been making for years—*if you go to therapy, your children won't need it.*

Of course, that is said for impact. There is no guarantee that when parents attend therapy their children won't need it as well. But, when children whose parents are at odds go to therapy, what do you think they talk to the therapist about? Their parents' fighting. Their parents' being cruel to each other. Their parents' new family. Their parents' drinking or mental health. Their parents' problems become theirs. That's why I say if the parents attend therapy and become proactive in addressing their issues, their children may not need to attend. By attending therapy, parents are assertively confronting the problems that are ultimately affecting their children.

In the present, if you want to help, be on the lookout for a change in mood or attitude around family milestones, like holidays or birthdays. Parents can minimize the flare-ups, or at least reduce their intensity, if they do their best to keep each other informed when they see their children struggling. Then together the co-parents can discuss and come to agreement for what is the best approach for their child.

Two Parents, Two Homes, No Secrets

Because you most likely have joint custody and share the children's time, both parents must accept that their children now have two homes. Not one real home and another that they visit, but two homes that are equally important to them. Your children will naturally share what goes on at the other home with both of their parents. That means, if you are dating, your children will pass it on.

My ex and I broke up 3 years ago. I have been dating when the kids are with their father, never mentioning anyone because I've never been serious until now. I would like to date someone. Actually, more than exclusively. We are planning a life together. My kids are young, 6 and 9, and know him as a friend. He has been at our home for dinner quite a few times over the last 6 months, but my co-parent has no idea I'm seeing someone. I'm trying to get the timing right. Who do I tell first that we are a couple? The kids or their dad?

If this mom's children have kept it a secret that her boyfriend has been to dinner quite a few times, they are the only ones I have met that don't pass on information to their other home—unless they have been instructed not to say anything and that's a problem. Don't be one of those parents who says, "What goes on here, stays here." Abusers tell children not to tell, and if you are telling your kids to keep a secret from their other parent, you are asking them to choose you over their mom or dad. Just remember, although your kids stay at your home half the time, maybe more, maybe less, their life doesn't stop when they leave your side. It continues at the other home and when they talk about what happened at Mommy's or Daddy's house, they are talking about *their* life. Not yours.

Your Dating Ground Rules: Things on Which You Must Agree

How long after the breakup before each of us starts to date?

It's not the length of time prior to dating, but how forthcoming you are with your co-parent and how you portray dating to the children.

I don't really want to talk to my ex about my dating.

This can be a difficult conversation, especially if one co-parent continues to have feelings for the other. But dating is inevitable after a breakup, and the way you manage it is important to your children's emotional and mental health. It is hoped that coming to an agreement about your dating approach will reduce conflict because you will then both know what to expect. There will be no surprises.

How open should we be with the kids about our dating other people?

Professionals caution parents about involving their children in their dating lives. You often hear, "Don't introduce the children until you know it is a serious relationship." The thought behind this is that serious relationships last longer than casual dates. Children crave consistency, and if they become attached to a date who quickly moves on, each time there is a breakup they will feel as if they are facing another life-changing split. The psychological impact of introducing multiple partners to your children has been documented in countless studies. While you are attempting to move on, your children may still be in mourning and need your calm understanding to guide them through the emotional upheaval of your breakup. This is an important distinction. Just because you are ready to move on does not mean your children are ready.

In the early stages after a breakup, it's not uncommon for children to take it personally if you choose to spend time with someone other than their parent. So, when you know you are serious about someone, that's when you say something to the children. Before that, it's not necessary to mention dating at all. Most parenting plans offer parents enough alone time to socialize when the children are with the other parent. That's when you date.

You have the kids around Jenny. It's too soon!

Age and emotional development have a lot to do with how well your children accept someone new. Each child is different. Some may be able to accept a new partner sooner than others. Be careful not to push *your* dating agenda on your children. If you broke up with their other parent 6 months ago, have been dating someone for 3 months and decide that this is the new love of your life, that is moving faster than most children can process. It will sabotage your children's relationship with both you and your new partner if you move too fast.

As a personal story to pass on, my own father died when I was 36. He was 12 years older than my mother, who was in her early 60s at the time of his passing. About a year and a half after my dad died, I dropped by my mother's home to say hi and I walked in on her embracing her new guy in the kitchen. He was a lovely man and she had mentioned that she was dating someone, but I had no idea it was serious, and I was thrown. I was 38 at the time and she had checked in with me to get my opinion of her dating. I was supportive and told my mother that I wanted her to be happy and she should get out there and meet someone new. But when it happened, I wasn't prepared. Can you imagine how a young child might feel if their parents move too fast? A year and a half after a breakup is certainly not too fast to begin seeing someone new, but it's the feelings I felt that I am trying to call to parents' attention. In my case, I dropped by without warning, and that was on me, but this story clearly demonstrates that parents must take note of how they portray their dating to their children . . . no matter how old their children are.

Conscious Dating

Conscious dating is being mindful about the kind of partner you're looking for and intentionally setting boundaries to ensure your needs and the needs of your children will be met. As a parent, even though meeting someone new can be intoxicating, you still have to keep your wits about you. The goal in conscious dating is to approach dating honestly—with yourself, your potential new partner, and your co-parent—so that all know what to expect and you can then reinforce respectful co-parenting boundaries.

Establishing Conscious Dating Boundaries

Conscious dating boundaries are your personal deal breakers that will just not work for you this time around. They can be anything from personality traits to lifestyle preferences.

To zero in on what you are looking for, I often suggest clients make a Conscious Dating List. Take out a piece of paper and draw a line down the center vertically. On one side, list your desire. On the other side, list the reason. This will help you think it through and analyze your deal breakers.

One of my clients, Suzanne, allowed me to include her Conscious Dating List as an example. It includes her personal boundaries, plus other desires compiled from her experiences. Suzanne was 42 years old at the time she made this list. She had been married for 10 years and had two children, ages 6 and 8. Her co-parent struggled with addiction, and her oldest child was diagnosed on the autism spectrum and occasionally had emotional meltdowns. Remember, these lists are individual and personal. Yours may not look anything like this, but most who have children and are dating will identify with at least some of her boundary points.

Desires	Reasons
1. They have to have a job.	I don't want to support someone. I want a partner with ambition.
2. They must have had children.	Because then they know a love bigger than themselves and can easily put somebody else's happiness firmly before their own.
3. They are tolerant of my children's struggles.	My son has ASD and occasionally has meltdowns. My partner must be patient and not judge him.
4. They don't have room-mates.	I'd feel like I was in college if I stayed over.
5. They are a problem solver and look for solutions, not arguments.	I will not date someone who argues for the sake of arguing. Been there, done that.
6. They get my jokes.	Laughing together is important.
7. They live a healthy lifestyle and feel staying in shape is important.	I like to be outside in fresh air and I want to experience that with my partner. I am attracted to people with fit bodies.
8. They are an occasional drinker, but not into marijuana.	Co-parent is a recovering alcoholic, and I do not want to take that on again. I'd prefer not to have pot around my children.

As Suzanne dated different people, she reported that she saw a major difference in attitude between those who had children and those who had never had children. She felt those who had never had children understood her parenting responsibilities intellectually, but when it came to putting that understanding into practice, they expected her to choose them over the needs of her kids.

Dating Red Flags

I told him I had to get home; I have a babysitter. He said, "You're choosing your children over me?" That was a red flag and I knew he wasn't the right person for me.

You know a red flag when you see one. They are indicators of concern and are warning signs of unhealthy behaviors in potential partners that do not mesh with your lifestyle. Many don't see red flags at first, or don't heed the signs, but the red flags below are common to those trying to combine families and parents should take note before moving forward.

Partner Says He Can't Accept My Child

I'm divorced and have a 6-year-old daughter. My daughter's father isn't in her life. My boyfriend of 2 years has a very difficult time embracing my daughter. He's told me that it's not my daughter; it's the fact that I have had a child with someone else. He admits that it's his ego preventing him from getting close to her. I believe I love him, but that little voice inside my head says, "Get out quick!" Do you have any suggestions?

If you are in a relationship with someone who has a problem with your child purely because you "have had a child with someone else," then you are setting yourself up for relationship failure—and you are really putting your child in a terrible position. Nothing your child could ever do will prompt this person to accept them. Consider the psychological and emotional impact this could have on a child. All their life they would be struggling for acceptance from the only father figure they know—and the only reason they are not accepted is because they are someone else's child.

Can you imagine the future family dynamic if this couple had a child together? Speculating, the new child would be openly accepted by the father while the older child continues to be disregarded. As bonus parents, we become role models and care for children who are not ours and never will be. We can build a child's self-esteem or quickly tear it down. That's why, in the best interest of our children, it is so important for parents to seriously consider the impact a new partner will have on their child before they make the commitment to date, let alone marry or move in together.

New Partner Is Rude to Co-Parent

> *My children's mother and I get along quite well, considering, and we have settled into a predictable routine. My new person loves my kids, and they love her, but she is rude to their mother, and it makes co-parenting difficult. Under the circumstances, I'm wondering if I should let this relationship get any more involved.*

Good question. This father is being mindful of the red flag he sees.

There are multiple reasons why a new partner could be less than polite to your co-parent, and you may be contributing to it without even knowing it. Let's examine what might be the root cause and then we will know the appropriate action to take.

First thing to ask yourself: Are you too close to your co-parent? Things like having flirty conversations about something other than the children or reminiscing about days gone by when you think the new date/partner's not listening all set the stage for distrust. Distrust in a potential partner looks like an angry, jealous, or moody person, and they lash out at the person they see as being the problem. This may be you at times or your co-parent at other times.

Second, children are extremely protective and territorial of their parents. If a bonus parent treats a parent poorly, it is sure to alienate the child. Parents notice when their children shy away from a bonus parent and question whether their date is the right person to add to the family. This is reinforced by the writer's observation: *Under the circumstances, I'm wondering if I should let this relationship get any more involved.*

Third, if you know it's not your behavior that is sparking the jealous reaction in a partner, and this is someone you still want to spend time with, then addressing the situation together is the answer. It could be that this new partner is simply holding an old-school breakup attitude and feels when a couple breaks up, that's the end of the relationship. If you want to continue, it's because you continue to be interested. In other words, the new partner sees the co-parents as former lovers, not parents of the same child and just doesn't realize how important it is for co-parents to stay cordial in the name of their children. Co-parents must be clear with their intent and establish strict boundaries to successfully bring a new partner on board.

Ultimately, if you can see that your date cannot adjust to your relationship with your co-parent, take note. A new partner must be cautious about imposing their views on co-parents who already have a healthy well-established co-parenting relationship in place. If co-parents are doing well problem solving together, exchanging the children without incident, and attending their children's milestones and special events, a new partner must be respectful and support their efforts. They can't let their insecurity or jealousy dictate a new policy. That's when a co-parent may feel as if they must choose—and, if forced to choose, most will not choose the new partner.

MORE RED FLAGS
When the Children Have Trouble Adjusting to Your Dating

> *I have met a guy with two sons, 3 and 7 years old. The 7-year-old son can't stand that his father and me are together. When we visit each other the boy cries and he just wants to sit with his daddy. We have no time alone. I just can't handle it anymore!!! I have started to hate that boy. I love his father so much, but his father is falling for all his son's nonsense.*

So many red flags—on both the writer's and dad's part. Let's start with the writer. Things cannot always be blamed on a child being spoiled. (I believe that was the implication since she referred to the child's behavior as "nonsense.") Of course that's a possibility, but more likely—and here's Dad's red flag—Dad has not sufficiently addressed the breakup with his child, nor has he properly prepared his child for the possibility of a new relationship.

So often, parents just expect their kids to fall into place. "I like her, so you should like her." *But* parents don't take into consideration how a child perceives a parent moving on. Never mind it's only been months, not years, since the breakup. Change is scary for a child, and with no preparation, it's doubly scary. Plus, to a child, a new partner may mean you don't like Mommy/Daddy best anymore. If you don't like Mommy/Daddy best anymore, there's a possibility you may not like them best someday. This child's actions may not be based in "nonsense" as much as plain unadulterated fear.

To prepare a child for a new relationship, start slow. A couple of hours at first, no displays of affection, then move to day visits going to activities that the kids will enjoy. Overnights are down the road when you decide to make a go of it—again, starting out slowly. Alone time? Most parents in an active relationship will tell you that you have to plan for alone time when you have kids. If you want alone time, get a babysitter. Alone time with kids? I'm laughing just thinking about it.

This is not to say that romance is a thing of the past. A new relationship with kids can be very romantic if you want it to be; you just have to understand that relationships with someone with kids are not like first-time relationships. You can't just drop everything and have sex in the kitchen. Little eyes are watching and personalizing every move you make.

Finally, combining families is hard work. There will be ongoing problems with kids and exes and the usual problems associated with any relationship. A child having trouble with their parent having a new partner is quite normal and only the beginning. If making a go of this relationship is important, the writer and dad must look for ways to make this child feel more secure.

If this is seen as a chore, these two are not right together. Loving your partner is not enough to make a family a bonus family.

Alcohol or Drug Use

> *I like to have a glass of wine with dinner. This was not an issue when my kids' dad and I were living together, but now that I'm single, my children have made it very clear it makes them uncomfortable when I have a glass or two of wine. I don't think one glass of wine is a problem, but I can see it in their eyes when I open a bottle.*

It's not the wine, children tell me; it's how unpredictable their parents act when they have been drinking. The mother in the quote above was talking about wine with dinner. That is different than drinking to excess when you are alone with the children. "I never know what to expect," a 12-year-old client told me. "Sometimes when my dad drinks, he is nice, sometimes he's angry. And when he's angry like that, he doesn't make sense."

"Angry like that." This child is talking about his parent getting angry when he's drunk. It's the unpredictability associated with too much alcohol that makes a child feel uncomfortable. They are afraid they can't depend on their parent to keep them safe. Plus, if you are drinking and there is a medical emergency, you will be unable to drive to urgent care. It's up to us as parents to model moderation and good judgment.

Will my drinking alcohol (or smoking marijuana) affect my custody of the children?

Drinking alcohol is not illegal and smoking marijuana is not illegal in quite a few states with more coming on board every year. However, it may impact your time with your children if you have a history of drug or alcohol abuse and it is documented by DUIs or in CPS reports. These kinds of reports imply the children may be unsafe when they are with you alone. Unsafe can be translated into many things. For example, questionable behavior like angry outbursts that scare the children, neglect, not having a place to live, no water or electricity, domestic violence or throwing things, even witnessing you drink or smoke pot and then get into a car and expect to drive them to soccer practice. The bottom line is not to track adult behavior, it's that if your children are reporting that they do not feel safe, it's your job to adjust your behavior so that they do.

When Your Date Doesn't Like Your Child

I have been dating a man for 4 months now. I have one son. Everything was fine at first but now he seems to really resent my son. When I ask him why, he tells me my son gets on his nerves. He said my son lacks discipline. Mind you, my son is 10 and has never met his biological father. I have been the only one raising him, but he is a good boy. Why does he feel this way towards my son?

That question is the one you should be exploring with your partner. If you are serious enough that you have introduced a new person to your kids, then you should be able to discuss things like this with them. If you feel you can't, it is a red flag that suggests you may be moving too fast and have not yet built the rapport you need with a partner to make them family.

Nevertheless, it's not uncommon for other people's kids to get on our nerves. We perceive that they act entitled, sarcastic, disrespectful, rambunctious, etc. Bottom line, the kids seem spoiled, and that's enough for many to retreat.

Here's another red flag: We all have different personalities, and personality types often run in families. Your family of origin may be agile, great at baseball or football, and physical contact is second nature. You were rewarded for excelling in sports and became an excellent athlete as a result. Your partner may have come from a more academic or musical background where the arts were reinforced. They received positive reinforcement for playing an instrument well or painting a beautiful picture. It is likely that your children follow suit, and when you attempt to combine your families, the differences in personalities don't immediately jell.

If a new partner has only been around children with a calmer demeanor, he may see a boy who is merely spirited as over-the-top. If this seemingly over-the-top little boy doesn't respond quickly to discipline—say it takes two or three times to get him to clear the table because he's distracted by a favorite TV show—now you may have a frustrated new partner mentally counting each time you have to ask your son more than once. That's a dangerous place to be. As the relationship continues, you may find yourself running defense for your child—which will ultimately pit you against your partner. And, I have to say it . . . beware of anyone who tells you that your kid gets on his nerves. Huge R-E-D flag.

Never be afraid to take a stand for your child. Granted, this parent has raised their child alone, could have been too lax and needs to step up. But take note: If you sense a new partner is being judgmental, and you have that conversation before more time is invested, you may realize it just won't work. This is the reason it's best not to introduce our children to our new dates until we know for a fact they are in it for the long haul—and that simply takes a little time.

HOW WILL YOU PRESENT YOUR SEX LIFE TO YOUR CHILDREN?

Fourteen-year-old Lizzy was remarkably close to her mother after her parents split. They had frank conversations about sex and her mother emphasized abstinence. Their relationship grew even closer when Lizzy's dad started to date. Lizzy thought her dad was "disgusting," and told her mother how uncomfortable she felt when her dad was openly affectionate with different women. When he finally found someone he really liked, Lizzy refused to talk to her. Dad didn't understand that his previous behavior actually sabotaged any relationship his girlfriend might have had with his daughter. He blamed Lizzy's mother for bad-mouthing him and the fact that Lizzy was an emotional teenager.

When Lizzy's mother started to date Jack, she thought she was being discreet. She remembered how Lizzy felt about her dad's dating and tried to keep her own affection for Jack under wraps. But one afternoon when Lizzy was at school, Jack visited Mom. Thinking Lizzy would not be home for hours, Jack and Lizzy's mother had an intimate afternoon together. When Lizzy came home, Jack and her mother were in the shower. Lizzy could hear the giggling in the bathroom, and she was horrified. She banged on the bathroom door, "You're doing exactly what you told me not to do!" Lizzy barely spoke to her mother for a week and her relationship with Jack quickly declined. Their close relationship declined because she felt mom and Jack were not honest with her—sneaking around behind her back.

How Can We Fix This?

Clear communication: Lizzy's parents did not realize that what they were doing would create a problem. They both thought their dating boundaries were fine and never saw the need to come to an agreement about how they would handle dating and integrating someone new. Unfortunately, their oversight not only undermined their own relationship with their daughter, but also slowed down their daughter forming a positive relationship with their new partners.

Consider the difference in the way Mom and Dad had presented dating to Lizzy. Dad appeared promiscuous while Mom was talking abstinence. It was no wonder Lizzy felt confused and betrayed. Who was she to trust? Who was right and who was wrong? It took some serious backtracking and the help of a therapist to convince Lizzy that Mom and Dad were still worthy of her confidence and respect—not specifically for their actions, but because they both did not tell her the truth.

Don't make your child your confidant: It's not uncommon for parents to confide in their children after a breakup. They may relax the rules now and then and believe their children will make the right choices because they are pals.

There's more: Because Lizzy thought of her mother as a friend, Lizzy felt that she and Mom were on the same level and what was fitting for an adult was fitting for Lizzy. Of course, what is appropriate for an adult is often not appropriate for a young teenager, but that was not made clear to Lizzy. That's why she was so upset when she found out that Mom was sleeping with Jack and Dad had girlfriends. She could not understand why it was ok for them to have that sort of relationship but not her. She felt the people closest to her had betrayed her.

Lizzy's mother had been talking about abstinence with Lizzy for months, but it was not something she was practicing herself, and Lizzy didn't know it. Teens see the "Do as I say, not as I do" philosophy as hypocritical, and that promotes distrust and disrespect. Plus, Lizzy felt betrayed when she found out her mother had been lying to her. She thought they were pals.

Once again, the answer is having a frank conversation (**C** is for **C**ommunication) with your co-parent regarding how dating will be managed. One cannot proclaim abstinence while the other demonstrates promiscuity. As Lizzy's parents found out, flaunting your sexuality, even inadvertently, will alienate your children. Put parenting first when your kids are around, and when they are with your co-parent, that's when you have private time.

SAME RULES FOR GRANDPARENTS

I have been widowed for almost 4 years. I have been in a relationship for a year with a wonderful man named Max. My grandchildren, ages 4 and 6, have become accustomed to seeing us together. I think the youngest one is jealous, even though Max has been very kind to her. She says mean things to him when I'm not looking and even though we have had little talks about her behavior, she continues. Last week she actually hit him on the arm. I sometimes have the kids stay overnight at my house and they usually sleep with me. He has started to sleep over. How do I handle him sleeping with me when my grandkids are here?

I advise grandparents the same way I advise parents if they asked me a question about their own dating: don't have someone spend the night unless you are confident the relationship has a future, and you have properly prepared the children for the transition. Since it is implied that her new love interest has a place of his own, this grandmother might want to consider that he sleeps there when the grandkids are around—at least for now. If the relationship progresses and they are confident they will be in each other's lives, that's when they would announce their intent to be together to the family—including the grandkids—and he spends the night.

Until that point, Grandma might consider weaning the kids from her bed. Grandparents' actions have an enormous impact on their grandchildren, and she is probably correct in speculating that there are jealousy issues to be addressed. Sleeping with an adult can be quite comforting for both child and adult—and a special treat if Mom and Dad don't let their child sleep with them, but they sleep with Grandma when they visit. However, when an adult allows a child to sleep in their bed regularly, then kicks them out when a new partner spends the night, they are putting the child in direct competition with the new partner. The child's perception is, "Grandma (or Mom or Dad) is making me sleep in my own bed because she likes this other person more than me." The child immediately equates the change, which they don't like, with the addition of the new partner—and that's probably why the grandchild says mean things when grandma is not looking. She doesn't want Max around. She feels as if she has been replaced.

So, what do you do? The same things I suggest to parents when integrating new partners. Lots of fun day trips, maybe some one-on-one time with and without Max, lots of extended family time together so the grandkids begin to see Max as part of the family and not an interloper. When it's time to sleep, even when he's not visiting, make sure the grandkids have a bed of their own. Then, when the relationship has progressed to, say, living together, the grandkids won't feel kicked out of grandma's life in order to make room for Max.

RESPECTING EACH OTHER'S TURF

It was the kids' weekend with their mother, and I felt comfortable inviting a woman I had been dating over for a drink. One thing led to another, and we ended up in my bedroom. As we lay in bed, I hear the front door jiggling. It was my ex. She thought I wasn't home because my car was in the garage. We used to live in this house together and she still had a key. My bedroom door was cracked open, and I could see her walk into our son's room and come out with his soccer bag. After she left, my friend got up and left, barely saying a word. And she would not return my calls.

This is where an agreement about BOUNDARIES is imperative. A co-parent should never show up at their co-parent's home unannounced. Too many things can be interrupted that may impact future co-parenting, particularly, as in this case, the co-parent has begun to date. You would never drop by a friend's house unannounced and walk right in if one of the kids left something behind. Why would you treat the mother or father of your children with any less respect than a friend? It's good manners to call someone before you visit. The same behavior should be extended to your co-parent if you expect courteous behavior in return.

I have had clients who have keys to their ex's homes just in case of emergency. You'd think they would relinquish the key when they moved out, but that's not always the case if the breakup was amicable, especially if the kids now live in both homes. That usually changes when someone new moves in, but amicable exes may not see the same importance in things like that as do their new partners. You know, the dreaded, "Now that Julie moved in, you better give me back the key" conversation may not be the first order of business—but it should be. Changing the locks might be the best alternative.

What if a child leaves something behind, the parent isn't home, but the child is old enough to have a key? Would it be appropriate for the other parent to enter the home with the child? Not unless that is the prior agreement. It would be better to wait until the parent returns and ask for their help in retrieving whatever was left behind. That is what is meant by "respect each other's turf."

DIFFERENT MORALS AFTER A BREAKUP

We were married for 9 years and split up 8 months ago. We share equal custody with no problems. Actually, we are very proud that the kids have settled in nicely. Yesterday when the kids came back to my house, Sammy, our oldest, announced that Daddy had a woman spend the night. He said he saw her in his bed in the morning. I was shocked! I've known him since college, and I never thought he would do that when the kids were around. What do I do?

Parents are often surprised by a co-parent's behavior after the breakup, thinking that they know them well and know what they will do in a given situation. In this case, the mother dated the dad in college and took it for granted that they were on the same page when it came to dating and morals—and they probably were—in college. How much discretion did they use when they started to date? Is it Dad who has changed his position or is it Mom?

It's not uncommon to become more conservative in your attitude about dating after you have children, but not everyone follows that rule. That's why it is important to have an idea for how you will problem solve in place, and then conversations about differences of opinion won't spin out of control. Discuss your mutual expectations prior to your dating and come to an agreement about how you want to portray spending time with potential dates.

In Chapter 1, we discussed the Bonus Family Problem Solving Model as a guide for addressing a touchy subject. Let's see how the above former college sweethearts implemented bonus problem solving when dealing with dad's questionable dating practices. This is a true-life situation faced by clients with whom I have worked. They never anticipated this, they agreed to date on their own time, but this did happen, and with the tools they learned in co-parenting counseling, they successfully maneuvered a potential disaster.

To remind you of the problem solving steps:

Step 1: Identify the problem

Step 2: Suggest a child-focused solution

Step 3: Negotiate

Step 4: Compromise

Subject: Child saw dad's girlfriend in his bed. Using the above model, it would be helpful to start with an observation offering no judgment, or Dad may get defensive and the discussion will end before it gets started:

Step 1: Identify the Problem
Mom: "I'm not making any judgments about how you are managing your life. I know you care about Louise. I'm concerned about Sammy, though. He was really upset when he came back to my home this morning. He said he went into your room and there was a woman in your bed. You weren't there. I guess you were in the shower. Did you know he saw that?"

Really good call. Rather than judge, the question, "Did you know he saw that?" was asked for clarification.

Next, make sure that you don't bring leftover feelings into the conversation. Say, if the person Dad had over was the person with whom he cheated. Mom must be extra tactful, or her observations will be ignored. She will be accused of "just being jealous," which might be the case, but that doesn't change the fact that Sammy saw what he saw and was uncomfortable. Mom must make it clear that her concern is that Sammy saw his father in an intimate setting with another woman so soon after the breakup. Give honest examples if the children have described something inappropriate. Don't exaggerate or make things up or speculate about what Sammy saw. And, then it's up to the parent receiving the news to accept it for face value, not turn this very important conversation into a defensive back and forth. It's not about what Dad did and if it was right or wrong at this point—it's about Sammy.

Dad's response might then be:

"No, I had no idea. I thought we were being discreet. She left at 6 am! He didn't say a word."

Continuing, Mom might say:

"Well, he saw her, and he said he was very embarrassed. He's afraid to say anything to you. He thinks you will be angry because you told him not to come into your room without knocking, but now he doesn't want to go back to your home."

Dad's next comment will make or break the problem solving plan. Some in his position would get defensive and be tempted to diminish the importance of what happened, "Oh, it's no big deal. He'll get over it." But, to Dad's credit, Dad took another approach.

Dad asked, "What should I do?"

Notice that this conversation is only about the child and that these parents are looking for solutions to help Sammy. Neither parent is discussing wrongdoing.

Step 2: Suggest a Child-Focused Solution

Mom: "I can only imagine how you must feel, but you better talk to him. May I make a suggestion? Apologize. Let him know you are sorry he was put in that position and that you are also embarrassed. He will be more open to returning if he knows you understand how he feels. Reassure him it will never happen again."

Step 3: Negotiate
Dad agrees and asks Mom's further advice—a good co-parenting step. Asking your co-parent's advice demonstrates respect and openness to work together.
"When do you think I should talk to him? Immediately, or should I give it some time?"
Mom continues with . . .
"Let's think about this. If you give him some time, I might be able to smooth things over."
Dad further negotiates but adds his opinion . . .
"I think it would be better to talk to him immediately. As much as I appreciate you offering to intercede, I think this is something he and I should address together, alone."

Step 4: Compromise
Mom continues, "Alright. I understand, but please let me know how it went as soon as you talk to him."
Dad: "I would prefer to keep it between Sammy and me, but I understand and will let you know the general outcome."
Dad is not committing to breaking confidence but is understanding about Mom's concern. It is important to note that these parents are discussing how to *help the child.* They are not caught up in assigning blame or passing judgment on questionable behavior. That approach might accelerate into a disagreement with the end result of Sammy refusing to go back to Dad's home. That's not what anyone wants—not Mom or Sammy, and certainly not Dad.

Mom Approached Dad With CARE

Communication: She explained her thoughts, prefacing that her observation was centered on the child.

Acceptance: She did not belittle Dad about his poor choice. She actually acknowledged that he cares for his new girlfriend, Louise.

Respect: She asked a question for clarification without blame. "Did you know . . . ?"

Empathy: She put herself in Dad's shoes. "I can only imagine . . ." And then she offered a solution that appealed to Dad's sensibilities.

When the Kids Start Asking Questions

Oh, honey, they're just a friend. . . . It's difficult to date casually in front of your children. No matter how innocent you portray the date, they will anticipate that this is a possible romance and need clarification.

Co-parents Michael and Julia broke up 2 years ago. They had a very observant 4-year-old daughter, Rachael. Michael and Julia had equal custody of Rachael, who lived with her mother for a week and her father for a week. Michael and Julia had done their best to compare notes and stay on the same page for their daughter. They did not worry about preparing her for their dating someone new, thinking that they had anticipated most situations and had a pat answer that they felt would support each other's attitudes and opinions. They thought they were on the same page.

Michael had been dating Lisa for 4 months. They had decided that they would date exclusively, and Lisa and Rachael enjoyed spending time together. They would do each other's nails and volunteer at the local pet sanctuary. Lisa and Michael had no plans to live together and had not discussed marriage.

One Sunday morning, Michael was sitting in his favorite chair with Rachael, talking about his affection for Lisa. Nothing that serious, but that he liked her very much. That's when the questions started to fly, and Michael was not prepared for two questions in particular. "Daddy, is Lisa part of our family?" and "Don't you love Mommy anymore?"

Michael understood that if he answered these questions incorrectly, it could complicate his new relationship with Lisa and confuse Rachael. If Michael automatically said, "Of course, Lisa's family" and "Of course, I still love Mommy," this would prompt all sorts of additional questions, like "If you love Mommy, why are you dating Lisa?"

So, at the spur of the moment, Michael said, "No, honey, Lisa is a very special friend for now." Thinking that was enough, Michael rose from his chair and headed into the kitchen, but Rachael wasn't finished.

OK, but do you still love Mommy? Professionals offer differing suggestions to answer this question, and rest assured, the question will come up when you start to date. The classic answer is, "I will always love your mommy/daddy. We just can't live together." But that response can be confusing. The word "love," in terms of relationships, implies "only" and "forever" and if used in context with their other parent just reinforces a child's hope that their parents will eventually get back together. Also, children weigh "love" in terms of how they feel about you and you feel about them, so thinking that you will always love and forgive them, they may not be quite sure why this breakup will be permanent and that's why they are always holding out for reconciliation.

In response, you may hear, "If you still love Mommy, will we be together again soon?" Since that is rarely in the cards, consider answering with something like, "Mommy and I made the decision as adults not to be married (or live together) anymore. There are lots of things about that decision that you may not understand right now. When you get older, we can talk about it more, but you should know that I will always *care about* (or *care for*) your mommy (or daddy), and you can rest assured that we both love you very much." An approach like this tells the child that their parents are in control and will continue to take care of them even though their life has changed substantially because of a breakup. It also explains that the decision was between the parents, the child was not to blame, and it leaves the conversation open for further discussion when the child is older. Using the words *care for* or *care about* tells your children that their parents don't hate each other and continue to consider each other's feelings. It puts the continued affection on a different level than forever-after love. Plus, when you emphasize that you both love your children, it reinforces that you both continue to be invested in their well-being.

COURTING THE KIDS

Have you ever heard of the term "court," as in, courting a potential partner?

"Courting" is an old-fashioned term, but the definition holds true for our purposes here. Courting is the process of getting to know someone to decide whether or not to pursue a more committed relationship. Even though the term "court" was usually used to mean *with the intention to marry*, when I use "court" here, I am calling attention to the fact that spending time getting to know a potential partner is commonplace, but new partners rarely spend time trying to get to know their partner's children. They are treated as if they just come along with their parents. However, if you analyze why most bonus families don't jell, it's usually because the kids don't accept the new partner or the new partner doesn't accept the kids. If partners spent as much time courting their partner's kids as they do their parents, I'm sure the bonus family success rate would improve expeditiously. People need time to get to know each other—and time to build a bond.

The way to build a bond with anyone, not just a child, is to take the time to learn about what they like and dislike. Let them know you see them and accept them for who they are, not because they are your partner's child, but because you like them and accept them for who they are.

SHOULD I INTRODUCE MY NEW PARTNER TO MY CO-PARENT BEFORE WE MOVE IN TOGETHER?

Lyle is 7 years old and my husband and his co-parent share custody. We see Lyle every weekend, from Friday after school to Tuesday night after dinner. I take care of him most of the time when he's at our home and we have a very close relationship. On Sunday, we dropped him off at his mother's house. I've never met her. My husband walked up to the door with his son, and they went into the house while I waited in the car. I felt very uncomfortable. Would it have been too aggressive if I got out of the car to meet her? Would it have been more appropriate if my husband introduced me?

If your child is invited to spend the night at a friend's home, it's common practice to talk to the friend's parent prior to the sleepover. You'd call them up and introduce yourself. You'd explain, my child has a real problem with horror movies and so we limit movies that might give him nightmares. You'd let the parent know your child is allergic to peanuts. But when kids spend the night with their parent's new partner, it's not uncommon to avoid discussion. Some parents have told me that it is because the child is with the other parent and so they trust the child is safe. But the parent isn't always present. They could run to the store or have to go back to the office for the afternoon and you have never even talked to the person who is alone with your child.

With that in mind, I would want to meet my co-parent's partner as soon as they are regarded as a partner—not to intimidate them, not to interrogate them, but to learn who they are so I can feel my child is safe when they are with them.

The best approach in this situation was for the child's father to introduce his fiancée to his child's mother when the two decided on a future together. That way his fiancée could have openly expressed her desire to support both parents in their efforts to make this child's life as stress-free as possible—and set the stage for working together in the future. As it is, this couple got married without meeting the child's mother—without even telling her that they were getting married, without including the child in the wedding plans, which is a huge bonus family faux pas (more on that in Chapter 7). As a result, no groundwork was laid for future communication or working together in the name of the child. Now Mom and Bonus Mom have to play catch up.

Truly, the biggest drawback to approaching a new relationship in this way is that without making some effort to familiarize the parent and the bonus parent prior to marrying or moving in together, the child going between homes is left to their own resources when navigating their allegiance to parent or bonus parent. The goal is for the child to feel loved and comfortable at both homes—and know it's ok to be close to both parent and bonus parent. It's doubtful in this case that this has been properly addressed.

My ex doesn't have to meet my new partner before we move in together. I'd prefer to keep it as business-like as possible.

Sometimes a secret strategy works in business, but that is most often when there is a strategic purchase and one company is being gobbled up by another. When the business is sales-oriented, and you must reorder or strategize together to build market share, a relationship based on trust is imperative. The more transparent you are in that kind of business, the easier it is to solve problems should a problem arise. Co-parenting is sales. It's how you present a problem and problem solve together. So, if you would like to keep it business-like, then be polite, be honest and open, and respect your co-parent and your new partner to be adults and look for ways to positively interact. The only reason they are meeting is because your children live with both of them. Standing in the way of their ability to get along will not benefit anyone in any way.

If you live a distance away and a face-to-face meeting is impossible, a phone call or email is in order—not a text. This information is far too important and may require further questions that cannot be covered properly in a text. All information should be passed on with the respect due all the parties.

The goal is to reassure your co parent that the children remain your first priority. Your co-parent may want exact dates, ask further questions about sleeping arrangements, and if your partner shares custody of their own children. Anticipate everything you can and be ready with answers. Your aim is to make your co-parent feel you respect them enough to keep them informed. Set the stage and you will get the same respect in return.

My kids like my new partner, but they tell me they aren't ready to live together. Should my partner still move in?

In a word, no. At least not yet.

In the name of not making any mistakes, many parents move in with a new partner just to see if it will work. This is not a test. It is the emergency bonus broadcast system issuing a warning. Although you may be ready to live together, kids move at a different speed. Moving in with someone is the last step before acknowledging their life with mom and dad under the same roof is over. This is to be taken seriously. If you move in, your kids get settled, they are doing their best to start over after a devastating upheaval, they get attached to your new partner, their kids, as well, and then you say, "Naw, not what I thought," that's emotionally abusive. You simply can't be that frivolous with your children's mental health. If you are not 100% certain that this is the right move, stay in separate homes until you are.

You're saying I should let my kids dictate my life?

I've made it very clear that children look to their parents for direction and will therefore follow your lead, unless they are teenagers, and most will make it very clear if they are unhappy with your choice—but most will still follow your lead, albeit kicking and screaming. Just remember, this isn't only your life. It's your children's lives as well. Your children didn't ask for the breakup, but they must accept it since this is what their parents have chosen. You are not letting them dictate your life if you slow down to allow them to adjust. You are being sensitive to their needs. This doesn't mean you never move in together. It means you don't move in now. In the big picture, the extra time before moving in together will allow your children and partner to be more in sync before they share a home. Then, everyone will be on the same page and can more comfortably anticipate the changes that we will discuss in Chapter 3, "Moving in Together: Planning and Preparation."

PART II
BUILDING YOUR BONUS FAMILY

CHAPTER 3

Moving in Together

Planning and Preparation

By failing to prepare, you are preparing to fail.
                                        BENJAMIN FRANKLIN

BONUS DYNAMICS OFTEN START WHEN A COUPLE FIRST BEGINS to date. Histories and goals for the future quickly intertwine. One or both of you may have children, and as you as a couple become more serious, both the children and the couple look to the union as their symbol of security and stability. As you develop a clearer picture of who you are as a couple, the intense feelings you have for one another can easily blind you to the possibility of problems that may arise in the future. That's why it is imperative parents moving in with a new partner have a PLAN to go forward.

PREPARING TO BE BONUS: WHAT'S THE PLAN?

In this chapter we will discuss all the things parents must take into consideration to properly prepare to combine their families. So many move in together with the expectation that love will conquer all—and sometimes it does, but having *a plan* in place will help you keep your focus and ensure that love flourishes throughout the family. That's what this chapter is all about—planning and preparation.

There are two parts to the plan I recommend. The first part always starts with mental preparation. What you envision for the future is what will be. To help you with the proper mental preparation and form that vision for the future, I like to start with an exercise I call the Before Bonus Exercise. It is an exercise that is done by the bonus couple before they move in together to ensure they have a clear idea of what they will encounter as a couple, as the leaders of their bonus family, and what they bring to the table to help their family to flourish.

The second part of the approach is agreeing on house rules. I call it "Setting Up House." I have included a checklist of the things you need to agree upon if your home is to run smoothly. There are some silly things included in this part of the exercise. Although you may not think of it when you are thinking about moving in together, choosing who cleans the toilets, who replaces the toilet paper, and who picks up the dog poop are the kinds of things families argue about. Right now you are floating on that love cloud, but as time goes by, it's the little things you did not anticipate that will be to blame for your family's frustration.

PART 1: THE BEFORE BONUS EXERCISE

I have included this exercise (with a few modifications) in every book and at the beginning of every Bonus Family Workshop or private preparation class I have taught for over 30 years. It's one of those things that is so important you really can't proceed without it.

As I mention all the way through this book, good communication and a cooperative mindset is an essential component to bonus family living. So, this exercise asks you to sit down with your partner and sincerely talk about what you envision and what you will bring to the bonus family table.

Step 1: Note how many relationships must be cultivated when you form this type of family. When I ask this of my clients, most write down the names of their partner and their combined children. But they stop there. Below is a list of all the relationships you create when you move in with or marry someone with children. It reaches out far beyond your new partner and your combined children.

1. New partner A

2. New partner B

3. Your children with your co-parent

4. Their children with their co-parent

5. Your children together

6. Your co-parent

7. Their co-parent

8. Your co-parent's new partner

9. Their co-parent's new partner

10. Any children your co-parent may have with their new partner

11. Any children your partner's co-parent may have with their new partner

12. Any children new partners had with former partners

13. Your extended family (grandparents, aunts, uncles, cousins, etc.)

14. Your partner's extended family

15. Your co-parent's extended family

16. Your co-parent's partner's extended family

. . . and we could possibly include more. Why are all these people included in this bonus family list? Because these are people with whom you and your children will have to interact when you form your bonus family, and doing your best to nurture each of these relationships will contribute to your bonus family running smoothly.

I'm always amused by a parent's shock when I bring to their attention how many relationships are created when they combine families. I believe that is a major contribution to why so many combined families fall apart—the bonus couple does not realize that a successful bonus family is more than the combination of two people who care about each other and their combined children. Most understand that any family extends beyond their immediate relatives to include grandparents, aunts, uncles, and cousins, yet only a small number acknowledge those same ties once the parents no longer live together. Very few enter a new relationship understanding and openly accepting that they may have to interact with, for example, their new partner's former-in-laws, or even their former in-laws, for that matter. Nevertheless, those former in-laws are your children and bonus children's grandparents, and it's your responsibility as a parent figure to reinforce those relationships. That's exactly what it means to "put the children first."

Step 2: Envision the relationship you expect with *each one of the people you have listed*, then list how you will foster a positive relationship with each one.

Considering each relationship separately and then asking yourself what you will do to make the relationship work puts the quality of that relationship in your hands. You have the power to create the relationship you want. I suggest you start with your new partner, and then work from there. The strength of the bonus couple relationship is the foundation on which this family is built.

For example:

What will I do to foster a positive relationship with my new partner?

- I will have reasonable expectations about our new relationship.
- I will not place my partner in the position where they must choose between their children and me.
- I will agree on disciplinary tactics and stick to the rules.
- I will do my best not to undermine my partner's authority in front of the children (no matter whose children they are).
- I will remember to set aside some time for just the two of us.
- We will design a way to problem solve between the two of us that does not involve the children.

I would like to put extra emphasis on the last bullet point. The thought behind the Before Bonus Exercise is that the two of you are discussing all these things with a rational mind and coming to an agreement for how you will address conflict should you find yourself in disagreement or have to make a decision together. Right now things are working harmoniously, but there will be a time when you are not as accepting, when you are disappointed and frustrated, and when you will need to talk something through. How will we make repairs when things go wrong? What are the rules of engagement that you both believe to be fair so that when you are faced with a disagreement, you know how to address each other?

Moving on, do the same with the next person on your list. To help you along, I have addressed some of the most important relationships you will encounter. But there are many potential relationship categories. To do this exercise in its entirety, you should look at each of the relationships and honestly consider what *you* can do to make each one the best it can be. Watch out for negative expectations or preconceived notions that could possibly sabotage your new life together. Take note of the positive things you may be ignoring.

What will I do to foster a positive relationship with my partner's children (my bonus kids)? How you see yourself interacting with your bonus kids is extremely important. If you resent them or see them as spoiled or contrary, those thoughts will prevent you from building a relationship. Here are some positive affirmations for this relationship:

- I will have a clear idea of my responsibilities as a bonus parent and compare notes with my partner before we move in together.
- I will accept my bonus children's individuality.
- I will respect my bonus children's past allegiances (to your partner's co-parent and extended family).
- I will try to listen more than dictate policy.

What will I do to foster positive communication with my new partner's co-parent?

- I will accept that I may have to interact with my partner's co-parent on a regular basis to help coordinate parenting efforts.
- I will not compete, on any level, with my bonus child's biological parent.
- I will do my best to support his or her parenting tactics when his or her child is in my care.
- I will be as cooperative as possible when interaction is necessary.

What will I do to foster positive communication with my new partner's extended family? Because extended family members form strong allegiances to past partners, these are among the most difficult relationships to anticipate. Decide what you will do to foster a positive relationship with people who are related to both you and your spouse's co-parent by marriage. Even though your husband, for example, is divorced from his co-parent, your husband's relatives might still interact with that co-parent because of the children.

Continue this exercise for each relationship. I know that at this point the exercise can get overwhelming. That's the reason I recommend it. I want everyone to realize the commitment they make when they are in a relationship in which one or both partners have children.

Step 3: Take inventory: Have a heart-to-heart talk with your partner. After you have compiled your lists, it's time for you and your new partner to have a heart-to-heart and compare notes. Know going in that there is no perfect how-to list on dating, moving in together, and, if you see it in your future, marriage. The choice is unique to each couple. But, *before* you make any move toward bonus, it will help to take an honest inventory of your relationship, finances, and mutual vision for the future. Take note of your negative or unrealistic expectations. Is what you expect for your relationship and your bonus family really feasible? Talk about everything—all your worries and concerns and discuss how you will care for each other's children. What will you both do to keep your relationship strong? What will you both do to keep this bonus family strong?

I can't emphasize the last two sentences enough. This is a collaborative effort. If you have never been a good team player in your life, now is the time to change your ways.

Be proactive. Anticipate what you can and put checks and balances in place that will empower growth in each family member.

Honestly address all concerns before you bring your children into a questionable situation.

The term "checks and balances" refers to the separation of power to avoid one party wielding too much power over another. Without checks and balances, one branch of government can grow too powerful and problematic. I use the term unconventionally. When I talk about "checks and balances" I mean putting things in place that will check behavior—like establishing a forum for conflict resolution within your bonus family—and then using that forum of conflict resolution when a family member faces a stumbling block. The check would be to establish a way to problem solve in your family and the balance would come from using it.

Preparing the Children to Become Bonus

In my work with families, I often hold sessions to help parents and their new partners prepare prior to moving in together. In this case I asked the new partner what she intended to say to convey to her partner's children how much she cared for them. She used a line I often hear, and I was glad I could head her off because, even though her intent was lovely, her words would have backfired.

She said, "I'm going to tell them, 'I love your dad, and because you are part of your dad, I love you.'" That's a sweet sentiment but think about what this is saying to the child. It's saying, "My attachment to you is because I care for your parent—not because I respect you as an individual and like you for who you are, but because you are related to someone else I love." You are telling the child the only reason you see them as special is because someone else to whom they happen to be related is special to you. That's not demonstrating respect. Basically, you just told them that if anything happens to their parent or to the union, they will be on their own. Respect for an individual is demonstrated by forming a unique relationship with that individual. Again, seeing them as an individual and building that relationship on genuine affection for that individual.

Bonus From the Kids' Point of View

Just as the new partners must have a vision for their future, so must their children. It is important to talk to them about the changes they can expect and what their life will be like once the family configuration they regarded as "normal" changes. In other words, in most cases, the child lived with both their parents in the same home, then the parents split up and the child divided their time between two homes. *That was one huge change.*

Next, one or both parents started dating a new partner who may have also had children. They were around all the time. *That's another huge change.*

Now, one or both parents are not only dating but have decided to live with this new partner—and maybe their kids. *That is a huge change, as well.*

That's a lot of changes in a very short time. All for which the child had very little input.

We have already seen how to improve our communication skills with adults using CARE as a guide. Let's look at how using CARE as a guide to talk to our children also works well.

Marni and William's parents recently split up. "Mom" moved 5 miles away while "Mommy" and the kids stayed in the house they all knew as "home." For the last 6 months Mom has been seeing Leanne and now Leanne and Mom have decided to live together. Leanne has a son, Derreck, who is about the same age as William. They are moving into a three-bedroom house in another school district. Mom wants the kids to go to school from her house, while Mommy is holding her ground and saying, "No." Mom mentioned to the kids that they might be going to another school and that's when the confusion started and the questions started to fly.

Approaching this with CARE, let's begin with:

C is for Communication: When there are questions that have not yet been addressed, like school choice or when exactly a move will take place, it's best to keep that information between the parents and other decision-makers and not involve the children until everything is known. Then, guard against surprises. Keep the kids informed of any big changes and give them time to process every step. Be available for comfort, if necessary, and answer questions *from the children's point of view.*

A is for Acceptance: Everyone processes change differently. While the kids may be kicking and screaming about the changes, the parents may be celebrating. And Marni and William are not the only children who must assimilate into this new lifestyle; Derreck is making the same changes, as well. Marni and William have each other to talk to about the adjustments they must make. Derreck does not have a compadre about his age who sees things as he does—or does he? Can these children identify with each other because they are experiencing a similar lifestyle change or will they resent each other's presence? The key is for the parents to move slowly—not at their pace, but at the children's pace. Moving too fast will not allow any of the children to adjust to the huge changes they are facing and the easiest way for them to cope is to reject everything—starting with Mom's new partner and then perhaps, Mom.

R is for Respect: Respect the children enough to allow them to make *age-appropriate decisions*, like pick a comforter in their room or where to put the picture of their dog. Something like, "We have narrowed it down to three homes. Would you like to see them and help us make the decision?" goes a long way toward accepting something new. Feeling as if your opinion is respected sets the stage for respecting others.

E is for Empathy: Even though adults think they are being thorough when offering information, children bring their own experiences to the table and may hear something completely different than what is intended. Put yourself in your children's shoes.

They are most concerned about how any proposed changes will affect *them*. The italics are what the child may be hearing and the question they want answered.

Leanne and Derreck are going to be living with us. *Where?*

I've found a new house. *Do I have to move?*

With room for all of us. *Will I have to share a room? Can I bring my pet?*

It's just 5 miles away. *Will I have to leave my friends?*

No big changes until school is out next month. *Will you make me change schools? What about soccer?*

Have decisions made and answers ready before you present anything to the children.

Part 2: Setting Up House

Once you have completed the Before Bonus Exercise and have a clear idea of the commitment you are making, you need to agree to house rules. House rules are the everyday workings of how you want to run your home. As you glance through this list, it should hit home how different your house rules as a bonus family are from a conventional two parent home. Notice how many times it says: How will you coordinate times with your co-parent and new partner? These are necessary decisions that if not taken into consideration will be the continued source of irritation.

Things to Consider: Basic House Rules

- Meals: Will you eat dinner together? If so, who is responsible for meal preparation? May the children eat in their rooms or in front of the TV? Do they have to ask to go into the refrigerator?

- Guests: Who is allowed in the home without adult supervision?

- Consequences: What are the repercussions when rules are not followed?

- Sleeping arrangements: Who shares a room?

- Decor: How will you arrange furniture and family heirlooms?

- Privacy: What does a closed door mean?

- Bedtimes and bedtime rituals: Discuss and decide what is appropriate for your home. Will you coordinate bedtimes with your new partner and your co-parent?

- Curfews: Teens have different rules and responsibilities than younger children. Will you coordinate times with your new partner and your co-parent?

- Chore assignments: How will we assign the responsibilities? Keeping their rooms clean, bathroom duty, care and feeding of pets, setting the table, doing the dishes, etc.

- Homework rules: Will there be a specific time for homework set aside? Will you coordinate completing homework assignments with your co-parent and their new partner?

- Screen and phone time: Discuss and decide how much screen time and phone time is appropriate for your home. How is social media regarded? How will you coordinate times with your co-parent and new partner?

- Discipline: Will you discipline each other's children?

- Rules: How will you coordinate the rules your partner has in place for their children with the rules you have in place for your children?

- Conflict resolution: How will you problem solve as a bonus family?

- Finances: Who pays for what? Will you assign separate responsibilities—for example, "You pay rent, and I'll pay for the other utilities"? What about miscellaneous expenses?

- Allowances: Do the children get allowance and who pays it?

- Contributions to each other's children: Discuss and decide what is appropriate for your home.

The Bonus Family Hierarchy

At the core of bonus family life is the bonus couple, the two partners now combining families and sharing a mutual vision for their life together. Their partnership and that mutual vision is the stabilizing force on which their family is based. Their combined children will look to them for direction and security. It's all about being prepared to live together with your partner, your kids, their kids, plus gracefully coordinating efforts with co-parents from previous relationships to raise *all* the children in an accepting harmonious setting. It's a well-choreographed dance with a lot of moving parts, based on positive communication, acceptance, respect, and empathy (CARE), and ultimately, *putting the children first*.

Who Has the Final Say?

The basic bonus home philosophy centers on "parents make the rules, bonus parents uphold them." If only one partner has children, then obviously the children's parent is the one with the final say, but it must be consistent with the morals of the bonus parent or a bonus parent is less likely to cooperate. A bonus parent who morally disagrees with a biological parent's rules will not uphold them. It must also be said that if a bonus parent wants to be accepted as a parent figure, they must move slowly into their new position of authority, taking the parent's lead and working together to refine the rules if need be.

Coordinating Efforts with Your Children's Other Home

My co-parent and I have both moved on to new partners and new lives. I would love to coordinate efforts with my ex's bonus family, but they have no desire to coordinate efforts with ours. We just can't agree.

We each progress toward bonus status at our own speed, and your desire to cooperate may not match that of your co-parent—or of your spouse's co-parent. So, what do you do when, no matter what you say or do, your co-parent and their new family do not want to listen or coordinate efforts with you?

To be honest, many don't even realize that there is another way. They cut off all interaction, thinking that none of this is affecting the kids as they go back and forth. That's not true. But you can only control your own four walls. You can pray that both your co-parent and your spouse's co-parent will begin to understand that it is also their obligation to put their issues aside and coordinate efforts in the name of the children. If they choose not to do that, however, you cannot control their home or parenting style. If you try to manipulate the situation by withholding time with the children, being late, or not being receptive to a request for a favor, it will only complicate the issue and possibly backfire. Your attempt to retaliate won't hurt your co-parent as much as it will hurt the children. They will be caught in the middle of your power struggle. Just remember, you cannot establish rules for the other family, but you can set the example. Choose your battles. As your newfound attitude of cooperation improves your ability to communicate with each other, a day might come when you can coordinate efforts. Make that your goal.

Dividing Bonus Family Responsibilities Fairly

It may be difficult to assign regular chores to bonus family members who go back and forth between two homes. To reduce resentment in family members that stay put, coordinate chores as best you can with your child returning to the other parent's home.

For example, let's say your child is with you every Monday through Wednesday and every other weekend. Tuesday is garbage night. Taking out the garbage might be that child's chore for the week.

> *During a co-parenting session with parents who were having trouble jelling as a bonus family, the father said, "There's this little blue thread on the rug next to the garbage can in our bathroom. It's been there for months. She's never picked it up."*
>
> *He was referring to his partner and he was irritated that she was not doing what he thought was **her** job, yet they both worked outside of the home, and both brought a child to their union. I asked him why **he** never picked it up. He looked at me bewildered. "I don't know," he said. "I guess I never thought it was my job."*

Here's something that is rarely acknowledged—when one of the parent figures has a more traditional outlook about who should do specific chores than the other. In the case above, the father figure just assumed the mother figure would clean the bathroom. Traditional responsibilities are a way of the past. When both parent figures work, chore assignments must be based on who has the time to do what needs to be done. And, if you assign those chores to one another, it is expected that you will make the time to complete them. It's the small things that become irritating and undermine your happy home. Come to an agreement and work together. If you both take up the slack with a gracious heart, you won't notice what your partner is not doing.

> *At the next session, the father proudly announced, "I went home and picked up the thread."*
>
> *"Ah," I said, "How did it feel?"*
>
> *"It made me feel good, and I wasn't angry at her anymore."*
>
> *"Hmmm," I said. "What did you learn?"*
>
> *"I think that thread was more a symbol than anything else. And it made me see I wasn't doing my part. But I really didn't know. I just figured that was her job."*

You would not believe the expression of surprise on his partner's face. This is what happens when you are both truly invested in making it work.

Stay Flexible

Sticking to the rules is important, but bonus children will be more inclined to respect you as a parent figure if they see that you are *flexible* after listening to their concerns and making judgments based on the information before you. This does not mean if the child is whining, you give in. It means that children, especially older children, view many issues within the family as "fair" or "unfair." If they perceive you, the bonus parent, as being unfair or asking them to do something their own parent may not ask, then you will seem "wicked" to them, a stepparent. If they know that you will honestly assess the situation based on the rule in place and make your judgments accordingly, they will be more willing to accept your decisions.

Using CARE to Navigate the House Rules

Communication: Let family members in on the reason why a house rule is being implemented and remember to be flexible.

Acceptance: House rules will be followed if they take into consideration the family members' history, culture, and individual backgrounds. "My way or the highway" doesn't work in bonus families.

Respect: Cooperation is ensured when family members' opinions are heard and considered with equal importance as your own.

Empathy: Put yourself in their shoes. Would you want to do what you are asking them to do?

Decor in the Bonus Family Home

I am preparing for life with a new man. We plan to marry in a few months. We bought a new home after his marital home was sold. His daughter still wants all the pictures of the "family" to be rehung. The family pictures were taken before her dad and I met. They include her mother. She is preparing for marriage herself and will be gone in 9 months. Do I just let them hang the pictures when it really bothers me and keep my mouth closed, or do I ask that I am to be respected and only allow them in her room? I am terribly upset, but I am at odds as to what to do . . .

Pictures of past unions need not be openly displayed in a common bonus family area—but it is completely acceptable, and understandable, if the children of the former union wish to display family pictures in their own rooms. As a matter of fact, I often suggest just that to children who have trouble adjusting to back-and-forth life. Pictures of dad in their room at Mom's and pictures of Mom in their room at Dad's often makes the transition from house to house easier. But it also can drive home the fact that their parents no longer live under the same roof, so approach this with CARE.

It's not uncommon for this type of thing to become problematic when a new partner moves into the former marital home. Then removing pictures is obvious to the children who still reside in the home, and it could cause resentment—but you take this one step further. Your fiancé has sold the marital home, and his adult child wishes for you to display pictures of his former marriage in a home that her father and you have purchased together. In that case, it is inappropriate for her to ask that the pictures of Mom and Dad be rehung. It was never her mother's home.

When decorating your new home, do your best to blend past and present by including pictures of your current life together. Remember to include pictures of all the children—and if they live nearby, you may want to ask them for their input about where to display the pictures. The more you can "normalize" the new environment, the better.

Finally, if your fiancé's daughter is adamant about displaying pictures of her divorced parents, it is completely fitting for her to display such pictures in her own home once she moves out.

Sleeping Arrangements: Who Shares a Room?

When parents combine families, those families instantly grow larger than we might have originally planned. "Growing up I always wanted three kids," a new bonus mom confided. "Well, I have three, all right. Three boys and three girls!"

Rarely can families afford six or seven bedrooms, so it's likely that some of the children will share a room. You may be one of the lucky ones who has a home or the ability to buy or rent a home large enough for each child to have their own room, but that isn't always the case. This problem becomes exaggerated when a child has their own room at one parent's home but must share a room at the other parent's home.

How do we decide who shares a room? There are a few things to take into consideration when deciding who should share a room:

- Gender identification or sexual orientation
- Biology (how the children are related)
- Age of the children
- How long the children have known each other

Gender Identification or Sexual Orientation

My ex has been dating a woman for about a year and they are talking about moving in together. Both her son and our son are 15 years old. Our sons have developed a friendship, and that's great, but my son confided that his new friend is gay, and his mother has no idea. This was brought up because of a discussion about sharing a room when they all move in together. The situation allowed me to talk to my son about his own feelings, which was great, but this knowledge also seems to add a new layer to their living situation and the boys' need for privacy. I don't know how to even begin a conversation with my son's father. I can't dictate their house rules, but they also don't have all the facts. Is it my place to say something?

The mother who drafted this email is right, this information does add a layer to their living arrangement—teens and privacy—plus, situations like this also emphasize the importance of good co-parent communication.

Let's address the first concern: sharing a room. This is a concern parents have for all genders and age combinations when setting up a house, and it is important to be sensitive to all concerned. This is your children's home, and their bedroom is their sanctuary. They need a sanctuary at both homes. Make sure they have a comfortable room, or at least a space, they feel is their own.

This is when I hear, "We can't afford a four-bedroom house! My son and his daughter are only 5. I don't think we will have a problem." And then you walk in on them innocently playing doctor behind closed doors. This could happen with any child—even biological siblings play doctor—but you are setting your children up for failure if you forget that your 5-year-olds are human. It is imperative that parents who wish to combine their families are logical about who shares rooms and have an open conversation with their children about house rules and what is expected.

If there isn't enough room in the home, put off living together until you can make other arrangements.

The second issue here is co-parent communication. Co-parents and their kids are in this together. As difficult as it is to get used to, your ex's girlfriend is now part of the narrative. The secrets that brew in families do not improve when no one talks about them. Combining families brings this to the forefront. This is why I say there is very little privacy when you share custody of your children. Their problems become your problems because the children live in both homes.

The adults in this situation can help guide two young people through possibly the most difficult time in their lives. It is understandable that the gay teen may not be ready to openly discuss things with his mother, BUT, to co-parent and create a safe environment for all the children concerned, there should be a discussion about how the stresses of facing this in secret will affect both your sons.

Therefore, start with encouraging the child to talk to his mother. If he can't do it alone, direct him to engage a trusted, unbiased third party (like a therapist) that will assist him in confiding in his mother so that she has all the facts and she and her husband can make an informed decision. Once it is known, make sure you are available to openly discuss how you can support all of them. You are doing this for your son—and her son. That is putting all the children first.

Biology and Age of the Children

> *My 9-year-old daughter recently told me her 11-year-old step-brother tried to get in bed with her. His mother and I have been together for 5 months. They moved into my two-bedroom home, so the kids share a room when my wife's son is scheduled to be with her. I think he should stop sleeping at our home, but his mother disagrees.*

Of course this mother disagrees with not seeing her child, but there is more to consider here than a parent feeling bad. These parents must protect *both* children. That begins by not putting them in a position for which they are not emotionally equipped.

Parents see their adolescent children as their innocent little ones and may not be prepared for those hormones kicking in so soon. The child may also be surprised how quickly their body is changing and be unprepared for those changes, as well. This is the reason many school districts introduce sex education in the 4th or 5th grade. It's meant to ease the child's curiosity and answer common questions. Add the sexual content regularly seen on the TV, the internet, and in the movies, and it's a lot of information for an adolescent to process all at once, and it could easily lead to experimentation. This doesn't mean that all children will experiment, but it also does not guarantee that they won't. Children as young as 3 or 4 years old may experiment when left unattended, but more importantly, parents must be mindful that experimentation is not exclusive to children of a different sex, and it is a normal part of maturing. With that in mind, it is important to stay available to your children and listen without judgment when they confide in you.

Considering all this, assigning rooms to our children is not to be taken lightly, and if there is not enough room in the house in which you currently live, in the best interest of their combined children, parents may have to wait to move in together.

Let's look at how one bonus family solved the sleeping arrangement dilemma.

When Robert and Jackie combined families, they suddenly had six children living in the same house—one boy and five girls. Robert had a boy and a girl. Jackie had four girls. They all moved into Robert's three-bedroom house. Their first priority was to find a bigger house, but until they could, they had to make do with the bedrooms they had. Logic would dictate that girls share with girls and boys share with boys, but in this family's case, this would mean one boy would have his own room, while five of his female siblings (some biological and some bonus) crowded into the other room. In this family's case, gender could not be the tiebreaker. They decided that Robert's daughter and son would have one bedroom, while Jackie's four daughters slept in two bunk beds in the other room.

The most important aspect of bonus family room sharing is to make sure that each of the children, no matter how small the room, has a wall—or at least a shelf—that is all their own. This is especially important if the child has a room of her own at one

house but has to share at the other. In these cases, privacy becomes
the issue, and bonus families must take special care to be respectful and allow family members private time if they want it.

Request for Private Time Using CARE

C is for Communication: Decide how family members will
communicate their need for private time. Does the family need a
schedule, or will family members simply honor the request when
asked?

A is for Acceptance: Accept that each family member may not
require the same amount of alone time. Introverts need far more
quiet time than extroverts. Be aware of their different requirements. Everyone is not the same.

R is for Respect: When a family member requests alone time,
respect their need and help them to achieve it.

E is for Empathy: Can you imagine the need for quiet time to
center yourself, but you are unable to find it? This can make family
members jittery, anxious, and short-tempered. Be sensitive when
family members request alone time.

Staying Flexible

My bonus family also had similar decisions to make when setting up the children's rooms. We lived in a three-bedroom home,
which was fine when it was just my husband, my daughter, and
me, but when his two children came home every other week, it
was crowded. Then we added a child, and it was time to move. This
time, we ended up in a four-bedroom home, but this still required
two of the children to share a room when my bonus son and
bonus daughter came home. My bonus daughter, Melanie, shared
a room with her youngest sibling until she turned 18 and moved
out. Her sister was then 7 years old. Many would think that the
age difference could present problems when sharing a room, but
in our case, Melanie was extremely nurturing and kind to her little
sister. They formed a lovely bond that continues to this day. I have

to admit, there were times we brought our little one into our room so that her sister could have privacy with her older friends, or we let the older girls camp out in front of the TV. There were also times we coordinated efforts with her mother, which allowed Mel to adjust her schedule to match her social life.

For example, although Melanie was scheduled to sleep at our home the week of her junior prom, her siblings were also at our house, which required her to be very quiet when she came home—something she did not want to do after all the excitement. So, she spent the night at her mother's where she and her friends had a party afterward. By that time, it was 11 years into the bonus family experiment and there were no "my time, your time" disagreements between co-parents. Coordinating efforts between Mom's house and our house was commonplace.

It's More Than Just Sharing a Room

> *My husband has a 6-year-old daughter from a previous marriage, and together we have another, [a] 3-year-old daughter. My bonus daughter sleeps over twice a month and shares a small room with two single beds with her half-sister. The room is really too small for two beds, so I suggested buying an air mattress that could be stored away, but my husband won't hear of it; he thinks his daughter will feel slighted. My feeling is my stepdaughter has her own room at her mom's house, why does my daughter's room have to be cluttered with an extra bed that only gets used twice a month? I love my family very much and want everyone to be happy and comfortable.*

I am going to speculate about the battle this father could be waging on a subconscious level. He's probably trying to go out of his way to include his first daughter in just about everything that concerns this family. Although his wife may feel this to be an intrusion, at the same time, he feels that this shows his oldest daughter that he loves her as much as he loves this family. He wants to make sure that his daughter knows that she holds a permanent place in his heart. Therefore, this bed is symbolic of more than just where she sleeps while at his home. It's a way to make sure she feels included.

Let's take another look at the original inquiry; the language is very telling. The writer says, "my stepdaughter has her own room at her mom's house, why does my daughter's room have to be cluttered with an extra bed that only gets used twice a month?" Something new partners forget is that their partner, in this case the father, is father to both children. It's impossible for him to choose between the two. A bed may seem like a small thing to this stepmother, but in his heart, this daddy is juggling his babies. It would not be surprising if he felt guilty that his daughter had to visit instead of living with him. He could be struggling with guilt about the divorce. Like so many other divorced parents who must share custody of their children, he may secretly fear that he abandoned his child when her mother and he divorced. His wife is very clear in her reasoning, but that reasoning does not take into consideration how her husband might feel (**E** is for **Empathy**), possibly because she has no idea. There are lots of things he may not be voicing, which just makes this situation worse. It is his responsibility to confide his insecurities (**C** is for **Communication**) so she can be more sensitive to his concerns and both can better address the needs of the family.

Discipline: Who Disciplines and How?
One of the most common questions I am asked is if bonus parents should discipline their partner's children. My comment is always, "Parents make the rules; Bonus parents uphold those rules," but that does require an amendment because there are certain times when you cannot take this rule literally.

In a bonus family, one parent is the biological parent, while the other is the bonus parent. Being careful to stick to this rule as stated may automatically put the bonus couple in an adversarial position—the biological parent is the boss, and the bonus parent isn't. But, when both partners have children, then they are both parents and both bonus parents. Following this same line of reasoning, they are both bosses. The caveat comes when both parents have established rules for their children prior to uniting forces—and those rules don't line up.

For example, Chad and Nancy both had two children prior to moving in together. Chad's children had chores before his divorce, and to stay consistent, he wanted the kids to have the same chores at his home after the breakup. Nancy's kids were 5 or 6 years younger. She said she felt it was a good day when her kids flushed the toilet. Chad's children became resentful because they had chores and Nancy's children didn't. They did not see the age difference. They just saw, "It isn't fair."

The parent and bonus parent must coordinate efforts or there will be nothing but resentment and chaos. That's why approaching this lifestyle with CARE—good communication, acceptance, respect, and empathy—is essential. All the players must listen to each other's concerns (**C**ommunication), take each other's backgrounds and history into consideration (**A**cceptance), respect each other's opinions (**R**espect), and put themselves in the other's shoes (**E**mpathy) when a different perspective is needed.

In this case, the younger children were assigned age-appropriate chores, but to ensure "fairness," the older kids were in on the assignments because they were previously assigned these chores, and they are now being redistributed. Both the bonus parent and the parent should be present for a discussion like this because we are addressing bonus siblings, and without both parent figures present, there may be a perception of prejudice.

The child's parent should initiate this conversation. "Miranda, you are 11 and have quite a few chores assigned to you. Let's sit down and figure out what chores Laura can handle to help you out." (Laura, her bonus sibling, is 6.)

"I think Laura should pick up the dog poop!"

"Really? Do you think she is old enough to handle that chore? I know it is messy, but let's think about it."

"Well, it's disgusting."

"I understand, but do you think Laura will be able to manage the scooper?"

"Probably not, but I hate doing it."

"I understand, and we really appreciate your help with it. What's another chore you can share?"

"Clear the table after dinner?"

"With your help, I think that's an excellent suggestion. I will help, too."

Since the older children were feeling slighted, it's a good idea to get them involved in the chore distribution so they could be part of the decision and no longer feel singled out. When they felt the chores were divided more equitably, they saw it as a family responsibility rather than a chore they were stuck with because they were "the stepchild" or "the oldest."

Discipline in Your Immediate Bonus Family

A crucial part of forming a bonus family is the adults deciding on and then presenting the rules in a fashion that lets the children see the bonus couple as a united front. If the bonus couple openly contradicts each other in front of the children, aside from undermining each other, it will also undermine the children's feeling of security. They won't know who to believe, and when feeling uncertain, they will feel as if they must align with someone. Most of the time, it's their parent, but conflict can make them question who is right and who is wrong. When there is open hostility between bonus family members, the family tends to split into factions based on blood relations. Once that happens, it is very difficult to regain middle ground.

In most cases, biological parents do make the rules for their children, and the bonus parents should uphold those rules. But there are times when bonus parents need to be able to offer input into establishing policy. One example is when the bonus parent is the primary caregiver and must have the authority to make decisions for the safety of all the children in their care. A second example is when the bonus parent is also trying to coordinate house rules and disciplinary tactics with rules that were in place for their own children prior to living as a bonus family. And finally, when bonus parents are trying to coordinate house rules with their partner's co-parent or their own co-parent.

Problems arise when the bonus parent attempts to establish policy and then is unwilling to compromise when confronted. As a result, the biological parent feels threatened, resulting in power struggles that are difficult to resolve unless everyone stops, takes a deep breath, and remembers once again to remove their personal self-interests and put the children first.

Keeping Discipline Consistent

> *My husband and I have been married for a year. We both have 15-year-old children—he has a boy, and I have a girl. My husband shares custody of his son with his co-parent. Recently, when school progress reports came, my daughter presented hers to me, but my bonus son told his father that progress reports were not due for another week. It appears that my bonus son has not been doing his homework and was afraid to tell us; however, his mother knew. My husband did not punish my bonus son for lying or for the bad grades, and he did not check in with his co-parent. This would not have been the case if my daughter had acted in the same manner.*

It's not uncommon for parents to feel guilty about their divorce—and their inability to live with their children full-time. Parents who feel this way tend to be extremely lenient whenever their children visit. To further complicate the issue in this case, there is a child who follows the rules. She sees the inequality in the way she and her bonus brother are disciplined. Soon her bonus dad will wonder why his relationship with her has deteriorated.

What often happens next is that the bonus parent calls her husband's problematic parenting to his attention. He then tries to change his ways, but he's inconsistent because he's fighting his guilt. His son gets angry because he can now only manipulate things some of the time and sees it's because the bonus parent is helping his parent stay consistent. He starts to resent the bonus parent; he may even threaten to move in with Mom full-time. The father panics and punishes poor behavior even less, which in turn infuriates the bonus parent.

For the child's benefit, his father must accept his choice to leave the relationship with his child's mother. It's done; vacillating between guilt and responsibility will not solve anything. He will not be able to make it up to his child by not confronting the child's poor behavior. Guilt-ridden or not, for the sake of the child, this father must stand his ground and do the best he can to coordinate efforts within his own home plus his co-parent's home. And that lesson does not stop with the son. His bonus daughter is watching, too. If this bonus dad wants to maintain a loving relationship with her, he must be as consistent as possible with *all* the children in his care.

Discipline When Only One Parent Has Children

> *My partner has never had children. When we first started to date, he was polite to my son, who is now 7, but recently my partner seems to discipline not out of love, but out of a need for control. We just don't see eye-to-eye, and he's my son. I want this relationship to work, but I'm ready to leave. I don't know how to make my partner see he's approaching this all wrong.*

A difference in disciplinary techniques is one of the biggest problems plaguing combined families, and the turmoil this causes seems to be exaggerated when only one parent has children. To complicate the issue, it sounds like this new bonus parent has fallen into a very common trap—attempting to take over and discipline far too soon.

There is a difference in how bio parents and bonus parents approach discipline, and it seems biology might be the determining factor. Biology allows us to forgive many of the mistakes our children make along the way, while bonus parents tend to look at things more objectively—they form their allegiances through acts and deeds. If there is unrest among the ranks, bonus parents are less likely to take it in stride unless they have had practice and have built a bond with the bonus child. This takes time, which is something that biological parents have on their side. The bonus parent-bonus child bond is built at an accelerated rate, beginning when the parent and partner get together, not at birth, and when people are forced to move too quickly, they often resist.

"You're Not My Parent!"

To demonstrate this point, let's look at a typical bonus family scenario and examine the different ways a biological parent and a bonus parent approach the problem.

Let's say the house rule is no eating in front of the TV. The biological mom comes home from work very tired, sees her teenager eating in front of the TV, and assesses that it's no big deal—there's no food on the rug—so she decides to take a shower and relax. The bonus parent walks in, sees the teen eating in front of the TV, and yells very loudly, "You are breaking the house rules!" The child says, "Wait a minute. Mom saw me eating in front of the TV and didn't say a word. Who the heck are you? You're not my parent."

The only alternative the bonus parent has is to confront the biological parent. The biological parent is thinking, "Look, I'm exhausted. I've had a terrible day at work. All I did was let the kid eat in front of the TV. So shoot me." But the bonus parent sees it as betrayal: "You set me up! You aren't supporting me! You are letting your child break the rules, and it makes me look like the bad guy. You are choosing your child over me."

This example demonstrates the different attitudes held by biological parents and bonus parents. Biological parents learn to pick their battles with their kids. Everything doesn't have to be a big deal, and they may simply let some of the small stuff go. Bonus parents, particularly those who have never had children, see this as inconsistent parenting. They often try to step in to compensate for what they feel are the biological parent's failings. This is the quickest way for a bonus parent to lose their bonus status and appear "wicked." The kids resent the interference because they are being disciplined when their own parent would not have disciplined them. The biological parent resents the interference because it implies their bonus parent does not respect their parenting skills. The bonus parent is simply trying to help organize the household, feels frustrated, angry, misunderstood, and worst of all, betrayed by their partner.

There's something else to consider. Arguments between biological parents and their kids may be soon forgotten, whereas a new partner may view arguments with their partner's children as "disrespectful." Respect is very important to bonus parents looking for acceptance. Biological parents don't see arguments as a direct affront to their sensibilities; bonus parents often do.

In the end, hugs, kisses, "I love you" or "I'm sorry" are great ways to end an argument. These signs of affection occur more naturally and freely between biological parents and their kids.

Because of these differences, it is imperative that the biological parent and bonus parent agree on disciplinary rules and tactics before they move in together. This is the very reason I created the Before Bonus Exercise.

It's important to establish your house rules together and then stick with them. All rules should apply equally to all family members—even the adult family members. If only one partner has children, then obviously they are the one with the final say, but it must be consistent with the morals of the bonus parent, or you will not have the bonus parent's cooperation. A bonus parent who morally disagrees with a biological parent's rules will not uphold them.

By the same token, if a bonus parent wants to be accepted as a parent figure, they must move slowly into their new position of authority, taking the parent's lead and assisting to refine the rules if need be.

Setting the Example

Initially, we learn how to communicate with our partners by watching how our parents interact with one another. If you manipulate with hurtful words, slam doors at the end of a disagreement, refuse to talk, or are unforgiving, there is a very good chance your children will mimic your behavior in their relationships. And don't think you are off the hook if you are their bonus parent. All parent figures are role models for the children in their care.

Offering and Accepting an Apology

We all know we aren't supposed to argue in front of the kids. Yet even the happiest of couples catch themselves loudly disagreeing enough for the kids to hear. To worsen the situation, when these couples realize the kids are nearby, they might move to a private room to finish the argument and make up behind closed doors. The kids are not witnesses to the concessions made to end the argument. They see the outcome—their parents are no longer fighting—but the kids have no idea why the argument ended. This approach gives your children a model for conflict but no guide to successfully solve disagreements.

For this reason, when offering tools to help bonus families resolve conflicts, I have gone so far as to suggest that the bonus couple stage an apology for the children in their care after a disagreement. This tactic works for co-parents, as well. While going through your regular routine and the kids are within earshot, casually apologize again. While there is no need to bare private matters or try to justify your position, offering the words "I'm sorry" and "I accept your apology" or "I'm sorry, too" offers children a positive model for conflict resolution they can use in every relationship throughout their lifetime.

> *My mom and bonus dad were arguing. Both were really angry and yelling loudly. All of a sudden, it went quiet. My mom had noticed I was in the other room listening and I heard her go over to my bonus dad and say, "I'm sorry I lost my temper. I shouldn't have spoken to you like that." I could tell my bonus dad was still mad, but they hugged and a little while later it seemed like things were okay.*

What did this mother's simple apology teach her child? It demonstrated firsthand how to assess a situation and respond constructively rather than merely react because you are angry or your feelings are hurt. It modeled how to accept responsibility for one's actions and to respect another's feelings. It taught love and acceptance rather than retaliation; the list of positives is quite long.

There's more to this story. This mother's former husband had lied to her about how much money he owed prior to their getting married. They divorced because of it. The reason for this argument was that the mother had received a notification of insufficient funds from her bank. Her husband was supposed to make a deposit, and she was shocked when there was no money in the account. She was reminded of her past problem, and she immediately accused her husband of stealing the money. While arguing, they figured out that he had deposited the money in the wrong account.

Based on that, a more complete apology, using it as an example for the children, might have included how she should have approached the situation. "I'm sorry I lost my temper. I shouldn't have spoken to you like that. I should have asked you about the notification calmly and you would have easily explained what happened. I sincerely apologize."

Now the children know that approaching a problem calmly is the preferred mode of action.

What if this parent had taken the opposite approach? What if they had noticed the child watching the argument, screamed at the top of their lungs, and then stomped out of the room while slamming doors? What a different message that would send to their child. Now the message would be, "I can control someone with my anger. If I act displeased, withhold communication and affection, and act out, I can manipulate this person into feeling bad enough to give me my way. Anger gives me power. When I am angry, I will win."

Retaliatory behavior promotes resentment, holding grudges, and teaches our children to be vengeful and unforgiving. Furthermore, it makes family members less likely to want to apologize to us in the future. No relationship can survive with such feelings at its base.

Does this mean that we should teach our children to shrink in the face of conflict? To shy away from family members when they disagree? Of course not. Apologies are important, but there's more to it than that. The bigger lesson may not be the apology, but the gracious acceptance of an apology when we are angry. Openly accepting an apology teaches our children the power of forgiveness—an important tool to help make our bonus families a happy, safe, loving place to live.

Bonus Family Problem Solving

From talking to thousands of bonus families over the years, it is clear that the families that really work have a way to solve their disagreements in place from day one. That way, when a problem arises, there's no guesswork. The family members know exactly what to do. This approach prevents the family from breaking into factions when there are disagreements, each partner and their kids against the other partner and their kids. If one of the partners doesn't have children, that partner most certainly becomes the outsider. With no way to resolve conflict, if the factions continue, the family will eventually break up. With a method to solve bonus family problems in place, each bonus family member can depend on an organized way to resolve family conflict.

The principle behind family conflict resolution is to teach our children to look for mutually agreed-upon compromises within the family structure. This negotiation can go by any name the bonus family chooses. At my home we called it "the family discussion," but other families call it "the family meeting" or "discussion time." One bonus family I worked with chose "family peace time." I liked that. Each family should personalize their choice, picking a name that evokes a feeling of peaceful, loving conflict resolution from within their bonus family unit.

Does This Cooperative Approach Give Children Too Much Power?

Parents attempting to combine families have expressed a concern that a cooperative method of resolving conflict may appear that they have given up their parental power. They are leery of offering an open forum to solve bonus family problems for fear the children will think they run the show. On the contrary, because bonus family members are often overly sensitive about issues of fairness and favoritism, having a forum to air misunderstandings offers family members an equal opportunity to discuss their differences. If parents present themselves as the leaders, they will remain the leaders as the bonus family matures.

By the same token, after a breakup, children have expressed that they often feel powerless. Their parents have made the decision to split up and then become involved with someone else, all without consulting them. Family discussions, when approached correctly, give children a forum to be heard; therefore, they feel as if they can once again have some control over their own lives.

But it remains understood that the parents have the final decision while acknowledging the children's input.

When handled properly, family discussions can serve as problem solving vehicles to air differences without assigning blame. By setting up rules for these discussions, families can often avoid the allegiance and betrayal issues that are so common in combined family disagreements.

Rules for Family Discussions

The following guide is an outline resulting from years of working with bonus families. It has been tweaked over the years as we learned more about bonus family conflict resolution. You will notice it follows the Bonus Family Problem Solving Model listed in previous chapters. That model has been incorporated into this forum for family problem solving.

Step 1: Identify the problem

Step 2: Suggest a child-focused solution

Step 3: Negotiate

Step 4: Compromise

Preparing for the Family Discussion

Family problems are too important to be left to spontaneous outbursts. Conflict resolution works best when family members remain calm and come to the table with an open mind.

Make an appointment with family members to talk things over. Asking family members to make formal appointments for family discussions shows the significance of constructive conflict resolution within the bonus family unit. Any family member may initiate the family discussion, children or parent figures.

The family member calling the appointment decides on the date and time, scheduling it far enough in advance that all family members can attend. Suggesting that any family member, no matter his or her age, may call a family discussion promotes feelings of equality and fair play. When something is bothering a family member, they should make a formal appointment to meet: "I am calling a family discussion for 5:00 p.m. on Sunday afternoon." Ample time must be offered so that family members can reorganize their plans to attend. It is understood by all family members that they should schedule social events for after the family discussion.

All family members living in the home must attend. Attendance is a requirement of bonus family membership.

All must come prepared with a positive outlook and a desire to solve the problem. The presenter makes the observation and comes to the table with a proposed solution. The other family members must come with an open mind, ready to negotiate, compromise, and problem solve as a family.

No outbursts, no interruptions. Anger with a family member may be the reason behind the need to call a family discussion, but don't let emotions get out of hand. If raising one's voice or insulting other family members is allowed during the meeting, it will not teach children how to solve problems in a respectful manner. Require those who have the floor to be direct, but not insulting. No interruptions from those who are listening.

"I Messages"

In Chapter 1 we discussed using "I messages" to help co-parents more effectively communicate their feelings. Family members can also use I messages as a constructive tool when speaking to each other during family discussions. Remember to start your sentences with "I feel" to reduce a defensive reaction in the opposition. This sets the stage for an openness to negotiate and ultimately compromise.

As you recall, there are three basic steps to successfully using I messages:

- State the feeling.

- State the offending behavior.
- State the effect it has on you.

After you state the effect it has on you, request the change in behavior that you would like to see.

Let's look at the interaction between two bonus brothers, Mark and Timothy. Their arguing was getting out of hand and causing tension in the home. It got to the point that no one wanted to be around them, and there were three other children in the home besides their parents. Out of frustration, Mark's mother called a family discussion. Rather than fight back and forth, they were instructed to use I messages during the meeting.

Five children and two parents sat at the dining room table. Mark was the one who called the meeting and was the one to start.

"I feel angry (feeling) when Tim takes my tablet without asking (behavior). He plays my game, loses, and I'm not on the level I should be. It's so frustrating (effect)! I would like Tim to ask to borrow my tablet. I don't really care if he uses it when I'm not home, but I would like him to sign on using his own name so he doesn't mess up my game. And I want to be able to say no if I don't want him to use it (change)."

Tim's excuse for the behavior was that his tablet was broken, but he was honest and admitted that he shouldn't have signed on to Mark's game. He knew it bothered him, and he did it anyway. He made a formal apology to Mark at the family meeting.

There's more: Evidently, Mark had purchased the tablet using his own money. Tim wanted a new tablet. Mom didn't realize the root of all this was a broken tablet and set up some special chores for Tim so he could earn extra money for a new tablet. Until then, it was decided that he must ask to use Mark's tablet, and if Mark says no, Tim needs to respect that.

The ability for Mark to say no ensured two things:

1. Mark regained his personal power.

2. Tim now had the incentive and a way to get a new tablet.

By expressing himself in a calm fashion at the family discussion, Mark was finally able to get through to Tim and Tim changed his offending behavior. Until that point, Mark's ranting had no effect on Tim's actions. Tim thought it was funny.

If the family had not found Mark's solution to the problem acceptable, the family would then search for a solution to the problem—together.

The culmination of the successful family discussion is that family members feel comfortable working together to find solutions to perceived problems. When family members openly consider each other's suggestions as solutions, it reinforces family unity and mutual respect.

What Family Discussions Are Not . . .

A family discussion can easily turn into a shouting match when family members, specifically the parents, use it to chastise a child in front of the entire family. That's not the purpose of these discussions, and if that's what they become, family members will be reluctant to sit still while others point fingers.

In successful family discussions, there is a leader but no boss. The person with the grievance calls the meeting and usually serves as the leader or moderator unless that family member is too young to maintain control of the meeting. They are the one to begin the discussion once all are in attendance. If the discussion goes off track, someone, usually a parent figure, redirects family members to look for solutions to the problem up for discussion. Family discussions are a way to solve problems, not air dirty laundry.

Financial Contributions to Each Other's Children

My daughter Michelle is 16 and has asked to go to cheerleading camp this summer. It is very expensive, and the cost is well above what her father pays in child support. My husband said when we move in together next month, we will find a way to send her. But my bonus son also wants to go to soccer camp. How can we send one child and not the other?

These are the things you must discuss and decide on prior to moving in together. Agreeing about splitting rent, utilities, and groceries is expected. Are you open to helping your partner with expenses for their children? If not, figure out an alternative. Do not move in together without an agreed-upon solution. It will come up and it will drive a wedge between you.

Sometimes child support just isn't enough and I have to pitch in. This isn't what I signed up for.

Unfortunately, child support doesn't always cover all the children's expenses. Bonus parents (bonus moms and bonus dads) must understand that child support pays for necessities, but it doesn't cover the extras—and there will be extras. If we want our children to be well-rounded, we must expose them to as much as we can. This means things like soccer during soccer season, horseback riding in the warmer weather, cheerleading, or drama workshops. As the child gets older, the demands only increase. Child support does not cover phones, phone bills, prom dresses, tuxedo rentals, yearbooks, senior pictures, cars, or car insurance.

All these things require a discussion with your co-parent. But what if your co-parent says no? Or can't afford it? That's when the bonus parent may have to pitch in with finances—or understand that if they don't want to help, their partner may not be able to help with the utilities for a month because they are paying for their child's baseball camp. It's important that all bonus parents understand this when they move in or marry someone with children; otherwise, there is likely to be resentment.

* * *

All the things we have discussed in this chapter are tools designed to help parents and bonus parents prepare for moving in together and create a cohesive loving bonus family unit. Starting with creating the proper mindset to having a plan for how to handle unexpected financial considerations—all must be anticipated before you take the plunge.

The next step is learning how to coordinate efforts with your co-parent as well as your partner's co-parent to form your Bonus Family Team—it takes a village—and that's what we will address in Chapter 4.

CHAPTER 4

Building Your Bonus Team

Sitting in my office trying to keep my mind on my work, the phone rang and distracted me. "Oh geez, who could that be?" I wondered. I was on deadline and did not want to be bothered. It was Sharyl, my bonus kids' mom. She was part of a carpool taking the kids to after school practice and she realized she would not be able to do it next Thursday.

"Would you do it?" she asked. "Please? I'll be out of town. Sales meeting."

"Sure," I said. "Thanks for the heads-up. It will give me plenty of time to plan."

There was silence for a second and I could tell she was collecting her thoughts.

"Jann . . . " she said matter-of-factly. "How do people do this without three parents?"

Working parents need help, and the last person most think to ask is their co-parent, let alone their co-parent's new partner. Jealousy, anger, hurt feelings, and territorial behavior are what is expected—all of which are part of "just being human."

I've heard the "just being human" excuse many times while in session with co-parents. They rely on it when there is no other excuse for their bad behavior. However, studies clearly show what parental "bad behavior" does to their children. It's time to take a different approach, a cooperative approach, where co-parents and their new partners unite in support of all the children in the care. But most scoff at the suggestion. *That's impossible.*

Before I start with what is necessary to build and maintain your Bonus Team, let me explain that by the time the above conversation took place between me and the kids' biological mother, we were about 4 years into our bonus family experiment. I firmly believe the reason it took so long to work together was because we didn't know any better. At that time no one was talking about the need to cultivate a working relationship with former partners, their current partners, and extended family to raise healthy children after a breakup. Parents were still getting used to sharing custody with each other, and they had no idea that to do that well, they must coordinate efforts with past and present.

What eventually brought us all to our senses was that we realized we were in this together. The kids, all of their parents, new partners, grandparents, and extended family, whether we liked it or not. I lived with Sharyl's children, and even though my biological kids didn't live with her, they were witness to her life. The decisions she made for her children affected my children. Why? Because *her* children (who were also my husband's children) went back and forth between our homes every other week. Our children were being raised as siblings. Her children's grandparents interacted with my kids. Their aunts and uncles and cousins interacted with my kids. My extended family interacted with her kids. We were clearly raising each other's children, and that set the stage for what is now regarded as a bonus family. It literally takes a village.

That's how you get in conversations like the one at the beginning of this chapter. After years of butting heads, you unite with your partner and your partner's co-parent in the name of the children you all love. To make it simpler, I call this the "counter-partner" relationship. It's based on the word "counterpart," which refers to a person holding a position or performing a function that corresponds to that of another person. Most commonly, that's a mom and bonus mom or a dad and bonus dad, but the term "counterpartner" is not gender specific.

FORMING YOUR BONUS TEAM
The Bonus Triad

The triad relationship juggles the co-parents and one of the co-parent's new partners. For example, in my case, I joined the co-parenting club and that changed the co-parenting dynamic to a triad. In the beginning, it's common for the co-parent who has not re-coupled to feel as if it is two against one. The new couple is often of the same mind and the other person feels left out of the loop. When a two-against-one dynamic is present, it can easily interfere with the ability to successfully co-parent. That's why it is so important to put boundaries in place prior to the entrance of the new partner that will allow them to successfully approach child-rearing as a team. But, even in the most amicable co-parenting relationships when one re-couples or remarries, it changes the balance of power, and co-parents and their partners must make a special effort to remain respectful of each other's position and point of view.

The Bonus Attitude as Opposed to Two Against One

The following question was posed to me by a client who had so completely moved on with a new partner after his breakup that he forgot his responsibility as a co-parent. Their co-parenting interaction during a session demonstrates firsthand how a two-against-one attitude can impact your co-parenting relationship and how unreasonable one can become as a result.

> "I just asked my girlfriend to marry me. We have been together for
> 3 years and have lived together for 2. I have a 5-year-old son who
> adores my fiancée." I watched the child's mother cringe when the

father said that. "For some reason," the father continued, "my ex will not allow my son to participate in our wedding. My son is very upset. I'm pushing to elope."

Let's analyze what might be happening here, and then it will be easy to find the solution.

For years, the co-parents in question had been sharing equal custody of their child. They were very young and did not choose to marry, but now this father is planning to marry his girlfriend. Although the mother had not expressed her contempt for the father, you could feel her anger. She was upset that she had this man's child 5 years ago, but now he's marrying someone else—and to top it all off, her child "adores" the woman he has chosen to marry. When a co-parent feels overlooked and disrespected, it should not be surprising that they become uncooperative. The mother felt overlooked and shoved aside, and to exercise what little control she had, she felt she had to forbid the child from taking part in the wedding. The father, not realizing how he had contributed to the problem, offered a flip solution, "I'm pushing to elope." His response just reinforced how little he was invested in the co-parenting relationship.

This situation is a perfect example of why I take the stance I do when working with co-parents. If a co-parenting relationship is to flourish, they must adopt an attitude of acceptance, collaboration, and respect. The ex-relationship must be left in the past and the parents must now openly respect each other as the child's parents. Their common ground is not their ex-relationship or all the years they spent together. Their common ground is their child. This mother must know in her heart that no one will take her place—and if Dad and his fiancée have made her feel as if someone could—in this case, his fiancée—then I'm not surprised mother was digging in her heels. She was reasserting the importance of her position.

So, was this mother putting the child first in all this? No, because she was too involved in her hurt when the father so easily moved on that she didn't realize she was using the child as a pawn to make her position known. But I also had to call to the father's attention that he may have so completely moved on that he had overlooked his responsibility to the co-parenting relationship, as well. This child had two homes. Two allegiances that must work together in his name. Dad forgot about a major member of the team—Mom.

The answer? This father and his fiancée must cultivate a more secure co-parenting relationship with his son's mother. When Mom feels respected as the child's mother and not overlooked as an ex, she may not be as intimidated by the father moving on and the introduction of another parenting figure in her son's life. The child participating in the father's wedding will then become the natural order of things.

Create a Bridge, Not a Wall

The relationship dynamic changes again when *both* co-parents have new partners. I call this the "co-parenting tetra," meaning four people working together in the name of the children in their care. It is then that all the players must realize that a new member has been added to the team and be careful not to allow factions to form—one co-parent and their partner against the other co-parent and their partner. When co-parents perceive they have an ally other than their co-parent, it is easy to slip into an adversarial, "you two against us" frame of mind. The co-parents forget to consult each other and rely on their partner to make parenting decisions.

The example each co-parent sets—how to problem solve, how to respect, and how to cooperate with one another—can create a bridge between the two homes or a wall. A bridge connects the two sides, allowing the children to gently move between the homes. You can see it in your mind—the child smiling as they travel from one loving home to the other. A wall stops the loving interaction and checks the child's allegiance each time they walk out the door.

United We Stand, Divided We Fall

Don't misunderstand the above scenario. New partners play a significant role in the ease with which people co-parent and live life after the initial breakup. A bonus parent can contribute to stepfamily chaos or aid in bonus family problem solving. They can be a significant member of the team or a spoiler. A new partner's presence impacts everyone, from your children to extended family members to your co-parent. In my case, I was Mom to some and Bonus Mom to others in my care. I was also the primary caregiver of "yours, mine, and ours" kids. In these cases, bonus parents must be empowered to make decisions for the safety of the children in their care.

> *I was my bonus son's caregiver for the day and I caught him playing with a pocket lighter he found in the junk drawer. Of course, a lighter shouldn't be in a junk drawer where there are kids who could play with it, but it was, and there he was in the backyard trying to light a stick on fire. I was so grateful that his dad, mom, and I had already discussed what to do if something like this happened. I disciplined him as we agreed and then called my husband and my bonus son's mom to let them know. No one was angry and I didn't end up the bad guy.*
> – LEEANDRA, BONUS MOM TO SALEM, AGE 5

It simply makes more sense to present a united front and cooperate with each other so that you can offer the same morals and ethics to the children than to compete with each other and confuse the children as a result.

Biological vs. Bonus

So many co-parents have confided that they are afraid their children might prefer their co-parent's new partner over them. Then when a child calls a bonus parent Mom or Dad, it affects the parent the same as an arrow to the heart.

I remember one co-parent's sad voice whisper under her breath while attending co-parenting classes. Up to that point she had been fighting and arguing with her co-parent, so angry he had met someone and moved on. After throwing up all sorts of imagined reasons as to why she would not allow her co-parent's new partner to be alone with the children, she finally just broke down. *What if they love her?*

I've heard the same fear from fathers, as well. The vulnerability parents feel about their children after a breakup is difficult to explain. Even the most secure parent has confided they feel less at peace in their parenting role after a breakup. Breakups change everything.

The truth is you want your children to care for their bonus parent. You want their bonus parent to care for your children. There is not either/or in a bonus family, there's *also*. Children love their parents, but they can have a special place in their heart for their bonus parents—if you all take the pressure off them having to choose. Because there is no choice, really. The parent is the parent. But you can't have too many people love your child, and if they aren't traumatized by leaving your home because they love the people at the other home, as well, thank goodness. You've all done your job.

It's important to point out that years ago, parenting roles were often defined by gender—as a blanket statement, moms were the nurturers and dads were the providers and protectors. Today, gender no longer determines the role of the nurturer, provider, or protector in the family. Each family assigns those roles to the appropriate parent figure, regardless of gender. However, a divorced parent who is feeling insecure about what they perceive as the loss of time with their children and a new bonus parent who may be feeling insecure about their newfound parenting responsibilities can be a volatile mix. Both may not understand their role and may struggle for control. Without an open line of communication between them, this can lead to disaster.

To drive this observation home, let's look at an exchange between a dad and a bonus dad from a private co-parenting session. It will explain their different points of view and help to illuminate the inherent animosity felt by both men.

Luis (biological dad): "The divorce nearly broke me, and I could barely make ends meet. Then Jack (Luis's ex) moved in with Mark, a guy with money, and although my son (Jason) had everything he wanted, I wasn't the one who was buying the things for him. I felt like a failure. Every time I tried to save up for something special, this guy went out and bought my kid something bigger and better. I could never compete."

Mark (bonus dad): "I knew Luis was having financial problems. His child support payments were often late, and Jack felt bad asking him for the check each month. Rather than wait for the money, I just bought Jason what he needed. I didn't realize it was undermining Luis. I thought I was helping."

Luis: "It's not so much the things that are purchased, but the value put on the things. Mark makes a lot more money than I do. He drives a newer, bigger, faster car. Everything is designer label. My son is so swayed by the glitter—his values are now completely different. How can I say, 'Mark, I think you are very materialistic, and now you have made my son just like you.' I can't."

And so, Luis said nothing to Mark, but all the while he was feeling inadequate as a provider and worrying about the values that were being instilled in his child. Every time he saw Mark, he was reminded how he no longer had control over his son. And Mark, just living his life, had no idea what he'd done to make Luis so angry. Meanwhile, Jack, Luis's co-parent, was stuck right in the middle of his partner and the father of his child.

Parents want to control their children's environment, but it's difficult to do so when your child lives for weeks or months at a time with your co-parent and their new partner. The values imposed at the other home have just as much influence on your children as do your values. As a result, the competition can become so intense that the competing parties lose sight of their original goal—instilling positive values and raising well-adjusted children—and spend most of their time trying to undermine each other's influences.

To further complicate the issue between Mark and Luis, Mark's attitude became almost arrogant. He began to refer to Luis as a "deadbeat" dad, and even though Jack tried to intercede, Mark's animosity grew because he felt his contributions were not being appreciated. "Look at what I do for his child, and he never has a civil word to say to me."

Once again, approaching this with CARE was the answer.

C is for Communication: There's a reason for Mark and Luis's misunderstanding; they never talked! Not even polite hellos for Jason's benefit. Even though Luis's child lived with Mark half the time, neither Luis nor Mark initiated a conversation. They had no idea how the other felt. If left unchecked, their unexplored points of view would continue to contribute to hurtful misconceptions. This had to change immediately.

A is for Acceptance: We all come to relationships with a past and an individual point of view. Accepting each other's backgrounds and histories will enable parent and bonus parent to be more supportive of each other's contribution to the care of the children. Luis and Mark had to accept and respect each other's chosen profession. It had to be made clear to Jason that neither job was better. The positions were just different, and both men loved Jason very much.

R is for Respect: Although Mark supported Jack as a co-parent, Mark's role needed to be more clearly defined. Without clarification from both Luis and Jack, Mark would continue to step on toes. Mark had to learn to respect Luis's place as Jason's father.

E is for Empathy: I always say, "Empathy is the great equalizer." It was determined that Luis and Mark needed to have a guided heart-to-heart in my office to air their differences. That is when Mark heard firsthand how Luis felt inadequate as a provider. That's also when Mark realized perhaps he was doing too good of a job picking up the slack. Luis was not a "deadbeat" but anxious and embarrassed about the discrepancy in wages. He had no reason to be. Luis was extremely competent and worked very hard.

Mark asked Luis point-blank what he would like him to do. "I just want to be kept in the loop," Luis explained. "I may not be able to afford what you are offering all by myself, but I can certainly contribute." From that point on, each time Mark and Jack wanted to buy Jason something special, they checked with Luis to confirm his possible participation. They were careful not to put him on the spot and agreed that participating was up to him, depending on his ability to contribute. It was always presented to Jason as a collaborative effort. No one mentioned how much was contributed. Luis appreciated the cooperative approach, and this helped to heal his resentment. Feeling included, rather than resenting Mark's contribution, Luis then became grateful for the help.

Parents and bonus parents are often guilty of misreading each other's intent, but you can see by this example that it can easily be explained by a lack of communication. Over time, parents and their bonus counterparts develop preconceived notions about the other's motivations and avoid interacting. This can go on for years. They bathe the same child, feed the same child, tuck the same child into bed, but they duck talking to each other or comparing notes about the child they both adore. Luis and Mark's more relaxed interaction not only better supported Jason but took Jack out of the middle.

BUILD A WORKING RELATIONSHIP WITH YOUR PARTNER'S CO-PARENT OR CO-PARENT'S PARTNER

Once again, this sounds good in theory—building an actual partnership with this unlikely collaborator, everyone cooperating for the sake of the children. However, the resultant relationship, the one with your co-parent's partner or your partner's co-parent, has been proven to be the most volatile within the co-parenting triad or tetra. Angry co-parents may compete with each other for their children's time or affection, but their role as parents is clearly defined. Bonus counterparts are often in the same parenting role when the children are with them, and this puts them in direct competition with each other. Mother against mother figure. Father against father figure. That's competition at the most basic level. However, if you agree to make the "best interest of the children" the criteria for all decisions, there will be no guesswork as to the right decision in a given situation. Once the adults remove their own self-interests, everything really does fall into place.

Approaching Your Counterpartner With CARE

Communication: At first, you may have to rely on the Bonus Family Problem Solving Model as a guide to keep your emotions under wraps when approaching your counterpartner. For communication to be effective, you must be clear, concise, and compassionate. Clear in your presentation, concise when offering a solution, and compassionate in order to reach a compromise.

Remember:

Step 1: Identify the problem

Step 2: Suggest a child-focused solution

Step 3: Negotiate

Step 4: Compromise

Acceptance: *Embrace your differences.* You do not have to have similar likes and dislikes or be friends to have a successful counterpartner relationship. Look for common ground but embrace your differences. That is acceptance in its truest form. You need not be too familiar. In the beginning, being polite and cooperative is all that is required. As your acceptance improves, you may build a friendship, but that is not the final goal. The final goal is to be a supportive and reliable person on whom all can depend.

This is not a competition. On so many levels, from worrying that they are a better parent to a better lover, counterpartners can easily fall into a comparison trap, and it is emotional sabotage for everyone concerned. Don't compare, don't compete, and don't fret over past intimacies. The key here is to remember when you are comparing, you are comparing what *you* think about the person to what *you* think about yourself. It's a closed conversation that sets you up for failure. Strive for your own sense of self and hold your head high. A secure person is the most attractive of all.

Find your niche. Many co-parents and their bonus counterparts with whom I have worked don't have a clear sense of their individual responsibilities. As a result, they can easily step on each other's toes and feel undermined by the other. Finding your niche means finding something you do well and offering that to the children—not in competition with your counterpartner, but as a way each of you can offer your best to the children.

For example, I am a perpetual student. I am constantly signing up for classes in something. Therefore, my helping the kids with their homework came naturally. Their mother, on the other hand, was not a student and had a difficult time making them buckle down to do their homework. Instead, she instilled in the kids a pride in their appearance. She was the one to make sure the kids had regular teeth cleanings and haircuts when they were little. The times we unconsciously crossed over to each other's niche, the kids did not get as good a grade on the report, and Steven went back to her home with the haircut from hell. Each of us was furious with the other when we crossed over into the other's territory. So, we assigned each other responsibilities and respected that was their job to complete without interference.

Here's an important caveat to that point, however. One dad told me, "My kid's bonus dad cares for my son. I know it. I can see it in his face when he talks to him, and truthfully, I am appreciative that my child is safe with him. But he just tries too hard. He is always the first one to volunteer, whether it's as soccer coach or to organizing a kid event. I'd call to volunteer, and he had already put his name in. I had to finally explain to him that while I appreciated his devotion, he needed to bring it down a notch. Include me, don't ace me out, or we were going to have problems. He appreciated that I just came out and told him what was on my mind. Now he and I have an understanding. This year I am the soccer coach and just yesterday I got a phone call. He asked if he could be an assistant coach. He *asked*. So far, so good."

Respect: *Cultivate mutual respect.* Respect must be earned; it just doesn't happen. But take note, I said, "*cultivate* mutual respect." That means baby steps. So, for our purposes, the word "cultivate" means "slowly move toward respect by using small gestures." Just as you would plant a small seed, water it, and watch it grow, building a relationship with your counterpartner is a slow but rewarding process. Allow your interaction to grow slowly into a cordial relationship. Don't push yourself before you are ready. Rome wasn't built in a day. Neither are bonus families.

Ask their opinion. I have used "ask their opinion" as a tool to initiate compromise in my business relationships, co-parenting relationships, friendships, and even smoothing things over with my own children. When communication breaks down, *ask their opinion.*

My co-parenting sessions are all on Zoom these days and the parents appear before me on two separate windows. I don't only work with co-parents. Sometimes I meet with just the counterpartners—bio and bonus. The issue at hand for the following clients, Gloria and Madeline, was that there was a problem at school. Gloria's son was suspended for throwing a rock and breaking a window. Madeline was off from work that day and got a phone call asking the child to be picked up. Gloria didn't get a call. This had occurred previously, as well, and Gloria was furious when that happened. Because of Gloria's reaction in the past, Madeline was afraid to call her. She just knew she would lose her temper.

Ironically, this event happened in the afternoon prior to our appointment, and it was the first time these counterpartners had spoken about the incident. It was a safe environment and so Madeline felt safe volunteering that she had to pick up the child from school early. Gloria did start to get angry, but I instructed her to stop, take a breath, and let Madeline explain. Madeline explained and then asked Gloria, "How would you handle this, Gloria, if Scotty was at your house this week?"

I don't think Gloria could believe her ears. The fact that her counterpartner asked for her opinion completely overshadowed the fact that the school hadn't called her. Madeline looked at the camera so I could take note. "I'm completely sick to my stomach right now. I was so sure she would be angry *at me*." Gloria then explained how she would handle it. They had a very similar approach. They were both surprised by the outcome.

I asked Gloria why this time was different. She laughed and said, "You're watching." But then she snickered, "She asked my opinion. She's never done that before."

If you are not sure how to handle a situation about the children, consider asking your counterpartner what they would do in the same situation. Many are afraid to ask because they feel it gives up control to the very person with whom they are struggling for power. Understandable, but it also breaks down walls, and it is an excellent vehicle to open a discussion about how to ensure rules are consistent from house to house. Asking your counterpartner's opinion is a simple way to put the relationship on a new and more equal footing.

Offer appreciation. The most consistent complaint I hear from both parents and bonus parents is that the other does not appreciate how hard they work at doing a good job. Neither thinks the other gets them. Acknowledgment of each other's hard work and dedication goes a long way. It lets them know, "I see you," and places you on equal ground. I know conversations that started with "I am really grateful for how kind you are to the kids" or "I truly appreciate that you pitch in to help when I can't" meant a lot to me and put me at ease before we had to have a more pointed conversation about what really happened when the kids said the sky was falling. A sincere compliment or observation is a genuine way to offer respect, particularly in this uncommon relationship. It enables you to both let down your guard and repeat the cooperative behavior in the future.

Empathy: Misunderstandings and breakdowns in communication will happen if you are not willing to look at a problem from a point of view other than your own. Putting yourself in the other's place to understand a particular behavior may be all that may be needed to get a fresh perspective and resolve conflicts.

Here's a story of two of my clients' personal evolution. They chatted comfortably in my office now, but when I first met them, they were seriously at odds. Their names have been changed. We will call the mother, Holly, and the bonus mom, Giselle.

Holly and Giselle explained that they were never jealous of the past or present relationship with their ex-husband/new partner. It was their individual relationships with Holly's children, Giselle's bonus children, that conjured up those jealous feelings.

Giselle was far more animated than Holly by nature, and the kids gravitated to her antics. They would make crazy hats and wear them as they went on scavenger hunts around the neighborhood. Holly just wasn't that kind of person. The kids would go back to their mom's home with stories of their excursions and Holly would be green with envy. She could not compete with Giselle's energy. To make matters worse, Giselle never referred to

Holly as "your mommy" when she talked about the kids' mother. She called her by her first name, which subconsciously undermined Holly's role as mother. This went on for months, making Holly feel more inadequate as the days ticked by. Then one day, Holly's son said, "Bye, Mommy!" to Giselle right in front of her. Giselle was thrilled. Holly was heartbroken. This did not pave the way for working together. Holly hated Giselle.

It may be difficult to keep all the players straight but let me preface the next part with the explanation that Giselle's ex-husband had also remarried, and Giselle was a mother also dealing with her ex's new partner. Everyone was wearing lots of hats . . .

None of this even registered with Giselle until her own child referred to her own co-parent's partner as "Mommy" at an exchange. "When he said, 'Bye bye, Mommy!' I lost my breath," Giselle confided. "I yelled without thinking, 'That is NOT your Mommy!' and I scared him."

She, too, was heartbroken, and it clicked so quickly what she had been doing to Holly that she confessed embarrassment. "Honestly, it was sort of a game until that second," Giselle admitted. "And I was winning. But then I realized what I was doing. I recognized how badly I felt in that situation and couldn't imagine that I would do that to another mother. Who had I become?"

E is for Empathy. It is truly the great equalizer.

Blurry Boundaries Breeds Contempt

My ex and I got along fine co-parenting our 6-year-old daughter until I remarried 6 months ago. My wife, who does not have children, does not want my ex and I to talk at all and requires all communication be done by text or email. She must do all the drop-offs and pickups, or she throws a fit. Although I want my marriage to work, I'm surprised by her attitude and worry that her controlling nature will get in the way of my co-parenting with my child's mother, not to mention our life together. What do I do?

Unfortunately, this father has made a common mistake that many parents make when they move in with someone or remarry—they forget to have that all-important conversation that makes their boundaries clear. The new partner, intimidated by all the ex-interaction and kid concern, creates boundaries of their own that they believe will prevent their partner from running off with their ex.

And, to top it off, new partners who have never had children often see having a child as an almost spiritual bond between the parents. *They* are the ones who feel that way. Most divorced parents do not. But, if you hold that belief, that's a pretty hard act to follow—and they have created the situation by comparing how they think they'd feel in that situation to how they think others feel. The comparison is in the mind of the new partner—not necessarily in reality.

All must be aware that counterpartners are not rivals. Your spouse is your lover and partner through life. Your co-parent is your partner in raising your child after a breakup. These are two very separate roles. Remove fear from the equation and you'll be surprised how quickly things will fall into place.

Finally, communicating by text or email is only for parents who can't get along. It keeps arguments to a minimum and provides written documentation of the interaction—but it's the least effective form of communication. Currently, the new partner requires this sort of communication because she wants to reduce the parents' interaction, but it's not her place to dictate the preferred mode of parental communication. That is up to the parents.

WHEN THERE HAS BEEN AN AFFAIR

Before we get started with dealing with an affair, I want to acknowledge how difficult it is to continue in the suggested partnership under these conditions. Co-parents and counterpartners each have their own point of view. It is natural that all have trouble putting their emotions aside to interact as parent figures to the same children. Ultimately, however, no matter what has gone on, it does not change the adults' responsibility to the children in their lives.

Should we tell the children about the affair?

As much as you are dying to tell your children what a terrible person their other parent was for running off with someone else, both parents must consider how knowing all the details will help their children feel safe and secure during the most turbulent time in their life. If emotions have gotten out of hand and the children do know about the affair, it would not be surprising if the children resent the parent and their new partner, as well. Of course, there are times when children witness more than we want, and at those times, information must be clarified. But, for all intents and purposes, parents must protect their children from as much gossip or angry talk as possible. Why compound the hurt caused by parental indiscretions by talking about it in front of the children?

You're suggesting we lie to them?

Out and out lie? Absolutely not. But there are some things to take into consideration as you contemplate exactly what the children should be told.

First, their age. The younger the child, the less they will understand, so just answer their questions and don't volunteer information that will confuse and frighten them. Older adolescents or teens will weigh in with their opinions and possibly take sides. Younger children don't really care who is right and who is wrong. They just want their parents to fix things so everything will be okay. If you can project that everything will be okay when talking to them and make them feel safe, you have done your job.

Along the same lines, in taking this tack, you may think you are letting the parent who cheated off the hook. It would truly be sweet revenge to tell the children, and they would never want to talk to the cheating parent again. That's not what you want for your children, to validate your pain through them, and it's probably not what you want for your co-parent. As time moves on, the truth will come out. It always does. And hopefully your children will be old enough at that time to make their own judgments about what happened.

Second, parents tell their children harmless lies all the time. Santa Claus, the Tooth Fairy, the Easter Bunny, and every other fairy tale that you have told your child is not based on truth. So, if you must pass on information, don't let self-righteousness be your guide. Consider how that information will affect your child before you say anything.

Third, no matter how much you are hurting, it will not make *you* feel better if your children know exactly what happened. It's also doubtful it will make them feel better.

What if the kids don't want to visit the parent who had the affair?

That's a tough one. Here, we are most likely talking about teens and children old enough to understand the reason behind a breakup. Angry teens can be very unforgiving and will expect your humble apology—many times over. In your frustration, do not try to turn it around to make them feel guilty for not wanting to see you. Portraying yourself as the wounded party will also backfire. "I was unhappy for a very long time before I met Jillian" doesn't fly with teens. They will feel manipulated and don't want to hear bad things about their other parent. That will only alienate them further. Don't pull the parent card, either. Letting impatience get the best of you and exclaiming that you are still the parent and deserve to be respected will not get you what you want. Teens have a very discerning eye and feel respect must be earned. They will see demanding respect when your behavior was so questionable as hypocritical and out of place and they will reject you and anything you say.

Unfortunately, some rejection is predictable under these circumstances, albeit it is directly proportionate to how badly the child feels betrayed. In the end, an unfaithful parent must accept their part in the infidelity and hopefully trust will eventually return. Don't be surprised, however, if it takes a while. Forgiveness is a process, and you may have to express your regret a few times over the next weeks or even years before the child fully forgives you.

Will I lose custody of my children because I had an affair? In most states, infidelity is not illegal; therefore, technically in those states it should not affect the decision of when the children will live with each of their parents. However, custody is decided "in the best interest of the children." If your co-parent is planning to immediately live with an extramarital partner, the court may decide that throwing children into that environment right after their parents' split is not in their best interest. So, if you have had an affair, be prepared. The parenting plan you are assigned may not be the one you expected.

Dealing with Your Own Feelings About the Affair
How long will it take to stop being angry?

I don't know. There is nothing more difficult than to try to have a civil relationship with someone who has cheated on you. Time does help to heal, but how long it will take is really up to each individual facing the struggle. Believe it or not, finding forgiveness may be the key. I know this sounds incredible to some—after all, the hurt can be extreme. However, *once you release those painful thoughts* you harbor, they will no longer have a hold on you, and you will be able to forgive.

What part does forgiveness play in our ability to move on?

That is up to the individual. However, when you can forgive, hurtful memories no longer plague you in the same way. They appear less and less until, hopefully, they have been reshaped, you release the negative thoughts, and moving forward becomes more important than moving on.

I know that "once you release the negative thoughts" is an easy statement to make. Let me explain the process and hopefully you can start to put hurt and resentment behind you. Learning how to forgive aids us in every aspect of our lives.

I want to set the stage with my favorite quote about forgiveness: "Forgiveness is giving up all hope for a better past." After doing research, I cannot tell you who coined that phrase; so many people have used it. The saying resonates, however, because it is so true.

You see, you pull up the same old terrible emotions each time you think about a bad memory in the past. You picture whatever happened in your mind, and it feels like it's happening again in real time. But it's not; the past can't be better or worse. It was and is gone, but the pain is etched in your brain as a memory, and this is what makes it difficult to move on.

By concentrating on the present moment (what's good and what you are grateful for NOW) and not allowing yourself to conjure up those thoughts and emotions from the past, you break the negative thought/negative response chain reaction to your painful memory. When you do this enough times, you're no longer governed by the negative emotions associated with the memory because you've moved your attention away from the pain. And, when you finally pardon someone for their indiscretion against you it frees you, to move forward again.

You make it sound so easy. Like, "just do this and it will be gone." Do what? What thoughts do I think? What church should I attend? What therapist should I see? How do I get on the other side of this anger and resentment?

I call this the "Makeup Mirror Story." It is my own personal story, and I tell it all the time because it so clearly chronicles how changing your thoughts changes your behavior. If you have read one of my previous books, you've seen it there. It was a while ago, but remains relevant, and each time I tell it reminds me how strong our mind really is.

My husband and I were married for 6 months, and during that time, Sharyl, his ex-wife, and I were constantly at odds. Every morning I would sit in front of my makeup mirror, and as I put on my makeup I'd rehearse exactly what I was going to tell her the next time she did something that made me angry. As I put on my foundation, I was a little irritated. As I progressed to the blush, I was angrier still. By the time I was adding the finishing touches with my mascara, I was livid—and I hadn't said a thing to anyone! With each step of my makeup routine, the adrenaline kicked in more and more until I was seething.

This went on day after day. I thought I was keeping it all inside. I didn't think anyone knew how angry I was until one day my husband timidly tiptoed around the corner of the bathroom.

"What are you doing?" I snapped.

"Well," he said. "I was checking to see how much makeup you're wearing. It seems the more makeup you have on, the angrier you are with me."

That stopped me right in my tracks. I had no idea my husband was so perceptive, and I was very impressed. Truly, if it didn't have Harley Davidson printed on it, I didn't think he would have paid any attention. But here he was making this insightful observation. His comment made me realize that I was the one making me angry, not Sharyl. As soon as I sat down in front of my mirror each morning, I started the same vengeful angry thought process day after day. My anger was simply learned behavior. I had taught myself to be angry!

Since I had learned to be angry about my predicament, I decided I could learn *not* to be angry. Rather than rehearse all the bad things in my head each morning, I made myself think about the good things—really *made* myself. I did not allow my mind to deviate from positive thoughts based in gratitude—how grateful I was to have met my husband. How grateful I was that the kids had accepted me and seemed to be adjusting so well. Everyone was healthy. Every time a bad thought came to my mind about what Sharyl was going to do, I pushed it out and replaced it with a more positive thought about how grateful I was at this time in my life.

This is going to sound unbelievable, but I swear it is true. The next time my husband crept around the bathroom corner, I said,

"Hi, Honey!" rather than growling at him—and I didn't even real-ize it. But, equally as important, the next time I spoke to Sharyl I didn't have one bad thing to say to her. And oddly enough, she didn't have one bad thing to say to me, either.

This story is a perfect example of how changing your thought process changes your behavior and releases you from the hold those angry vengeful thoughts have on you. I was thoroughly convinced that it was Sharyl's fault that we were at odds. She was causing all the problems. I was the victim. If I had not made the necessary changes to break the negative thought/behavior chain reaction and change those negative expectations into positive affirmations, I would still be furious, sitting in front of my mirror and snapping at everyone who crossed my path.

CHECK THE LANGUAGE

It really gets me when my ex refers to himself and his new wife as "we." And when he refers to her as "my wife," it makes my heart pound. I have no idea why. I have no desire to go back to him, so that can't be it. Our divorce was final 2 years ago. We have 2 kids, and we have to talk to each other. I think he does it to make me angry and it makes it very difficult to have a good relationship with his wife for the sake of the kids.

– FAITH, MOTHER TO JACOB, AGE 9, AND MARTA, AGE 7

Because this mother feels overlooked, it's difficult to be part of the Bonus Team. After a breakup, many don't like to admit their vulnerability and they go out of their way to act like something doesn't bother them, when it really does. So, let's look at what's really going on here so people in this position can hopefully let it go once and for all.

What I believe this woman is responding to is not the desire to reconcile, but the feeling of being so easily erased from her co-parent's life. A mere 2 years ago, she was the other half of "we." Now he barely references her. Emotionally, she's feeling over-looked. "Was I nothing to you that I can so easily be replaced?"

So, when he refers to this other woman as "we" or "my wife," the emotion wells up inside of her.

I remember a time when one of my clients came unglued when her co-parent referred to his current wife as "we."

"Weeeeee?" she whined. "We?" We were just *we* a few months ago!!!!"

Interestingly enough, I have found that these semantical references seem to bother women more than men. Some women have told me that they feel referring to a new partner as "we" or "my wife" or even "my family" is flaunting the new relationship. "He's just trying to stick it to me, make me see that he can be happy with someone else." I've heard this from men, as well. Just not as often.

Although we have all seen selfish, spiteful former partners, and sometimes we feel they do things on purpose to hurt us, we all must acknowledge that getting over a breakup is a process.

You might easily be jealous of an ex's new partner. You might compare homes or cars or even how they look. "He's stronger." "She's prettier." You might be hurt when your ex refers to their new partner as "we." But, as your co-parent, none of that comes into play. Your relationship is built on your mutual love for your children and your mutual respect for one another as your children's parents. It's a whole new way of looking at your relationship. It's like you give each other an upgrade. You are co-parents. Same family, just a different family configuration.

Reframing the Labels

> I truly believe my co-parent's partner hates the ground I walk on, but honestly, I have barely spoken to them in the 3 years they have been with my co-parent.

I hear comments like this all the time, and it just takes a few more questions to help them reframe their thought process. Reframing is about looking at the big picture and thinking of the problem from different angles. So, I start by asking, "Do you think it's *you* this person hates, or is it just your label? Would the person hate *anyone* in your position?" Everyone I have ever asked those questions has answered, "It's the label. The person doesn't even know me."

So, by reframing or changing labels, you change the perspective in which the label is viewed. Change "ex-husband" or "ex-wife" to "co-parent," and now you aren't enemies, you are allies in raising the children. Change "ex-wife" or "ex-husband" or merely ex to "counterpartner," and you are part of a team. Change "stepparent" to "bonus parent," and now you aren't wicked or evil; your label embraces a loving, cooperative, inclusive spirit.

When we put aside the labels and start relating to each other simply as people who want the best for the same kids, it makes it easier to let go of the anger automatically associated with the label. It allows you to then relate more civilly.

HANDLING UNEXPECTED EMOTIONS

My co-parent and I have been divorced for 4 years and we have a 13-year-old daughter. We've had our ups and downs but have worked through many of the common pitfalls co-parents face after a breakup. My co-parent recently remarried, and the three of us have settled into a comfortable routine. I just found out they're expecting a baby boy. To my astonishment, I'm feeling jealous, resentful, and angry, with no idea how to deal with these feelings. How can I handle my emotions and keep my daughter positive about her new baby brother?

Possibly the most common questions I am asked are questions about how to overcome troublesome emotions, specifically, jealousy first, anger second.

It seems no matter how much a person initially wanted the breakup, most have conflicted feelings about the failed relationship. I see this most often in cases where couples were married for many years. In this case, hearing that their co-parent's wife is going to have a baby prompted this co-parent to revisit feelings she'd thought she buried long ago.

Other parents in this position have confided that there is a certain mindset behind their jealousy. It was explained that even though the parents split up long ago and both parents have moved on, there was always one thing that set the first partner apart—they were the other parent of their co-parent's only child. Now that the co-parent's partner is expecting a baby, they are equals, peers, so to speak. As a result, *now* the first partner feels angry, resentful, and jealous.

Ironically, although the writer confesses their untimely emotions, they could not be in a better place to overcome the feelings with which they struggle. They already attribute their feelings as a result of jealousy, and they are asking the right questions: "How can I handle my emotions and keep my daughter positive about her new baby brother?" This parent is putting the children first.

It is also commendable that this parent refers to her co-parent's new child as her daughter's baby brother. It's not uncommon for some to try to convince their children that the children born of the new partner are not their "real" brother or sister. They present the first family as the "real" family, and the bonus family doesn't count. You want unity. You want to promote love and acceptance. Sabotaging the siblings' relationship is emotionally and mentally abusive. Children need to feel as if they belong—both the existing children and the one that will be born soon.

If you find yourself feeling jealous, start by doing a bit of soul-searching. Consider why you feel the way you do. The key, as in the Makeup Mirror Story, is to go break the negative thought/negative behavior chain reaction by mentally listing the positive aspects of your life. You can even write them down if you think that will help you make the connection. Ultimately, the goal is to break the neural pathways that generate jealous feelings every time you think about a situation. Through repetition and attaching new, more positive, thoughts to when you feel jealous, the jealous feelings will eventually diminish.

Never dwell on what you secretly feel are your inadequacies—and certainly don't compare yourself to anyone else. Reaffirm what you know to be true about yourself. If you find yourself drifting into comparison mode, stop! And start the positive thinking process again.

Losing Sight of the Ultimate Goal

I have been married to my husband for 4 years and we are having a terrible time with his co-parent. My bonus son goes back and forth between both parents' houses. We like to have some nice clothes set aside for when we go out as a family, but his mother always wants to borrow his nice clothes and will not return them. His mother has been told that his nice clothes stay at our house, but she doesn't want to have to buy her own. It's something like this every day. What do I do?

This Bonus Team forgot they were a team. The houses have broken into factions over dress pants.

Let's look at how this bonus mom phrased her explanation so that we can understand her mindset: "We like to have some nice clothes set aside for when we go out as a family, but his mother always wants to borrow his nice clothes. She has been told that his nice clothes stay at our house, but she doesn't want to have to buy her own, so she doesn't return them."

I've seen parents in this sort of tit-for-tat go as far as making the child strip before returning to the other home.

"Those are *my* clothes, they stay here."

No, they are not. They are the child's clothes. Making a child change their clothes before they return to the other home humiliates them and reminds the child that their parents are no longer together, they don't like each other, and they would rather keep the vendetta going than set an example for their children.

The players in the above example have a long way to go before they settle into a cooperative counterpartner partnership and are regarded as members of a Bonus Team. They can stop this absurd scorekeeping, but all of them must do their part to make peace. Rather than looking for a way to solve the problem, they are stuck in a reactive state where they simply respond to the other's bad behavior. Without knowing it, they are setting each other up for failure.

Let's examine how this type of interaction evolves into a problem on multiple levels: It's time for the child to return to Mom's. As he is packing up his stuff, throwing his clothes into his bag, his stepmother says, "Honey, we bought those nice slacks, so they should stay here. Tell your mother to buy slacks for her house." She says it very matter-of-factly. She doesn't sound as if she is trying to be mean. But think about what she's doing. The child is right in the middle. He returns to his mother's house. She says, "Honey, we are going to church tomorrow and it looks like you forget your good clothes at your dad's." The child explains, "Oh no, Mom. Rhonda said they bought the clothes, so they have to stay at Dad's." Even the most even-tempered person would not be able to hide her disgust.

Plus, the child knows he's the one to pass on the bad news. His mom is angry at his dad and his dad's new partner, and it feels to the child as if it's all his fault. If he hadn't passed on the information, they wouldn't be fighting. Next time something like this happens, I promise you the child will not be forthcoming. He's in the middle and he's in trouble. This kind of craziness is not exclusively reserved for mothers and bonus mothers. Fathers and bonus fathers can take part in this negative behavior too. The behavior can be started by either home.

To defuse this situation, my suggestion is to reach out to your co-parent. Initiate a conversation by saying something like, "I have been thinking about it, and these are really Billy's clothes. To make things easier on him, and to equitably share in the extras, let's send his good clothes back and forth and when he's ready for a larger size, we can alternate who buys things for him. What are your thoughts?"

Dad used the Bonus Family Problem Solving Model. He made an observation (they were Billy's clothes), offered a child-focused solution (send the clothes back and forth and alternate buying them), and initiated negotiation (*What are your thoughts?*) that will hopefully lead to compromise.

Then let it go. Allow your co-parent some time to calm down and consider your suggestions. By asking her opinion, when she comes back with an idea, it allows her to do the right thing, plus have it look like the suggestion was her idea. Rather than set her up to fail, her co-parent has set her up to succeed. Round 2 . . .

TESTING ALLEGIANCES

My wife's co-parent (my counterpartner) and I have slowly become friendly, which makes things much easier when it comes to co-parenting the kids. Unfortunately, he confided that he recently got cited for driving under the influence of alcohol, and I am sure that he hasn't told my wife this. I know that she will not let the children in the car with him if she thinks he drinks and drives, and I agree with this. I feel very conflicted. On one hand, I'm worried about the safety of my bonus children; on the other, I hate the idea of betraying the confidence of a friend and upsetting the cooperative lifestyle we have come to enjoy.

Counterpartners walk a fine line when they become friends. That's because there may be times when they learn things about each other that they wouldn't necessarily have known had they remained simply your partner's co-parent or your co-parent's partner.

The best course of action is to create an atmosphere where the parents in question can tell each other the truth. If it is a safety issue for the children, as in this case, this bonus parent may have to suggest a specific date by which the information must be passed to his wife. He might say something like, "I believe it is your responsibility to tell Gracie (his wife) what you have told me. Please tell her before you are scheduled to pick up the children next week. You have put me in a very awkward situation. I am glad that you and I get along. It's much better for the children. But please don't put me in a position where I have to intercede. The responsibility to tell her is yours, and you should do it right away."

You might want to brainstorm about some possible solutions. If he has lost his license, he won't be able to take the children to school or extracurricular events on his scheduled time for a while. Perhaps offer to help with transportation until he gets his license back. If he hasn't lost his license, ask him to offer some sort of restriction about drinking when the kids are present. And finally, make sure he is the one to present these ideas to the children's mother. She will not like that she was the last to know when she should have been the first to know.

Too Close for Comfort

> *Since we sort of get along, it was amusing when I would go to spin class and my husband's co-parent was also there. We live less than a mile away from each other because of the parenting plan and go to the same supermarket and gym. It's not so amusing now that she has struck up a friendship with the instructor, who is also my best friend. I'm afraid to confide in my BFF anymore because she might unknowingly break my confidence. She's my go-to person, and now I have no one I can go to.*

When you co-parent as a team, you publicly acknowledge your acceptance of each other. This is fine within the parameters of parenting, but once it reaches outside of the parenting boundaries, it can feel as if you are testing allegiances. Ironically, we work very hard to accept the co-parent's partner or partner's co-parent within our familiar stomping ground, but when our friends and family start to invite them to social gatherings like they are family, some say, "Hey. Wait a minute. You didn't check with me!"

I remember one Christmas, we were about 75% into the bonus family experience—not all the way, but almost there. This particular Christmas, the kids were scheduled to be at their other parent's home, and when we didn't have the kids with us, we spent Christmas Eve with our best pals. They always had a huge party, and it was really fun. We walked in and the kids came running over to us, excited to say hi. I noticed their mother chatting with another friend over in the corner. As our friends took our coats, jokingly, I whispered, "How dare you invite my husband's ex-wife to Christmas Eve!" Without missing a beat, he said, "We did that for you."

It was a collective you. For all of us. Now the kids could be with both parents on Christmas Eve in a neutral location and there were enough people around to diffuse any awkwardness. Just remember, if you set the stage for acceptance, your friends and family will follow your lead. We had set the example, and although we weren't really to the point where we could spend a holiday together, our friends thought we were and were trying to get on board. So, we got on board, too, and we realized that our Bonus Team reaches out past our immediate families to extended family and friends, as well. That "village" is your community, the people who surround your family and for whom you set the example.

Building a Bonus Team in the name of your children goes against everything we have been taught about breaking up and starting over. But I can tell you that I have seen thousands of children raised this way over the years and, when done correctly, it has been a stabilizing force in the children's upbringing. I have never seen fighting, arguing, lying, or bad-mouthing ever be a stabilizing force or a positive influence—ever.

CHAPTER 5

Living the Day-to-Day of It

Bonus Is Beyond Step

A house divided against itself cannot stand.

ABRAHAM LINCOLN

UP TO THIS POINT, WE HAVE BEEN LAYING THE GROUNDWORK for creating your bonus family. Chapter 1 offered tools to better co-parent after your breakup; the principles discussed are the foundation on which creating a bonus family is based. In Chapter 2, we discussed a new, more cooperative approach to dating once parents are no longer together. Then, Chapter 3 explored the necessary preparation for moving in together once you finally meet someone you feel would be a good partner—and if you have children, a good parent figure. Chapter 4 takes a different approach—again cooperative, reaching out to your children's other home and building a team to help raise all the children in your care. We are now here, in Chapter 5, the chapter that will incorporate everything we have learned so that you can comfortably navigate day-to-day bonus family life.

There are some core challenges for bonus families, beginning with the very real fact that bonus families must create a completely new family structure while navigating the back-and-forth life previously created by the parental breakup. Most bonus couples, namely a co-parent and their partner (who may also be a co-parent) most likely have no formal model on which to rely and may struggle to create their own identity as the primary couple keeping their bonus family strong.

In this chapter we are going to take a typical problem often faced in blended families and approach it from a bonus family state of mind—a state of mind that rejects the old way of combining families with no plan for problem solving and co-existing for a future rooted in cooperation and acceptance of each family member's individuality.

This chapter also takes for granted that the bonus couple has read Chapter 3 of this book and has discussed their goals and have a universal vision for their family and future. Starting with the bonus couple as the leaders of the family, if you and your partner do not have a plan for the everyday workings of your family, go back to Chapter 3 and review the Before Bonus Exercise.

A IS FOR ACCEPTANCE

If someone asked me, "What is the most important tip you could offer parents attempting to combine their families?" I'd have to reply, "**A** is for Acceptance." The most important component for successfully combining families is the understanding that each family member's individuality must be nurtured and their history respected. Too many try to squish everyone into a perfect little blended family box modeled after a conventional two-parent family. Even though that is the way it has been done for years, I think that is the primary reason many combined families simply don't work. It's like trying to force a square peg into a round hole.

Here's an example of discounting a family member's history and individuality. I call mistakes like this "Bonus Blunders." We will talk more about Bonus Blunders later in Chapter 9, "Bonus Blunders and Course Correction," but it is important to discuss this here to drive home how important "Acceptance" is to bonus family life.

> *Shane Troop has a son Micah, 11. Jessica Johansson has a son, Joe, who is 12, and a daughter Madison, 13. This bonus family has been navigating bonus life for a year. When Madison was 11, she went to a slumber party at the home of a girlfriend. The girls watched an old scary movie that was rated PG-13, where the main character, Pennywise, terrified the neighborhood. Believing that a PG-13 movie would not be "that bad," Madison's friend's parents did not check with Jessica prior to showing the movie and Madison was traumatized by the Pennywise character. Clowns now scare her, and she hates images of them of any kind.*
>
> *It was movie night at Troop/Johansson home and, thinking it would be funny, Shane picked a Simpson animated movie called* Krusty the Clown *as the movie choice that night. Madison was the last to sit down to watch and as the movie began to play—even though it was animated—she jumped as the clown image came on the screen. She covered her eyes and eventually left the room. Jessica, trusting Shane's choice, was furious. "How could you do that?" she screamed. "I was just playing around," he laughed. "I thought it would be funny."*

Shane knew of Madison's fear of clowns. He did not honor her history or take her fear seriously. Do you think the choice of the movie brought her closer to him or undermined trust? After the incident, Madison refused to again join the family for movie night. That single seemingly silly act was a wedge that began to pry away at the family unity. Without a quick interception, the Troop/Johansson family could easily slip into factions—me and my kids against you and your kids. To make matters even a little more complicated, it sounds like Micah was in the middle of the whole thing. He had become quite close to Joe and thought of him as a brother/ally. That would leave his dad without an alliance. Who does Micah side with?

Each family member sees themselves as an individual and wants to be accepted for who they are, particularly teenagers who are just learning about independence and respect for themselves. All too often everyone in the family thinks everyone else will line up to their expectation—and when they don't, they get frustrated and resentful. The adults see the children, whether they are theirs or not, as disrespectful if they don't conform. The children resent being expected to act a certain way that does not coincide with who they were prior to their parent meeting someone new. Don't acknowledge each family member's individuality—parent figures and children, alike—and they will not be invested in being an active member of the family. Children, in particular, will just bide their time until they can get away—once they are grown, they will not be invested in the family because they felt the "family" was not invested in them.

Allegiance and Betrayal in Your Bonus Family

We left Micah trying to decide to whom he should pledge his allegiance—Shane, because he was his dad and who, because of what might seem like a silly blunder, is now shunned by the rest of the family. Or should he unite with his bonus mom and bonus siblings because he understood his father's choice was insensitive? Standing back and looking at what happened, the act might seem small, but these are the kinds of choices bonus family members must make minute by minute.

When kids go back and forth between their parents' homes, *everything* is perceived as allegiance to one and betrayal of another.

From the bonus child's perspective, Micah has a big problem. How is he supposed to navigate this Bonus Blunder without alienating one or the other side of the family? Shane expects allegiance because he is Dad, but Micah agrees with his bonus mom and bonus siblings and believes they are right.

Although Micah is the one in the middle, Shane can easily take the pressure off his child by accepting that he did not use good judgment when he chose the movie and offer heartfelt apologies to everyone. He will have some backtracking to do with Madison because she no longer trusts him. But that can be addressed by openly doing things to build trust. Things like spending relaxed time together with predictable outcomes. Key word: predictable. Madison will learn to trust Shane again if she can depend on what he will do.

For example, ask her to join him in picking out a movie and discuss the choices together prior to choosing one. This might be something Shane could do with each child on a rotating basis.

What if Shane believes "this is a lot over nothing," feels Madison is just being dramatic, and that Madison's mother is coddling her? That attitude is not uncommon in bonus families—parent and bonus parent do not always agree on an approach to parenting and discipline. This could definitely interfere with these parental partners working together in raising the children. Plus, if he doesn't take the phobia (coulrophobia is the fear of clowns) seriously, it will make it difficult for Shane to find the sincerity necessary to communicate a heartfelt apology.

When decisions like this arise, although each situation is different, one has to weigh how important it is to put the bonus family back into working order or stand your ground, especially when all it will take is an apology to set things back on course.

Finally, those who are not affected by a phobia often do not understand the person who suffers profound fear. As Shane even explained when confronted, "I thought it would be funny." A quick Google search would help Shane to see that although the incidence of coulrophobia varies across studies, the largest and most recent survey to date, including 987 adults from 64 countries, reported that 53.5% (528) of their sample manifested some degree of fear of clowns.[1] Madison may have been truly traumatized by the movie and needs help.

Shane Can Use CARE to Address the Problem

Communication: Apologies all around with the explanation that he misjudged the seriousness of the situation.

Acceptance: Acknowledge that Madison's fear is real.

Respect: Demonstrate true regard for Madison's feelings. The goal is for Madison to regain trust and once again depend on Shane to protect her. This can be improved by Shane modeling respect for Madison and helping her to deal constructively with a possible diagnosis. This could include initiating therapy and offering to attend sessions if the therapist deemed it appropriate for the treatment.

Empathy: Shane may not only want to put himself in Madison's shoes to understand her fear, but also try to understand how Jessica felt when her daughter had such a strong reaction to an animated movie. Jessica may not have understood the seriousness up to that point and was surprised herself.

The best course of action is for Shane, Jessica, *and* Madison's biological father to work together to support Madison in addressing any problem Madison is experiencing. That's a bonus family approach.

BONUS FAMILY AUTONOMY

A bonus family embraces a loving, cooperative, inclusive spirit, but it is not communal living. It's a cooperative approach to merging families. Each co-parent's family is autonomous and can be separately referred to as a bonus family. However, as both families begin to comfortably interact, the extended family is also referred to as a bonus family as the whole. Bonus is a state of mind.

With all this back-and-forth and everyone in everyone else's business, how do we establish a sense of privacy for our individual family?

First, all parents know that privacy after children is not the same as privacy before children. How many times have your little ones followed you into the bathroom? As the children go back and forth between their parents' homes and all the parental relationships improve, it will be very easy for boundaries to become blurred unless co-parents make a special effort to communicate what they think is appropriate in no uncertain terms.

> *I came home from work the other day to find my co-parent and our 9-year-old daughter chilling on her bed at my house. Evidently, her mother had picked our daughter up from school and planned to drop her off for my custody time, but I was home late from work, and she didn't want to leave her alone. We have not been together for 3 years and my co-parent does not have a key, so I know our daughter let her in. There she was when I came home, lying on our daughter's bed just chatting about the day. My girlfriend is moving in next week. I can only imagine the scene if she was with me and my co-parent was cuddled up on our kid's bed.*

Most would think that you would start with a conversation with the child. But it's uncomfortable to say, "Honey, don't let your mother in the house. Now that Stacy lives here, it just wouldn't be right." A child doesn't understand "why it wouldn't be right," and that explanation tells the child the reason Mom shouldn't be in the house is because of Stacy. Stacy is keeping Mom away. That explanation is not only inaccurate, but it will drive a wedge between the child and the new partner, Stacy. Some parents might secretly think, "Good! I don't want my kid to like Stacy, anyway." That's the parent putting their own feelings first, not the child. The truth is, you want your child to feel loved and cared for at both homes. If they don't, that's an indicator the parent figures have missed something, not the child.

It would be best in this scenario to start with Dad initiating a conversation with Mom. She is the one who must respect Dad's space and monitor her own behavior. Can you imagine the position the child was in trying to figure out if it was appropriate to ask her mother into dad's home? Respecting the other home is an important component to bonus family living, but it all starts with the example set by the co-parents.

You can picture what probably happened in this case. Mom picked up the child from school and normally delivers her to Dad's, but no one was home. Not knowing what to do, Mom may have wondered out loud, "Your dad's not home and I don't want to leave you alone." So her daughter said, "Why don't you just come in, Mommy?" Mom figures, "What the heck. It's only for a few minutes." The next thing you know, Dad comes home to the ex curled up with their daughter talking about their day. Even for the friendliest of co-parents, this would seem too familiar and be a lot for a new partner to digest.

Co-parents with bonus families must be clear with what they expect at each home. At a minimum, each parent should ask permission to visit the other home rather than come by unannounced. Even when parents get along well, children tell me that these kinds of unexpected visits upset the new rhythm they are trying to establish when living in two homes. If a child is having fun at one parent's home and the other parent shows up without warning, the child often wonders, "Will it make my parent feel bad if they know I'm having fun here?" A child simply does not know how to navigate that situation unless their parents set a very clear example of what is expected.

COMPARING BIO TO BONUS

Although it's human nature to sometimes compare in certain situations, I've mentioned the importance of keeping the bio and bonus relationship separate in your mind. I counsel my clients to beware of comparing and to be vigilant in guiding their children not to compare their lifestyle to anything or anyone.

Years ago, while teaching a Bonus Families Workshop, I met a teenager, Sam, who shared an interesting view of comparing that has always stuck with me. He was actually frustrated that others wanted him to compare how he felt about his parent to how he felt about his bonus parent. He said, "My friends are always asking me who I like better, my mom or my bonus mom. It's such a stupid question."

He explained that his father remarried when he was 4 and he really has no recollection when his bonus mom entered his life. It was very clear in his mind that his mom and bonus mom each had a special role. They couldn't be compared. He knew who his mother was, and he had always been close to her—and he explained that his bonus mom, although different, was always good to him, and she held a special place in his heart, as well. He had no trouble telling the difference and resented when people asked him to weigh in. And this is the truth of it—when parents have a clear understanding of the role biological and bonus play in their children's lives, the children will also. This child was not compelled to compare bio to bonus because he was raised not to.

Sam's attitude is also a reminder of the importance of teaching our children to see their relationships with their parent and bonus parent as two separate entities—not either or, but also. More importantly, if a child has permission to form a loving bond with a bonus parent or to openly discuss his love for his parent, he will not feel caught in the middle. It will teach him to avoid those gut-wrenching allegiance and betrayal issues that ask him to choose between two people he cannot compare. When parents and bonus parents truly put the children first, their roles become very clear. Jealousy falls to the side. You cannot have too many people love your child.

OUTSIDE LOOKING IN

The kids walk in, and I no longer exist. I understand that's when Jerry is on dad duty, but I feel like an afterthought. He barely talks to me; he's so focused on his kids. The other night his kids came over for their Wednesday night dinner and no one even acknowledged I was there. The kids didn't even say hi. I was completely ignored.

There is a song from the '60s, "I'm on the Outside (Looking In)" by Little Anthony and the Imperials, that plays in my head each time a bonus parent tells me how they feel left out when their partner's children come over.

I picture someone standing outside in the cold peering through a window and people inside a warm house. This is reinforced by their partner's understanding that they might feel that way but not knowing what to do about it. Parents in this position often feel like a failure as a parent and as a partner. In an effort to defuse the situation, they may seem insensitive, "Oh, come on. No one is ignoring you," when they know they are, but they are only one person and can't heal everyone's problems. "I can't be all things to all people all the time!" one frustrated parent confided. Meanwhile the bonus parent wonders, "Will I ever feel like part of this family?"

The answer is, maybe not part of *that* family, but you certainly are an important part of your bonus family and that's the one on which to focus your attention.

THE KIDS HATE EACH OTHER

My kids and my partner's kids hate each other. They are always fighting. What do we do?

First and foremost, parents should not make their children feel guilty that they don't like each other. The reality is not everyone likes everyone else, and there may be times that bonus family members just don't get on. This is when the bonus couple must intercede and offer tools to teach the children to openly accept differences and agree to disagree. The bonus couple must model acceptance and a nonjudgmental attitude for their family structure and not allow the children to gossip or bad-mouth each other at any time. This includes times when the kids complain in confidence and you want to identify with their feelings. Don't deny their feelings. Hear them out but redirect them toward accepting someone who is different from them.

FINDING ONE-ON-ONE TIME WITH YOUR KIDS

In the name of family blending, it's not uncommon for parents to lose sight of the need to spend one-on-one time with their biological children. But bonus families don't have to spend every waking minute together to successfully build their bonus bond. One-on-one time with your biological children does not take away from the whole. It actually strengthens it. It offers the kids the individual attention they need to continue to feel connected to their parent. Combined time reinforces the bonus family ties. Don't be afraid to take your kids to pizza and allow your partner alone time for a few hours. If they have children, that's alone time with their kids, as well. Be flexible. Your ability to "roll with the changes" marks a successful bonus family.

FINDING "JUST US" TIME

We've all referenced enough pop-psychology to know the importance of "us time" in any relationship. The caveat is where to find it. Cultivating a loving passionate coupling is difficult while juggling parent-child plus new partner relationships. As the kids come and go and the family configuration changes, for example, two kids this week, five kids the following week (one partner has two children, the other has three), private moments with your partner can easily become few and far between.

That's when you have to get creative. "Just us" time does not have to be secluded getaways to exotic locations, although that would be nice. Look for private time *within* your hectic schedule. Things like private jokes that make the two of you giggle, a quick telephone call "Just to hear your voice," or a text and emoji can distract you from the stresses of bonus family living and ease the challenges of a hectic day.

Also, don't be afraid to trade an evening or weekend with your co-parent. They may appreciate the extra time with the children. Plus, this lays the groundwork for a cooperative spirit when they need a favor.

An Unconventional Bonus Family Solution

When I was doing research for this book, I asked visitors to the Bonus Families website to give me some examples of unconventional bonus family fixes that made their family unique. I had never heard of anything like this, but it goes to show that bonus families can find an answer when they work together.

> *My co-parent and I have both remarried and we try to coordinate efforts as best we can. My co-parent and I have twins, plus my husband and I had another set of twins. My co-parent and his wife also have a 19-month-old. We both need a rest from the chaos and found ourselves asking each other to trade weekends so we could have some alone time with our partners. When we realized we asked each other about every other month we decided to just assign weekends where one of us would take all the kids and let the parents at the other home have some uninterrupted time. I know it sounds unconventional, but it works for us. I take all the kids on the fourth Saturday evening in even months. He takes all the kids on the fourth Saturday evening in odd months. Sometimes the kids sleep over and pop popcorn and sleep in the living room at my house. It's sort of a Bonus Family Slumber Party. We don't do this in the summer, June through September, because things get too hectic, but the fourth Saturday in October does not come soon enough.*
> — NADINE, MOTHER TO TWINS JOSEPH AND WILLIAM, AGE 6,
> TWINS HADDIE AND HENRY, AGE 3

BONUS PARENTING

Bonus parents live a sort of paradox. They are told they are not the parent, yet there are times when they find themselves in a parenting role. To complicate the paradox even further, some bonus parents also have children of their own, and this means they must constantly juggle their personal parental responsibilities with their bonus parent responsibilities. Many, both parents and bonus parents alike, don't understand exactly what those responsibilities are.

> *"When do I take my parent hat off and put on my bonus parent hat?" a confused bonus dad asked me. That's really a tough one. "I know my boundaries with my child, but what about my bonus child? I really don't know what I'm supposed to be doing. Am I supposed to be treating this child as my own or am I his friend? Every decision I make, I feel like I'm stepping on someone's toes. I'm doing the best I can, but I feel like I'm missing the mark. This is so much harder than I thought it would be."*

These words echo the sentiments of just about every bonus parent with whom I have worked. Now that joint custody is the most common custody solution after a breakup and most children go back and forth between their parents' homes, it's easy to see why a parent's new partner might question their role. Rarely do a child's parents outline their expectations, so the bonus parent is left to fill in the blanks. Bottom line: A bonus mom or bonus dad supports the parents' rules, looks for ways to promote cooperation, and is a loving third voice in the bonus family.

BUILDING BONUS PARENT/BONUS CHILD RAPPORT

> *I have an 11-year-old son, Bradley. We get along great. We have so many private jokes others sometimes don't understand what we are laughing about, but we do. I thought I got 11-year-old boys, but I cannot even have a civil conversation with my bonus son. We've been living together for 3 months, and it is miserable. He's nothing like Bradley and we both walk on eggshells when we are home together. I can see how uncomfortable he is, and I have no idea what to do.*

Here are the red flags derived from just the seven short sentences above:

1. *This parent is comparing their child to their partner's child.* He's a completely different person with individual likes and dislikes. All 11-year-olds are not the same, just as all adults are not the same.

2. *This parent has not built a connection with the child before attempting to correct him.* Too much, too soon. The child will either resent the discipline—"You're not my parent!"—or possibly ignore the request altogether. Over time, if parents agree, the bonus parent can step into a disciplinary role, but even then, they support the rules the parents set; they don't establish protocol.

3. *This parent has lived with their child for 11 years and her bonus son for 3 months.* Building a rapport with anyone takes time. You have to put the time in to build the relationship you want.

4. *Private jokes can alienate those who don't get them.* They do not feel included and it will distance the bonus child because they feel like an outsider. Private jokes come about by sharing experiences, laughing about something that happened on a trip, or the line of a movie that made you both laugh. Create shared experiences.

Will I Ever Love This Child?

I am [a] bonus parent to a 5-year-old boy. I'm worried because I do not feel the love toward him I thought I would feel by now. Will I ever love this child? I keep my distance from his biological mother because she is condescending and bossy, and I get mad at my husband

for not standing up to her. Help! I don't want to be angry all the
time, but every time I look at this boy it reminds me of his mother!
— SUSAN, BONUS MOM TO DOMINIC, AGE 10

There is more than one troublesome issue here, but like so many
who cope with the anger and frustration of breaking up and
starting over, the writer is running them all together in her mind.
She is allowing how she feels toward the child's mother to affect
her feelings toward her bonus son, thereby creating problems in
her relationship with her partner. Angry and confused, the writer
wonders with time whether she will ever feel the love she hoped
she might feel for this child. Until she has the ability to stop
running the issues together and approach each problem individually, it is doubtful. She will continue to be caught in the negative
thought/negative behavior cycle and be predictably moody and
angry with those close to her most of the time.

Building a bond with a stepchild is not easy. They are a constant reminder that your spouse has a past that did not include
you. But that's the challenge you accept when you connect with
someone who has children. As a bonus parent, you have the
opportunity to make a difference in a child's life. You can act like
the stereotypical example of a stepparent you read about in fairy
tales, or you can help mold a child by setting an example of love
and mutual respect. You can be someone that this child holds in
high regard and goes to for advice and comfort, or you can be
someone who causes additional pain. If you harbor animosity for
a bonus child, it will eventually color every aspect of your married
relationship, and that's when another breakup looms.

What to Do . . .
As I have said throughout this book, you control your thoughts,
and your thoughts influence your behavior. Stop the angry
thought associations. Instead of dwelling on the fact that this
child is obnoxious, look for something positive he brings to the

family. Start with just one thing—even if that one thing is that it makes your partner happy when his child is around. That means something to your partner, and witnessing your tolerance and acceptance will bring your partner closer.

People, like this writer, who are in the midst of blame and fault do not realize how their actions contribute to the problem at hand. Blaming actually stifles the person with whom you are at odds. Rather than look for solutions, the blamed person, in this case her husband, is compelled to defend himself and his child; couples cannot maintain a loving relationship when they are on the defensive. This bonus mom must take note that her contempt for the child may backfire and actually distance her partner.

So, bottom line, once the writer mentally addresses her frame of reference, literally changes her thinking, her relationships with all three people—the mother, father, and child—will improve.

Maintaining a Loving Relationship with Your Bonus Child: But She Used to Like Me

I need help with my 11-year-old stepdaughter. In the last few months she seems out of control. She won't do anything I ask unless her dad makes her and I can't seem to spend any quality time with her. I've tried to set up activities for us. I've even let her pick some of the activities she would like to try, but nothing seems to work. Nothing seems good enough. Her natural mother has little to nothing to do with her. She will call about once a month and makes promises she never keeps or to complain about her own problems. My question is, should I take a step back and let her father deal with things? (I hate doing this because I've taken care of her since she was 5) or should I continue to try to spend time together? I feel a lot of her problems have to do with puberty and trying to find her place, but I hate tiptoeing around her thinking she might explode any minute. Plus, each time she lashes out, it really hurts my feelings.

– KATHY, BONUS MOM TO RHIANNA, AGE 11

So many bonus parents have confided that they feel exactly as this bonus parent feels. They prided themselves in this wonderful relationship when their bonus child was younger, then *pow*—puberty—and that lovely relationship becomes a faint memory.

"What happened?" they ask. "What have I done?" The answer? Probably nothing.

Let's take a look at what could be happening here.

When a child reaches puberty, which we all know is confusing in itself, the new hormone fluctuations can make them extremely moody. If you are the primary caregiver, you are receiving the brunt of the mood changes. Even more important to consider is that children of divorce often live with an unwarranted adoration of the non-custodial parent. As they get older, they realize for themselves which parent they can depend on, and this realization can put an adolescent into an emotional tailspin. At 11, this child is finally old enough to see her parent's failings for herself. She can understand that her mother isn't around by her own choice, and this can be very upsetting.

At the same time this bonus parent is working hard to offer stability and camaraderie, her bonus daughter may simply resent that her biological mother is not as attentive as her bonus parent. In her disappointment she could be wondering, "Why can't she (mom) be like you (bonus parent)?" And the nicer the bonus parent is, the more angry the child becomes.

The writer mentions that each time her bonus daughter lashes out, it really hurts her feelings. This is a trap lots of bonus parents fall into because they are trying so hard to be the perfect parent. When the bonus child doesn't respond to their efforts, the bonus parent often becomes resentful that all their hard work is for nothing and emotionally withdraws from the child. "That kid isn't going to hurt me again . . ."

This attitude will not help the situation. This bonus child was dealt something she did not ask for—her parents' breakup and a parent who is not invested. When a parent is not active in their child's life, it's even more important that the bonus parent continues to be a good role model. Bonus parents must stay as open as possible, be available when the child needs them, and reach down inside for all the patience they can muster. They should make sure that their partner (the child's parent) is also on the same page so that they can support bonus parent and child in their continued efforts to work toward bonus status.

If you find yourself at a loss as to why the big change in your child, consider reaching out to professionals, like teachers or the school counselor, to confirm a change in attitude. They may be able to offer some additional insights that could be contributing to the changes at home. Is the child struggling with new math concepts? Are her friends rejecting her or is she being bullied? And, finally, don't be afraid to suggest her parent initiate counseling for her. A little help from an experienced therapist may be all that is needed to get her back on track.

BONUS FAMILY INTIMACIES

My 10-year-old bonus daughter started her period when we were out to dinner. While we were in the bathroom at the restaurant, I realized she barely understood what was happening to her. No one had talked to her, and here I was having to explain her changing body. I wasn't sure that was my place and wasn't sure how to handle it.

When we got home, she immediately ran into the bathroom. "Come here!" she yelled. And after a few panicked exclamations, she asked me not to tell her dad what happened. I found myself wondering, "Do I keep this from her dad? Should I be the one to be discussing the female reproductive system with her? My husband, her mother, and I never broached this subject. I was in uncharted waters."

Life is different when kids go back and forth between their parent's homes, especially if one or both parents live with someone else. People that you may not have picked to be in your life may be intimate with your children. By intimate I mean bathing them, changing their diapers or potty training them, and talking to them about their changing bodies. All the intimate behaviors formally reserved for parents may also fall on bonus parents simply because of timing—they live with your children.

Yes, bonus children have biological parents, but their parents may not always be around when they are facing a crisis, and the bonus parent could be the caregiver. There will be times when the appropriate answer is, "Honey, I think you should talk to your mom (or dad) about that." And then pave the way for an easy conversation. But there will also be times, like the one mentioned above, when you are just going to have to trust the bonus parent to do the right thing—and you can ensure that will happen when you all anticipate a problem, get on the same page, and work as a team.

Finally, parents, both bio and bonus, must strike a balance between respecting privacy and keeping the other parent in the loop. The reason for the request to not tell Dad is that the child is simply embarrassed. Look for ways to openly discuss those feelings and let the child know it is a natural part of growing up. Let the child know their parent is fully aware that they are getting older and is not surprised that they are facing this. Use the same approach if you are faced with a similar discussion about a male's changing body. "We all go through it."

Family Nudity and Intimacy

> I didn't ever think I would have to face this, but my 4-year-old son walked into the bathroom as I was getting out of a shower and just as casually as could be, said, "Jenny's boobs are bigger than yours." He's four! What are they doing at that other house??? Is that woman naked in front of my child?

This question prompts another similar story when a mother came into my office very upset that her 5-year-old son was commenting on his father's girlfriend's thong underwear. The child had com-pared Mom's more conservative choice to the ones "Lisa wears," and she was very concerned Dad's girlfriend was "prancing around the house in barely nothing." Yet another mother complained that a bra was mixed in with her 15-year-old son's laundry and she was concerned that he was sexually active at dad's house.

None of these stories happened as they appeared. The 4-year-old did see Jenny in a bikini and ascertained all by himself the size of Jenny's boobs. This kind of thing registers even with 4-year-olds. Lisa's thong underwear was drip drying in the laun-dry room, and the bra in the 15-year-old's laundry was his bonus mom's. It had gotten mixed in the laundry by mistake.

As amusing as these stories might be looking back, when they are first discovered, they can be disconcerting. Parents wonder if their children are being put in a compromising position or if their other parent is just being very lax and cannot be trusted. Ultimately, the answer here is to have an information-gathering conversation with your co-parent—not accusatory, but informa-tive. Instead of, "Oh my god, Justin was talking about Jenny's boobs yesterday. Does she walk around your house naked??" try something like, "Something that Justin said yesterday made me realize that we have never discussed how we feel about nudity in front of the children now that we are no longer together. So, what are your thoughts?"

Truthfully, how you handle nudity in your own home is a very personal matter. What one person might feel is appropriate, another might feel is completely out of the question. Most parents tell us that they would prefer their children's bonus parents not appear nude in front of their children. Mental health profession-als also agree that it is best to be comfortably modest in front of bonus children. We all must acknowledge that because of very close quarters, there may be times when someone walks in on someone else while showering or changing, but this can easily be met by calmly saying, "Excuse me," and to minimize embarrassment or the novelty of it, the subject can then be dropped.

Sexual Attraction Among Bonus Siblings

> *She has a 16-year-old boy; I have a 15-year-old girl. Hormones are running rampant at our house. It's been about 6 months now and I'm a little worried they may be attracted to each other. We are afraid to leave them alone together, especially after school. They get home at 3:30 and my wife and I don't get home until around 6:00 p.m.*

Let's explore the reasons this is such an important topic to discuss for all concerned.

- First, concerns about sexual harassment: are the feelings mutually shared, or is one child intimidated by another?
- Second, if the answer is the feelings are mutual, how will this relationship affect the bonus family dynamic?
- Third, how will this relationship affect the younger children in the home?
- Fourth, physical intimacy . . .

If you are faced with sexually attracted teens, as alarming as it may seem, now is the time to keep your head. Stay focused on what is important; the teens need levelheaded guidance during a really confusing time. If you do not stay calm, we all know teens are rebels and the kids may end up in a relationship but keep it from you. If that happens, there is no way you can offer your help.

Teens must realize that romantic relationships carry heavy responsibilities and can have serious consequences. As we all remember, those heavy responsibilities are not what you are thinking about when you are a hot-blooded teen. Understanding that teens biologically find reason and decision-making trying (the frontal lobe of their brain which governs reason and decision making is not fully formed until someone is in their mid-20s), appealing to their ability to reason may fall on deaf ears. Even so, a conversation asking them to reflect on some thought-provoking questions may help them make better decisions.

- How do you feel about the impression your actions will make on the younger children in our home?

- How will you feel if you break up and still have to live in the same house?

- What will happen to your friendship if the romance doesn't work out?

- How will you feel about the negative reactions of friends who perceive your relationship as forbidden?

- How will you feel knowing that it might make all the other members of the household very uncomfortable?

Notice that most of the questions start with, "How will you feel . . . ?" That is designed to help teens consider the consequences of their actions and then talk about their feelings rather than feel as if the parent is passing judgment. If teens feel a parent is passing judgment, they won't say a word. If their feelings are being considered, they will be more inclined to open up.

It is during this question-and-answer period that you can let your feelings be known. Use discretion when voicing your unhappiness with the situation. It may be a good idea to suggest that they put the relationship on hold, but they may not see the necessity to do so. At that point, it may be time to look for subtle ways to limit their time alone. Suggest an after-school job, after-school extracurricular activities, volunteer work (most high schools require some community service work to graduate), or tutoring others. You may have to get creative.

If your teens still refuse to end the relationship, you will have to set some strict limits (which should have been anticipated when you moved in together). Be specific about house rules and the exact behavior you expect in your home. If you prefer no displays of affection in front of younger siblings, make that clear. This is not a time to be shy, but you must also understand that if you are too heavy-handed or demand that the involvement cease, the teens will probably continue the relationship secretly. A discussion about contraception may also be in order. This will undoubtedly make things even more uncomfortable, but it's better to face the discomfort rather than the unexpected consequences.

There is also an alternative that parents who share their children's time rarely want to consider—the other parent's home. If the relationship has progressed to a concern about physical intimacy, the child's other parent should be asked to weigh in and offer their ideas. Rarely do teens anticipate how complicated life can get before they get involved.

Professionals warn parents that they cannot control their teens' behavior, but they can become sought-after mentors or consultants in helping their children make their own decisions. If you listen and do your best to appear nonjudgmental, you will keep their trust and keep the lines of communication open.

It's important to note that this section refers to a situation in which the teens in question have a mutual attraction for each other. If you are faced with a situation in which one family member is sexually harassing another family member, get a professional involved immediately. All family members have the right to feel safe in their own home, and if they don't, more drastic measures may have to be taken into consideration. This may include the aggressor living with their other parent full time or even involving law enforcement. Take this very seriously.

ADDING A BABY TO YOUR BONUS FAMILY

We have lived in a bonus family for 2 years now. My husband has two children from his previous marriage, and I have one from my previous marriage. We are now expecting our first child together.

What can we do to ensure that the children see adding a child to the family as a joyful addition? I've read so much about jealousy among bonus siblings. How can we prevent it?

An important distinction, the child this mother is carrying will not be a bonus sibling to the children already in the family. "Bonus" is used in lieu of "step." This child will be a half-sibling to all the kids. Some will share the same mother, and some will share the same father as the newborn.

While some children may be ready for a new child in the family, others may see it as just one more person to steal away their parent's attention. Some children will not share their fears, and it may turn out that even though the parents think they have covered all the bases, their children's secret fears hit them by surprise.

A year after my youngest daughter was born, my daughter from a previous marriage, Anee, confessed that while I was pregnant, she had a secret fear that I would love the new baby more than I loved her. Her reasoning was that since I was no longer married to her father, I didn't love him as much as I loved the new baby's father because I was now married to him. That meant I probably loved the new baby more than her. I remember how sad I felt when she explained this to me. I was surprised that she felt my affection for her was somehow related to how I felt about her father and my husband. It seemed my obvious affection for my husband, in her mind, established a pecking order between her father and the other children's father.

Anee felt this way even though we strove to do everything the experts suggested. We included all the children in the preparations for the new child—we even asked them if they wanted to add to the family before we considered it. We took a bonus family poll on names.

I was grateful that my daughter confessed that after the baby was born, she realized her fears were unfounded, but I still felt like a supremely unconscious parent. How could I not have known how she felt? How could she have hidden her fears so completely? I pass this experience on as a warning to all parents considering adding a child to their bonus family. Don't take it for granted that your children are as excited about the new addition as you are. Like my daughter, they might be excited, but also harbor secret fears that they are afraid to talk about.

By the same token, my bonus daughter confessed that she overheard some of her adult role models talking about how things would change once the baby was born. Since she felt very comfortable with how things were, the thought of changing the status quo scared her. She overheard that I would not have the same time for her and would devote all my time to the baby. Like my biological daughter, she only confessed this after the baby was born and she could see that my affection for her had not changed. My daughter and bonus daughter said they never expressed their fears to each other. They suffered in silence until they could see for themselves.

The following points will help you help your children adjust to the addition of another child.

- Have open discussions with your children about adding to the family. Emphasize the positive ways a baby will change the family dynamic, but openly address the children's fears, as well.

- Include your children in the planning for the new baby's arrival. Good ways are to ask them for name suggestions or let them help in decorating the baby's room. Older children can be a great help with planning and giving baby showers.

- Anticipate what will upset the existing children most and make changes *before* the new baby arrives. Try not to make changes that the older child will equate with the new baby's arrival. In other words, don't preface a change with, "Now that the baby's here. . . ." An existing child may be inclined to think the change is because of the new baby and resent the baby's arrival. Most changes you will be faced with are actually age-related and should be presented as such. "You are so big now, you get a big kid bed!" Not, "Now that the baby is here, you get a big kid bed!"

- Emphasize each child's individuality. Although this new child is related to everyone equally, make the children know you see each of them as unique and that the new sibling will add happiness to their lives, not distract a beloved parent. Be careful that the new baby does not dominate the lives of the existing children.

- Don't expect older children to clean up after the baby or dump babysitting responsibilities on an adolescent. Until your existing children have accepted this child as a member of the family, try to maintain a babysitting swap with your friends and other parents. Watch how much you ask grandparents to watch the baby, too; older children might start wondering why their grandparents prefer the new baby to them.

- Remember one-on-one time with existing children. Even though a new baby will take up most of your time, existing biological kids and bonus kids still need private time with their parents and bonus parents. A great way to find extra time is to integrate existing children into your everyday routine. Let Dad watch the baby and Mom take the older child to the grocery store or vice versa. When it's time to change the oil in the car, ask one of the kids to come along for company. Grab a quick bite together while you are waiting. Use the time to talk and joke together.

NAMES FOR BONUS PARENTS

My father makes me call my bonus mom, Mom. It makes me feel weird, but if I don't, he gets mad.

Regretfully, misguided parents sometimes demand this, and that is unfortunate. It is said to be done in the name of family unity and is based on the notion that a "family" is a mom and a dad and children—all under the same roof. Now that there are all sorts of family configurations, parent figures may not be male and female, but in the families in which I have seen this to be a problem, the parent figures have a more conventional view of "family."

Although some divorced parents strive to put the past behind them, and that means attempting to eliminate their ex from everyone's life, including their children's, others have explained that when a parent makes the children call the new partner Mom or Dad, "it is understood that she (or he) may not be *their* mom or dad, but they are the 'mom' or 'dad' in the household and should be addressed as such." This is done in the name of "respect," but if you poll the biological parent, they see the practice as disrespectful.

By the same token, rather than promote a feeling of family unity, if a child is forced to call their bonus parent Mom or Dad, it could backfire because the child may feel disloyal to their parent and openly reject the bonus parent. If parents wish their children to accept their choice of a partner, they must remember acceptance is earned. When acceptance is demanded, resentment is sure to set in and it will be because a newly-coupled parent did not openly respect their children's other parent.

Finding a name that suits a bonus parent can be a difficult task. The goal is to find a name that is reflective of the relationship between the parent figure and child—or just a nickname the child feels comfortable using. Brainstorm with the child for a fitting special name used only for their bonus parent.

Legal Rights and Responsibilities
Knowing that I usually use the word "bonus" in lieu of "step," addressing legal responsibilities is one instance where the specific label really does make a difference. Stepparents have historically had few rights in regard to their spouse's children. And even then,

what rights they did have were because they were married to the child's parent. Marriage is a legally binding contract. Bonus parents don't necessarily marry their bonus children's parent. Therefore, legally, a bonus parent who has not married their bonus child's parent has even fewer rights concerning their bonus children than does a stepparent.

While laws regarding stepparent rights differ from state to state, after the year 2000 states began to restructure laws and pass legislation that recognizes the role of stepparents in their stepchildren's lives. Thank goodness courts now recognize that suddenly terminating a child's relationship with someone who's an important part of their life can be psychologically harmful.

What If the Child's Biological Parent Passed Away?
If a biological parent has died, custody of the stepchild legally reverts to the child's other parent unless the stepparent has formally adopted the stepchild. Then technically the child is no longer a stepchild. Adoption makes the child the legal child of the petitioner and any further legal proceedings would be based on visitation between two legal parents. In some jurisdictions, if a stepparent's legal standing remains as a stepparent, that stepparent may petition for custody of their deceased spouse's child, especially when the child continues to live with the stepparent after the death of the biological parent. The final decision will be determined in the child's best interest.

> My partner, Kevin, died last month of a long illness. We lived together for 5 years, and I helped to raise his son, Judah. Judah calls me DJ for Daddy Joseph. Do I have any legal standing to see Judah? We miss each other terribly, but his other parent will not allow it.

Once parents and bonus parents divorce or a parent passes away, bonus parents do not have any legal obligations to the children of a former partner. That means they are not automatically granted visitation rights. But moral obligations are another thing altogether. Many bonus parents do not realize the impact they have on a child who has lost their parent, and once the parent is gone, they move on. This practice is not in a child's best interest unless there has been severe tension between bonus parent and child while the parent was alive. Even then, it's best to check in with the child.

This was not the case with DJ above. He misses his bonus son and wants to connect. However, any contact must be initiated through the parent who now has custody of Judah. DJ does have recourse if the child has bonded with the bonus parent and no longer interacting with them will add to the trauma of losing their parent. If this can be proven, visitation may be granted based on what is called "psychological parent status." Psychological parent status does not grant joint custody to the bonus parent; it merely recognizes the impact of the bonus parent-bonus child relationship and declares that severing that relationship would be detrimental to the child's well-being. The previous custody designation remains with the biological parent(s).

This situation is yet another reason why maintaining a good relationship with your partner's co-parent is important. When open communication is part of regular interaction, Judah's other parent would automatically understand the importance of maintaining a relationship so important to their child's security and emotional development and the thought of terminating such a relationship would not even come to mind.

COORDINATING EFFORTS WITH YOUR CHILD'S OTHER HOME

The true test of your bonus family status is how well you work with the other home. Granted, just getting on the same page in your own home is trying, but then you realize that to complete the circle, you must coordinate efforts with your partner's co-parent— sometimes more than one co-parent. Someone may have children with two different fathers or mothers. The bonus couple may both have co-parents with whom they must communicate. Remember the Before Bonus Exercise we discussed in Chapter 3? There are 16 different relationships, just at first glance.

Before we even start to attempt to reach out to the other homes, the first thing on your list is to check your mindset. If you can see you are harboring resentment, guilt, anger, jealousy, or any base emotion you have not dealt with, understand that this will get in the way of you honestly communicating with the other home. This is the reason I stress so strongly that we must move forward from past hurts to form a new working relationship with our co-parent's home now. If you are stuck in the past, you will not progress, and your children are destined to be the by-products of angry divorced parents. Rather than shying away from a problem, consider feeling excited or even relieved that you will have help in finding a solution.

Too Close for Comfort

OK, I held out the branch of peace and made nice with my husband's ex. They co-parent their kids and it seemed like the right thing to do since the kids go back and forth every few days. As a result, we get along far better than she and my husband and she'd rather talk to me than him. But now she thinks she can walk into my house any time she wants. She doesn't knock, and yesterday she showed up while I was cooking dinner, went straight to my freezer and said, "I'm making spaghetti for the kids tonight and I am out of hamburger. Have any?" Now what?

This is a legitimate question I received from a visitor to the Bonus Families website—and a legitimate situation I have heard from families who are afraid to initiate clear boundaries now that the relationship between houses is better.

I don't want to upset things. Things are so good, but seriously. What do I do?

People only respect your boundaries if you are clear about what they are—and don't vacillate, making them unsure of what you expect. Holding out the branch of peace is great. Allowing someone to take advantage of your good nature as they make themselves comfortable in your home is another story altogether. If the boundaries from house to house aren't certain, it will not only make you uncomfortable, but it will also make the kids uncomfortable. Not to mention your partner, who is probably happy you aren't fighting with his co-parent but may not be happy that she now feels that she can make herself comfortable in your home. It's time to have a heart-to-heart. No insults, no innuendos, and tact and timing are critical. Use the Bonus Families Problem Solving Model in Chapter 3 as a guide, if necessary.

When Poor Communication Lingers

While teaching workshops and working in private practice, I have seen that one of the most obvious problems in communication is avoidant behavior. Most co-parents problem solve the same as they did when they were together, which is usually not existent. So, when one reaches out to the other, no one responds because they don't want to deal with each other. Neither will call the other back. Meanwhile, texts go unanswered, phone calls go to voice mail, and both parties' frustration increases by the minute. Ultimately, problems do not get solved. They are never even brought to the table because no one wants to talk to each other.

From a practical standpoint, responding is all that is necessary. You may be angry and not want to talk, and gathering your wits about you prior to responding may prevent additional arguments. But, if your relationship has been built on avoiding confrontation, silence will make things worse. So, yes, use the time to cool off or think about whatever is proposed, but communicate that is what you are doing:

"Thanks. I got your text. Give me 24 hours. . . ."

"Let me think about this. I'll text (or call) you tonight."

"Can't talk now, but this is something we should discuss. Thanks for reaching out. Call you tomorrow."

Notice how all the responses offer a time frame in which interaction can be expected. Now the other party (co-parent, counterpartner, mother-in-law, etc.) knows you received the text and you aren't avoiding the issue or them. By responding, you are offering respect as well as being a good communicator and partner in coordinating efforts between homes. Remember to respond within the time frame you offered.

The feeling we all want when we reach out to someone is relief. We are calling this person to get help, reinforcement, or ideas how to handle something creatively, and that's what I am appealing to all co-parents to project.

A REAL-LIFE EXAMPLE OF USING ALL THE TOOLS

My bonus kids' mother and her husband called a meeting, and the adults all congregated at the local pizza parlor. They did not bring visual tools, like a calendar, to discuss the schedule, so my husband and I knew this was a serious discussion about a new topic.

The kids' mother opened the conversation. She explained that Melanie, by then 16, had expressed that she no longer liked the week-with-each-parent parenting schedule. Mom reported that a week was too short for Melanie to stay organized at 16. When she was 8, it was fine, but by 16, her good jeans were always at the other house, and this drove Melanie crazy. Although the kids' dad was skeptical that these were Melanie's feelings, I had to tell him that she had confided years ago that she felt like she lived out of a laundry basket. I had even written an article about it for the Bonus Families website. Evidently, he didn't read the article.

In order to address this problem, we followed the Bonus Family Problem Solving Model:

Step 1: Identify the problem

Step 2: Suggest a child-focused solution

Step 3: Negotiate

Step 4: Compromise

The kids' mother placed a change in parenting plan on the table (identified the problem). She suggested 3 weeks with her, 1 week with their father (suggested solution). This did not fly with the kids' dad. The following things were then discussed (negotiation):

- Is this really how Melanie felt? She had not mentioned it to her father, which told me it was probably true. She did not want to hurt his feelings.
- If a change was made, would it include her brother, Steven, age 13, since he had no problem with the week-with-each-parent parenting plan?
- If there was a change, when would it begin, and would it be permanent or just a social experiment to try out the change?

Melanie's father's point of view:

- He was open to a change if that is what Melanie truly wanted, but he wanted her time with both parents to be equal.
- He wanted Steven to stay on the same schedule as his sister.

Something that was observed by both homes is how the change in the parenting plan would affect the other children. First, Steven, who had no problem with the weekly change, and then the other two children who did not go back and forth between these two homes—my daughter from a previous marriage, age 15, and our newest arrival, age 5. I was gratified my bonus kids' mother was sensitive to the fact that Melanie, Steven, and my daughters were very close and that any proposed change would also affect them.

What was a solution that would take all the kids' needs into account?

The Compromise: It was decided that the parenting plan would change to 2 weeks with each parent. Both children would follow the new plan. A Monday night dinner would be put in place on the second week so that children and their other parent and the other siblings would not go for 2 weeks without physically interacting, and a more open-door policy would be adopted so that if the kids missed each other or the other parent and just wanted to hang out, both families were alerted to being sensitive to that request. It was agreed that we would try the new parenting plan for 3 months and meet again for a reassessment.

In truth, it worked quite well, and we kept it in effect for the following 2 years until Melanie graduated high school. There were additional tweaks along the way, and this is where being flexible comes in.

Talking to Melanie about the change, both then and now, one of her biggest concerns was that she felt like she was abandoning her little sister, who was 11 years younger than her. It was a serious decision for her to make this change and that was the reason for so many compromises within the new parenting plan.

When Melanie was 18, her brother was 15 and was very close to each member of the bonus family, particularly his dad. The open-door policy evolved to mean he could spend the day at either home and both homes must be in the loop with permission and planning, but he was required to sleep at the assigned parent's home. This was the agreement until he graduated and moved out to go to college.

I must note there were reasons why these compromises were easier for us to make than for others in a similar situation.

First, this was not our first rodeo. These co-parents had been divorced for 12 years at the time of this discussion. I had been in the picture for over 10 years, and my bonus kids' bonus dad had been married to the children's mother for 2 years. We all had time to design a problem solving strategy that we knew could work within the parameters of the personalities of all the players. In other words, we knew each other.

Second, we lived about a mile from each other in a small community. Transportation was very easy and enabled us to be more spontaneous when adjusting a schedule.

Third, we approached it with CARE. Here's how:

Communication: Having a plan in place for problem solving and using a communication problem solving model such as the Bonus Family Problem Solving Model keeps the conversation on track.

Acceptance: Not taking a request for a change personally. Acknowledging the children's individuality, ages, and development would require adjustments over the years.

Respect: I'm proud to say on so many levels . . .

- Both parents were gracious in their treatment of one another. No one lost their temper or insulted each other when discussing this sensitive topic.

- Both bonus parents observed and only commented when asked.

- Any decision that was made took all children's feelings into account, bio and bonus alike.

Empathy: When discussing the change, both parents were sensitive to how difficult it was to hear that a child wanted to make a change. All the parent figures put themselves in the kids' shoes and realized that a change was an important consideration—the age difference in the children created special problems—and how a change might affect each child differently. Checks and balances were then put in place, like the parents taking a more flexible approach, adopting an open-door policy, and adding a Monday night dinner.

You can see that the day-to-day workings of a bonus family take lots of patience, ongoing communication, acceptance of each family member's idiosyncrasies, respect for their differences, and empathy for each family member's position. Sounds like the makings of CARE, doesn't it? It's a lot of work, but years down the road after the kids are all grown and have children of their own and they tell you they realize the time and effort you took to make their life better; it is all worth it.

CHAPTER 6

Improving Extended
Bonus Family Relations

When couples decide to combine families, they often forget to look past blending their immediate families to consider how they will integrate both sides of their extended family members. The children living in this new bonus family could easily have four sets of grandparents (two sets of biological grandparents and two sets of bonus grandparents). Not to mention additional aunts, uncles, and cousins, plus good friends who are not an immediate part of this new union. The family dynamic changes radically when bonus families are formed.

Extended Family Before Bonus Exercise

Similar to the Before Bonus Exercise mentioned in Chapter 3, where you and your partner get a clear idea of your expectations for your immediate bonus family, I have designed an extended family version of the same exercise to help create the proper mindset for both accepting and feeling accepted by extended family.

Step 1: Envision the Relationship You Expect

The Extended Family Before Bonus Exercise starts out in a very similar fashion to the original exercise. Again, sit down with your partner. But in this case, we start our conversation by discussing what you envision as a whole. What image do you want to project to your family and what are your expectations from them?

So, together, with your partner, ask yourselves . . .

What are your desires and expectations for this extended family relationship?

For example, your desires and expectations might be . . .

- I would like my parents and siblings to be accepting of my life and the people now in it.
- I would like my siblings to include my bonus kids when planning something child-focused.
- I would like my relatives to not openly distinguish between my biological children and bonus children. In other words, when my bonus children are present. I would like them to be inclusive rather than exclusive.
- I would like my relatives to be fair.

Negative Expectations vs. Positive Affirmations

Throughout this book I talk about the importance of a positive mindset prior to interaction and how that sets the stage for a better all-around experience. It can be surprising when you believe extended family will be supportive but find that they are not.

At my bonus daughter's eighth-grade graduation, we took turns taking pictures with my bonus daughter. First, with her dad and I, then her mom and her husband, then her sibling and bonus siblings. I was in charge of the pictures, and as I snapped all the combinations of extended family members, her mother's sister said, "Alright, that's enough. Can we take pictures with her real family now?" It was at that moment I realized my bonus daughter's aunt thought of my daughter and I as less important in the big picture and that was a shock. My daughter and I lived with her niece. I was the mother of her half-sister, which we never referred to as "half." She only saw my bonus daughter every couple of years, yet she did not see our importance nor acknowledge the life we were all trying to create for all the children in our care, including her niece and nephew. It was extremely discouraging.

– CYNTHIA, BONUS MOM TO NICOLE, AGE 13, AND
MOTHER TO HER HALF-SISTER, SHELBY, AGE 4

The above writer could sit in her discouragement or turn the now negative expectation (or a negative prophecy) into a positive affirmation. This is done by continuing on to Step 1 of the Extended Family Before Bonus Exercise and doing exactly what it says: "Envision the relationship you expect." You are foreseeing, and therefore expecting, a negative outcome. But you can take that negative thought or expectation and turn it into a positive affirmation. Here is an example of how you can use this change in mindset in your everyday life as a bonus family.

Let's say your bonus aunt drives you crazy. You see her as self-centered, unaccepting, and disrespectful. You know she is going to be at another family event, and when you see her, do you think you will greet that person with an open mind? Most likely, she will say hello, and although you try to be nice, she will pick up that you are not happy. Not knowing that you are still upset about the last interaction (which you never talked about), your behavior will just reinforce that she thinks that you are a nasty person.

Rather than dwell on the unproductive relationship you are having with your bonus daughter's aunt, visualize the relationship you want to have. Picture yourself talking to her in a relaxed manner. It doesn't matter what she has done or what she might do to reinforce the negativity—concentrate on *your goal for the relationship* and take steps to make that the reality. Do this for every relationship you have, and you will have turned your negative expectations into positive affirmations.

Step 2: Cultivating Individual Relationships

Make a formal list of the extended family relationships with whom you and your children will interact. Discuss how you will cultivate and reinforce positive relationships with each extended family member.

Consider the primary ones first. People like your mother and father and your partner's mother and father. These are the children's grandparents. The ones who love your kids as much as you do. How do they feel about your partner's children? They may be your fallback childcare. Will they also be the fallback childcare for both bio and bonus kids? You are not just bringing home a new boyfriend or girlfriend like you did in high school. You're bringing home a partner—a partner who has children. Extended family members will have an impact on those children, and the children will have an impact on your extended family members.

How will I foster a positive relationship with

- My parents?
- If they are divorced, my parent's new partners?
- My partner's parents?
- If my partner's parents are divorced, their partners?
- Extended family: aunts and uncles, cousins, and their new partners?

Again, there are lots of relationships to consider, and each one may need your individual attention.

What will you do to set the stage for this relationship you desire?

If you are having trouble integrating your partner's extended family with your new bonus family, consider that extended family members follow their relative's lead. How you act and how your spouse acts set the example for how your relative will in turn respond to this newly formed family.

Start with making sure you have your spouse's support. Without their knowing it, their statements may not suggest a feeling of bonus family unity.

For example, let's say someone who has recently combined families with a partner with children is talking to their parents. His mother asks where his partner is.

Listen to the response:

"Gabrielle took her kids to the movies."

"Gabrielle took the kids to the movies."

"Gabrielle took Billy and Mark to the movies."

All three statements are saying the same thing. Which statement does not imply bonus family unity? Some communicate less attachment than others, and this drives my point home.

"Gabrielle took *her* kids to the movies" clearly communicates two separate family factions. The other two approaches do not. How one frames the connection in conversation can set the stage for bonus acceptance.

Step 3: Discuss Expectations With Family Members

Have a heart-to-heart talk with your extended family member. Each of you should discuss your expectations for the future.

Because extended family members form strong allegiances to past partners, these are among the most difficult relationships to anticipate. Decide what you will do to foster a positive relationship with people who are related to both you and your spouse's former partner. In other words, your in-laws. Even though your partner, for example, has broken up with his former partner, his relatives might still interact with the former partner because of their relationship to the children.

CHAPTER 6

Do you expect your new relatives to sever all ties with your partner's former partner and their extended family? You will be asking your in-laws not to interact with their grandchild's parent.

LOYALTY ISSUES

The day before yesterday, my son's father picked up my teenage son for a special golfing trip they do every year for the last 11 years. My father and brother usually go as well, but they didn't go because I am now divorced from my son's father. They are usually gone for 4 days, and they play golf until they can't stand up. My son looks forward to it every year. After they'd left, my mother told me that my father and brother actually did go along! I can't believe they chose my ex over me! I feel completely betrayed. Once my husband and I divorced, that should have been the end of my dad and brother's relationship with my ex.

Let's look at this from another perspective—the child's. He loves doing this with his dad, uncle, and grandpa each year. Now that Mom and Dad are divorced, his mother believes his grandpa and uncle should not go. Granted, everyone understands the betrayal this mom feels, but if we are using the "best interest of the children" as the criteria for our decisions, then these relationships must continue. Mom divorced Dad. The child divorced no one.

A divorce severs the ties between two people who were previously together as a couple. It does not sever the extended family's affection for their family member's former partner. The same holds true when the couple did not marry. When there are no children produced from the union, then a decision to sever ties with extended family may be understandable. But when there are children, the relationships reach out past the two divorced parties. In the case above, the connection built over the years was enhanced by the grandfather and father's mutual respect and a love for the son/grandchild. Keeping the trip a secret was done in an effort not to upset Mom, but it actually made things more complicated. She explained, "I can't believe my dad chose him over me."

Choosing one over the other wasn't the real issue. Mom had put herself in that position when she asked her father to take sides. The tradition had been intact for years, and she expected it to stop because of the breakup. She had a very difficult time accepting that the relationship Grandpa, Dad, and son had formed didn't depend on her.

The only time we can really dictate policy about associating with exes after a breakup is when someone's safety is in question. For example, if history tells this mother that her son is not safe with Grandpa or his uncle, then it is understandable that she would intercede. However, it is simply unfair for the mother to expect family members to reject her ex when her son is present because her relationship with his father has ended.

There is something else to consider in this scenario. The divorced mother is not the only one who has not thought her reaction through. Grandpa and uncle also made a questionable decision. It goes without saying that divorced couples should always inform each other of their overnight destinations when they are with their children, but this is also true when extended family takes the children on special outings. In this case, it was the grandfather and uncle's responsibility to volunteer relevant information prior to going.

This was the epitome of avoidant behavior, and it was done for the same reason co-parents do not return a text or pick up the phone. Grandpa didn't want to deal with his daughter's reaction. Granted, keeping the golfing trip a secret was probably not done maliciously, but deceiving his daughter most likely made her angrier and feel disrespected. It also set a bad example for his grandson—someone who is learning to reason on his own and make his own value judgments. It places the child in the middle and tests his allegiance to his parents. If he tells his mother about the golfing trip, he is betraying his father, uncle, and grandfather. If he keeps the trip from his mother, he is betraying her.

In defense of everyone in this story, bonus family relations can be confusing for all concerned, and the right decision may not come automatically. Most people regard their parents as their parents first and their children's grandparents second. It would be completely understandable if the mother's first reaction was to be hurt by her father's apparent allegiance to her ex. However, in the midst of her hurt, she would do well to realize that her father's choice is not a betrayal of her, but a desire to maintain a relationship with his grandson and to at times share that relationship with his grandson's father and uncle. These relationships can exist comfortably without the mother's input. They are not a personal affront to her. They are based on her son's relationships with his extended family.

This golfing trip might produce lasting memories for father, son, and grandfather that would have been missed if the family members had abided by the mother's original wishes. By the same token, it is important that you approach every interaction honestly. Never withhold important information about a child because you are afraid of someone's reaction. That becomes a lie that perpetuates itself. You must keep lying to cover up the initial lie—and of course, your loved one will feel betrayed when they are faced with that kind of deception.

All the adults in this scenario need to change their approach for the sake of the child that is watching for the correct way to approach similar situations. Sneaking and then volunteering information to compensate for deceitfulness is not a bonus family approach. Honesty promotes trust.

Let's look at this same situation from another point of view.

My husband recently took his son on a special golfing trip. When they returned, I found out that my husband's ex-wife's father also went along! I feel uncomfortable with my husband associating with his ex's parents on such an intimate level. I feel like they are always comparing me to my husband's ex and what they really want is for my husband and their daughter to reconcile. This infuriates me. I want my husband to stop interacting with his ex's relatives!

Same scenario, same grandpa. Different perspective.

New spouses would do well to promote such relationships rather than undermine them. They should not expect their mates to cut off ties to the children's extended family members because of their personal insecurities. That needs to be understood before the couple calls themselves a couple—a perfect discussion point for Step 3 of the Extended Bonus Family Before Exercise.

New partners must also do their best to understand that former extended family relationships are perpetuated not out of disrespect for them but out of respect for the child and to offer him continuity and security at a very tough time in his life. Buying into thoughts such as "I feel like they are always comparing me to my husband's ex, and what they really want is for my husband and their daughter to reconcile" undermines their own existence.

What if she's right? What if a former extended family member does wish for a reconciliation? That is their prerogative, but it is her husband's place to make his intentions clear to his former father-in-law. If her husband sets the example, his former father-in-law will follow suit. If the former father-in-law does not follow suit and continues to be openly disrespectful of his former son-in-law's new relationship, it is up to the former son-in-law to calmly set appropriate boundaries. If this does not rectify the situation, it may be time to reduce the amount of personal interaction with the former father-in-law but continue to support a positive relationship between grandfather and grandchild.

Extended Family Favoritism

My husband and I have been married for 3 years. My husband has two daughters and I have one son from previous relationships. My husband's parents are great, but sometimes they favor their biological grandkids over my son. A year after we were married, the oldest granddaughter turned 18 and was given a generous sum of money for college. A year later, the second one also turned 18 and was given the same amount. My son, on the other hand, recently turned 18 and was given a token monetary amount. Although he was happy they remembered him, I could see how hurt he was. Should we say something to the grandparents about this?

Bonding takes time. The writer loves her child and has had years to nurture and raise him, and as a result, she loves him in spite of his faults. New bonus relatives who have not had that bonding time just don't feel the same way. Her son is simply new to them.

If an adult extended family member meets a child at 6 years old, by the time the child is 18, the adult and child may have had time to form a bond. If the adult meets the same child at 15, as in this case, the relationship between grandparent and child may still feel new to the adults, and it is unlikely a bond has yet to be formed. (Three years at 15 seems like a long time. Three years at 65 is a blink of an eye.) You can't change that. The best thing the parent in this case can do is to make sure the child understands it's not his fault. If extended-family members treat him differently than biological family members, it is based on circumstance and is their choice, not based on anything he has done.

Here's where the heart-to-heart conversation mentioned at the beginning of Step 3 of the Extended Bonus Family Before Exercise comes into play. You can head off a lot of misunderstandings and possibly speed up the bonding process if you have a formal conversation with extended bonus family members *before* new couples move in together or get married. It's a good practice to explain that there will be more members of your family and that you hope that as your mother, father, sister, or brother, etc., they will support you and accept these new members as part of their extended family.

You may even want to formally invite them to become members of your bonus family. For example, you might say, "We know you and the kids are not biologically related, but we value your place as a grandparent figure (or family member) in all of the children's lives and we want to include you." Without having this type of conversation up front, extended bonus family members may have no idea how you want them to interact with all the children in your bonus family.

BONUS FAMILY HOUSEWARMING CEREMONY: FORMALLY PRESENTING YOUR INTENT

Fewer couples are formally marrying, so weddings may be less prevalent, but couples continue to come together and combine families, often adding a child to the family themselves. For those into ritual and tradition, I have seen bonus families have a sort of Bonus Family Housewarming Ceremony that invited only close friends and family to a get-together soon after they moved in together. They treated it differently than a wedding in the sense that it was very casual, but they used the opportunity to offer those attending an invitation to formally join them in their new endeavor.

At one ceremony I attended, it was very important to the couple that their friends and family embraced their union. They had the get-together in their backyard and made a formal presentation in front of all who attended, saying something like, "Bridget and Tom, you are our best friends and enhance our life immensely. I would like to introduce you to my family, the family I have wanted for a long time. We invite you to participate with us as much as you would like. Family, this is Bridget and Tom." And they went around the room to all who attended, saying something similar to each person, couple, or family that they wanted to acknowledge. It was similar to wedding vows or a commitment ceremony and a really lovely tribute. That was the day they chose to be their anniversary.

While working with bonus families and their extended family members, I have found that grandparents may be even more afraid of displaying favoritism than the parents are. Grandparents don't want to hurt their biological relations' feelings (biological grandchildren, nieces, or nephews) by making a fuss over the new bonus additions. They worry that an all-inclusive attitude toward new bonus grandchildren will offend their beloved biological grandchildren. They are also afraid to overstep their bounds because it is rare that boundaries are clearly set for extended bonus family members. If you are a bonus relative and no one has said anything to you about how they would like you to interact with the kids, don't be afraid to initiate the conversation. Ask them what *they* expect from *you*. Discuss how you will all go forward using your mutual love and respect as a guide.

THE OTHER SIDE OF THE COIN: EXTENDED-FAMILY FINANCIAL OBLIGATIONS

I have set aside some money to help my grandchild through college. My son recently remarried, and his new wife has three children. There's just not enough to help my step-grandchildren through college. Am I obligated to provide for them, too?

It is important to clarify that when a family member marries someone with children, their financial obligation does not automatically become the extended-family members' responsibility. We all do what we can with the resources we have.

Once again, C is for Communication. Put your heads together. Talk about the possibilities. Pool your resources if that seems appropriate. The key is to discuss your available options and work together for the benefit of the children. However, if there are limited funds and your decision is to help your biological grandchild only, that is the way it was when you made the financial plan and may be communicated as such without fear or embarrassment.

I'm happily remarried, and my sister just doesn't like and won't accept my new family. We try to present everything in a positive light, but she's resisting. As much as you would like your relatives to accept your choices, there may be times that you cannot sway them. As much as it hurts that a loved one does not accept your new family, that is her choice. All you can do is continue to be polite and courteous to her and set the example by your words and deeds.

MULTIPLE PARTNER DILEMMA

How many times am I supposed to welcome new people into my family? My son has been married three times. I get close to his wife and her children and then they break up. Each time they come and go, it's an adjustment.

If this mother-in-law is like most in-laws I have worked with, her problem is not about welcoming new bonus family members into her family—it's about welcoming new family members into her heart. She hasn't experienced the arguments or betrayal issues that served as the catalyst for her son's separations, so each time there is a breakup, she is left mourning the departure of a beloved family member. Reading between the lines, she is questioning if she should maintain a relationship with her son's former partners and bonus children and if she is being disloyal to her son if she wants to stay in contact with these former relatives.

This is a hard call, and the grandmother's concern is completely understandable. However, if we are staying consistent in our reasoning, the answer is based on this grandmother's relationship to the children and if it would be detrimental to them if she no longer interacted with them after the breakup. Of course, weigh in with her son, but at the beginning of the next relationship, it must be understood if and how interaction will be maintained if there is another breakup.

ACCEPTING A NEW FAMILY MEMBER AFTER THE DEATH OF A LOVED ONE

I have been lucky to be in love two times in my life. The first time, with my wife of 48 years who passed away 6 months ago after a long illness, and now with Patricia, a lovely woman who also lost her husband. Patricia and I plan to eventually marry, but that's not our immediate problem. We both have grandchildren. Hers are much younger than mine. I have grandchildren that range from age 27 to 8 years old. All [of] Patricia's grandchildren call her "Grandma," and so I have begun referring to her as "Grandma" when I am in front of the kids. Yesterday, I spent the day with my grandchildren and referred to Patricia as Grandma when talking to the youngest. My oldest granddaughter overheard and was furious. Such a happy occasion turned into a mess, and I don't know what to do.

Unfortunately, this grandfather couldn't have made a bigger mistake if he tried, and I'm sure it was done inadvertently, but it's on the same level of demanding a child call their bonus parent Dad or Mom. First, the child may feel uncomfortable, but it can also be perceived as disrespectful of the deceased grandmother's memory.

Six months after someone passes does not really prepare family members for a new partner, but many times, it often happens, particularly when grandparents pass away after a long illness. Although many seniors start their mourning when they realize their spouse is terminally ill, other younger family members do not face the passing until it happens. The oldest granddaughter had the strongest memories with her grandmother and is just now facing her loss. She is simply not far enough into the mourning process, and when her grandfather inadvertently referred to another woman as Grandma, it sent up a red flag. As a result, rather than promote Patricia's acceptance, things like this can prompt grandchildren to go on a personal crusade to rally the other grandkids against the new partner in Grandma's memory.

What can you do now? There are some things this granddaughter wants to hear. First, that Patricia isn't trying to take

Grandma's place. Second, that you won't forget Grandma and how important she was because you now have Patricia in your life.

Your granddaughter knows she won't forget Grandma. At this point, she's not so sure about you. And, just saying, "I will never forget your grandma," may not be all you need to do for her to believe you and ultimately accept Patricia. You have to prove it to her by demonstration. This means presenting Patricia as a loving companion, but don't be afraid to reminisce about jokes between Grandma and the grandkids or discuss special memories. Be careful not to offend Patricia, as she should be careful not to offend you when she reminisces with her grandchildren. This is a two-way street. She should be having the same sort of conversation with her grandchildren, too.

Third, they are not betraying Grandma by accepting Patricia. Something this family must realize is that accepting someone new into the family betrays a deceased family member's memory *only* if one tries to replace their feelings about the relative who has passed with their feelings about the new relative. But, if one keeps the two relationships separate, respecting both people as individuals, they are then free to mourn one while befriending the other. They both live separately in one's memory.

Finally, it may be good to sit down with the grandkids and figure out a unique pet name they can call Patricia (and that Patricia's grandkids can call you). Keep the conversation lighthearted, and perhaps look to the older kids for suggestions.

TIPS FOR BECOMING A BONUS RELATIVE

How can I maintain my close relationship with my grandchild, niece, nephew, etc., and comfortably nurture a new relationship with a new bonus grandchild, bonus niece, or bonus nephew? The following tips are suggestions to get to know any new bonus children in your life, whether they are your own, your bonus grandchildren, bonus nieces, or nephews, even your friend's bonus kids.

Remember that no two children are alike. Make a special effort to get to know this child as an individual. Find out about his likes and dislikes so you have more to say than "Hi, honey, how's school?" Most kids do not like to talk about school. They prefer to talk about their interests—skateboarding, snowboarding, cool movies they have just seen, their favorite video game, the music they like to listen to, and so on. Ask them about those things and you will get an engaged answer. Ask them, "How's school?" and all they are likely to say is, "Fine." And that's the end of the getting-to-know-you conversation.

Look for ways to get to know them and for them to know you. Tell your new young bonus relatives special stories about your past, just as you would a young biological relative. Bonus grandkids like to hear those "In my day, I walked five miles in the snow to school" stories, too. And the more they know about you, the easier your interactions will become.

Go slowly into the new bonus children's lives. Don't push yourself on them or force them to kiss or hug you. Allow them to respond naturally to your kindness.

Don't say, "I love you" if you don't mean it. Kids can be skeptical of declarations of affection from people they don't know well. Start with things like "Aren't you a smart girl!" or "Great choice, Joseph!" Positive reinforcement makes everyone feel more accepted.

Don't play favorites. Don't sneak extra money for that little something special to the children who are related to you biologically. You can be sure your grandchild, niece, or nephew will let their bonus sibling know about the special gift, which will only reinforce the bonus child's feeling of lack of acceptance. To reinforce that special relationship with your biological grandchild, niece, or nephew, you might set aside a special day or time on a regular basis for just the two of you. If you live far away, send emails or connect via an occasional phone call.

If giving a grandchild extra cash is important to you, consider an individual bank account or college fund. You may never feel the same way about bonus relatives as you do about blood relatives but try to find a way to show your affection that does not make one child feel blatantly less cared for than the other. This is especially true if the bonus child's biological relatives are not in the picture. You may be the only chance at having a grandparent, aunt, or uncle this child has.

If you harbor any anger or resentment because of the breakup, discuss that directly with the parents. Never direct it toward innocent children or make comments about anything that can be perceived as negative toward a family member that they love.

Don't compete with your biological counterparts. Get to know the child's aunt or grandparent so that they don't feel like you are invading their territory. This could be the opportunity to make a new friend who cares for the same people you do. Children follow the lead of the adults who are setting the example. If an existing relative is your enemy, don't expect to be openly accepted by the child.

Try not to overcompensate. Being overly nice to the new bonus child in your life can cause jealousy in your young biological relatives. In other words, your grandchildren could get jealous if you are spoiling your bonus grandchild in front of them. This happens sometimes when adults try too hard. Just be yourself, and if you aren't sure what to do, be honest. Talk to the parents and talk to the kids. Talk to a counselor. Or write to me via the Bonus Families website.

Whose Side Are You On?

My husband of 10 years and I were just divorced. My best friend for 25 years has sided with him. I'm devastated about the divorce—and also about the loss of my friend, who is like family to me. Unfortunately, allegiances are tested when relationships dissolve, and losing an old friend can be part of the fallout after a breakup.

Chapter 6

When I divorced, I had two good girlfriends that I had known for years. The first had been my best friend since high school. The second I had met in college. My friend from college had been a friend of my ex-husband's before we were married, and I automatically assumed that their relationship would continue after we divorced. By the same token, I assumed that my old friend from high school would automatically choose to continue our relationship. I was wrong on both counts. My friend from high school, now married to a man who had become my ex-husband's best friend, felt compelled to choose one of us over the other, and because the men were so close, she felt she had to support her husband. My friend from college, on the other hand, the one I assumed would choose my ex-husband if a choice had to be made, stood her ground. "I love you both," she said. "And I want to remain friends with both of you." Thankfully, that is exactly what happened, but she also made her boundaries very clear. She told us both she would not pass on information or gossip about either of us. I was grateful that was stated, and it has been confirmed over the years. However, we made her life easy because we eventually held no animosity for the other and concentrated on raising our child. I say *eventually* because it was a process.

My daughter lived with her boyfriend for 5 years. We loved him and accepted him as part of the family. Two months after they got married, they broke up. We are all reeling. My daughter expects us all to just move on and forget about this person my husband I considered a son. The breakup was not expected and although my allegiance is to my daughter, forgetting about Jeffrey will be difficult.

Allegiance to past partners gets complicated when there were children produced from the union. The children bind the couple forever and extended family forever. If there were no children, as in the case above, if the former relative reaches out, never be rude, but consider your relative's wishes.

202

Unaccepting Bonus Relatives

> *My husband's previous wife passed 4 years ago and left him with two boys, now ages 7 and 9. We have been married for almost 2 years and also have a little girl who is 6 months old. To round out our family, I recently adopted the two boys. My problem is that their grandmother, his former wife's mother, is incredibly rude to me. Whenever I post things on Facebook about what our family is doing she comments, reminding me that I "am only the stepmom" and telling me about the things her daughter and my husband did before her death. I feel like I have to defend myself.*

What is being described is a mother who is still grieving the loss of her daughter, and with the arrival of someone new, is afraid that her son-in-law and his children will forget her beloved child. Unfortunately, her insecurity translates into rude interaction—and that's too bad, particularly for her grandchildren who have suffered a huge loss and need the adults in their lives to show love, understanding, and offer them as much security as possible. Undermining you in the eyes of your children, her grandchildren, does not offer them the security they need.

This family is hurting, and that hurt is fueling their negative reactions and bad judgment. That's the reason, but not an excuse for their bad behavior. As difficult as it will be, these are the times we must do our best to set the example for the children in our care. Plus, it will be easier for everyone if your husband sets clear boundaries for Grandma's interaction with the kids.

Something important to note—the writer is not the boys' stepmother; she is their adoptive mother. Legally, she is Mom, and it would be to her credit if in her devotion to their being well balanced and emotionally stable, she also helped her boys remember their birthmother. Grandma may also respond positively if she sees that her daughter is remembered and that this adoptive mother is openly teaching the boys to respect their mother's memory. However, it is also important that the boys are allowed to normalize their feelings and cultivate a loving relationship with their adoptive mom. Rather than raise these boys to miss their biological mother, raise them to be grateful she gave them life and that someone else also loved them enough to step in and offer them emotional stability after her death.

Godparents

> *My ex and I have been co-parenting our kids for the last 3 years. About a year ago she married a guy I really like and that has made things easier, believe it or not. Yesterday they both asked me to coffee, told me my ex was pregnant, and asked me to be their child's godfather. Sounds a little weird to me.*

This may sound like an unconventional request, but if you think about it, what it means is that this father is doing such a good job at co-parenting that his co-parent's husband believes he will also put his child first when called to do so. Impressive.

Before we go further, let's examine what being a child's godparent means. The duties associated with the request can vary culturally and from family to family. In some families, being a godparent is merely an honorary position. In others, the godparent is like a second parent and a fundamental part of the child's spiritual education. In essence, a godparent's role is to serve as a mentor and stay involved with the child should his or her own parents be unable to guide them. It is the godparent's responsibility that the children remain solid in their faith if the biological parents pass on.

More often, being asked to be the godparent signifies that you're the one the parents see raising the child if something happens to them. Get clear on that one. Openly ask what being this child's godparent means to them and what they expect of you. If it's more than you want to take on, be honest. Being a godparent is a huge compliment—but also a huge responsibility.

It sounds as if this man doesn't have someone in his life now, but he probably will. He must be prepared for possible pitfalls. Being someone's godparent will require him to interact very closely with the child—and with his parents. It's not uncommon for new partners to understand the need to interact with their partner's own children but not their ex's children—some distinguish between the two. That could upset the well-balanced apple cart these co-parents and his co-parent's new partner have worked so hard to build. Anyone he chooses will have to go along with the program from day one for them to remain successful.

Finally, thinking about it, he shouldn't be surprised that they've asked him to do this—he's actually the logical choice. There are other half siblings in the mix, and if he is designated the one to have the kids means that the siblings will be raised together. Personally, I remember the first time my bonus kids' dad and I went out of the country. As I returned the kids to their mother before we left (plus mine and ours—she was watching them all!), I realized we had no one designated to take the kids should something happen to us. It was a very sentimental moment that also made me laugh a little. Her words as we pulled away to drive to the airport were, "I don't know how I'll do it, but I promise they'll all go to college!" Luckily, she never had to make that decision alone.

PART III

NAVIGATING BONUS FAMILY SOCIAL OBLIGATIONS

CHAPTER 7

Bonus Family Weddings and Commitment Ceremonies

My youngest daughter just got married. It was the perfect wedding, outside in Golden Gate Park in October. At the wedding rehearsal, the seats are set up according to tradition, the bride's side of the family on one side, the groom's side of the family on the other. The wedding planner whispers to me, "Who is that woman sitting in the front row?" I glance to my left and see Sharyl chatting with the relative next to her. "Oh," I say. "That's the bride's sister's mother."

"Huh?" The wedding planner looks perplexed as she whispers under her breath. "Bride's sister's mother . . ." She repeats, "Bride's sister's mother . . . Wait, you mean your husband's ex-wife? Your husband's ex-wife is here at the wedding?"

"Well, yes. She's been in the bride's life since she was born."

"But, in the front row?"

I shrugged. "She's family."

Few weddings come off without a hitch, even in those rare families in which there has been no breakup or remarriage for generations. Breakups complicate just about everything, and weddings and commitment ceremonies are at the top of that list. Whether it's your breakup, your parents', or your friends', a breakup can turn the simplest decision into a huge challenge—and it's simply because the proper preparation has not been put in place to plan such an event with multiple players, bad memories, and hot tempers.

This chapter is designed to help you consider all aspects of planning the big day, taking into consideration whether you and your partner both have children, if only one of you does, and how the ages of those children impact how you approach your union.

Looking back at my own wedding, I wish I had done things differently, starting with communicating more effectively with the other side of my bonus children's family, specifically with their mother. I should have facilitated more effective conversations about the changes we would all face after we got married, particularly just keeping her in the loop so she could properly address what her children were feeling during all the preparation hoopla.
— SHARON, MOM TO ANTHONY, AGE 8, AND
MARCELLA, AGE 12

Do we even have to get married?

Life is not the same as it was even a decade ago. Social mores evolve, laws change, language changes. Although many still wish for a conventional wedding, others do not want to marry but want to make a public commitment to their partner. Many want to include their children in the ceremony. This means we need to establish a more contemporary approach to planning family celebrations, finding an easier way to incorporate past, present, and prepare for the future.

This more contemporary approach is not just for the couple looking to make the commitment. It is for anyone who must communicate with someone in the context of a breakup.

How can I plan a wedding when my parents are making what should be a wonderful time into a nightmare? My dad says he won't go if my mother and my bonus dad are there. My mother says she won't go if my dad is there . . .

Or

My partner has three children. His co-parent will not allow the children to participate in our commitment ceremony because she thinks it's stupid. She said it is not like it's a real wedding and she doesn't take it seriously.

Or

I would like my nephew—my divorced brother's son—to be the ring bearer at my wedding, but his mother says absolutely not. She does not want to have anything to do with this side of the family—and that includes her son. How is that even possible? His dad is my brother!

Each message is a plea for help from someone who has been touched by a breakup. All three people feel the situation is out of their control and that they are at the mercy of someone who doesn't respect them or their point of view. This chapter will help us address all these feelings and hopefully set the example.

PLANNING A WEDDING OR COMMITMENT CEREMONY
Is there an alternative to marriage?

That's a question more and more people are asking, and it appears many believe the answer is yes. In my work as a child custody mediator with the court system, I worked predominantly with parents under 35 and saw far more unmarried parents than married parents. This may be because their parents broke up and they did not want to re-create what they went through as a child. Still, a breakup is a breakup, whether the parents are married or not. It affects the children in the same way.

Domestic Partnership
For those who want to formally commit but do not want to enter a traditional marriage, a domestic partnership could be a good

alternative. This approach was more widely used prior to same sex marriage becoming legalized in 2015; however, seniors who do not want to marry but like the idea of a formal commitment often consider a domestic partnership to be the answer.

A domestic partnership is a formal, legally recognized union between two individuals who live together. It offers similar legal rights and responsibilities to marriage, but it is not the same. A domestic partnership allows you to inherit, have hospital visitation rights, and be added to healthcare benefits. However, a domestic partnership still requires separate tax returns, the parties may not receive Social Security benefits from each other, and it is not recognized in all 50 states. There are other legal benefits to marriage, as well. Many feel a label—marriage or domestic partnership—is not necessary, and living together without a formal document is all that is needed. Just remember, choosing not to marry does not ensure that your children will be protected from the fallout of your breakup.

Do you have a ceremony, like a wedding, when you enter into a domestic partnership?

Ceremonies are optional for both weddings and domestic partnerships. You can even opt and instead have a "commitment ceremony" to mark the personal commitment to live together. A ceremony is a public celebration acknowledging your union. Having a ceremony is the couple's decision.

Commitment Ceremonies

What is a commitment ceremony and how does it differ from a wedding?

Some partners want to declare their love and commitment to one another but do not want the legalities associated with a marriage license or domestic partnership. In these circumstances, a commitment ceremony may be the perfect choice. It is simply a ceremony or get-together that publicly acknowledges the couple's commitment to one another.

In the past, a commitment ceremony was the only option for partners who wanted to formally commit to one another but could not legally marry. For instance, if one or both partners have been in marriages previously and do not want to marry again but still want to make a public commitment. Or they may have a different lifestyle that does not lend itself well to conventional marriage. It doesn't matter whether you are straight, LGBTQ+, or in a polyamorous relationship; a commitment ceremony is often the answer for those who want to express their affection and dedication to one another but do not fit the conventional mold.

Commitment ceremonies do not follow any sort of formal protocol. You can exchange vows, offer gifts or rings to mark the occasion, and include anyone you like to support your union in the ceremony. You don't even need an officiant if you don't want one. You can simply express your feelings to one another—alone or in front of guests. As with a wedding ceremony, the parties' children or grandchildren may also take a special part in the celebration if they like. There are no legal requirements for a commitment ceremony, so no birth or marriage certificates are required. And, if you eventually choose to part ways, since a commitment ceremony is not a legally binding contract like a marriage license or domestic partnership agreement, there is no reason to formally divorce if you decide to part ways.

Announcing Your Bonus Family Engagement

Announcing an engagement should be an exciting time, but it can be tempered with anxious anticipation when family members are battling and struggling with familiar grudges. Many have expressed concerns because their own parents don't accept that the person they have chosen to marry already has children, or their co-parent doesn't approve of their choice of a partner. Couples with children from previous relationships wonder how they should tell the kids their life is changing. Then there's the appropriate wording on the ceremonial announcement invitations. So many live together prior to deciding to make a formal commitment that the approach to announcing an engagement is more relaxed and can easily be tailored to each individual couple.

Engagement Announcement Ideas
An engagement party is optional, and if you choose to have one, the key is to present the anticipated marriage as a family coming together, and the wording should reflect that.

If a family member or friend is hosting, the wording could be:

> *Mike and Lola*
> *Are getting married!*
> *Please join their family*
> *In celebration of their engagement.*
> *Saturday, [date] and [time]*
> *Location:*
> *Hosted by:*

Or add something like:

> *Jill, Michael, and their children would like*
> *to make an announcement!*
> *They are getting married!*

If you are announcing your own engagement, the wording would simply reflect that at the beginning of the announcement. Add something that acknowledges the combining of families, either the names of the combined children or "Please join our bonus family in celebration of our engagement."

Wedding and Commitment Ceremony Invitations
The language when inviting guests to a bonus family wedding is very similar to bonus family engagement announcements. Some other things to consider, however, would be how to announce who

is hosting the wedding when the parents of those getting married or making the commitment are no longer together and one or both have re-partnered.

When the remarried father is hosting the celebration and issues the invitation with their partner:

Mr. and Mrs. Steve Miller
[or whatever the partner's name might be]
request the honor of your presence
at the marriage of
Mary Rose Miller
to
Michael Kent Stuart

If the parents of both parties marrying have helped to host the wedding and all wish to be added to the invitation their names should all be listed. I have listed various ways to refer to the hosts below:

Mr. and Mrs. Brad Lawton or Ms. Lucy Smith
[if the parents do not share the same last name]
Mr. and Mrs. Michael Gimelli
[bride's mother and her partner. If they do not share the same name, their names should be listed individually.]
Mr. and Mrs. James Goldman
[groom's mother and husband]
Mr. Scott Blumberg and Mr. Luis Rodriguez
[groom's father and partner]
request the honor of your presence
at the marriage of
Jeanne Marie Lawton
to
Kenneth Michael Blumberg

When both the bride and groom's parents have divorced and remarried, and everyone, including the couple to be married, is pitching in, rather than list everyone's names individually, the invitation may begin with the marrying couple's names and follow with "together with their parents and bonus parents" before the request line.

I recently received a wedding invitation that used this straightforward approach:

> *The parents and bonus parents of*
> *Mary Rose Miller*
> *and*
> *Kenneth Michael Blackstock*
> *request the honor of your presence*
> *at the wedding of their children.*

WHEN THE COUPLE HAS UNDERAGE CHILDREN

I have been sharing custody with my child's father for 3 years. She is now 4. My work takes me out of town every weekend, so she stays with her dad each Friday to Monday morning. This Monday, she walked into the house with a huge smile on her face. "Daddy is getting married, and I am going to be a flower girl!" I didn't even know he was dating anyone. I don't want to get in a confrontation with him, but I'm furious that I had to hear the news from our child! I was so taken by surprise I yelled, "No way! That A******!" and my daughter started crying.

The reason behind withholding this sort of information is usually because one parent doesn't believe the other needs to know their business. But as I have mentioned previously, if parents are co-parenting and the children live in both parents' homes, then what happens at either home is equally important and it is vital that parents share the information. That way, when your child comes home with information like Daddy's getting married, your response can be "Yes, honey, I know! And you will be such a beautiful flower girl!" instead of "No way!" and scare your child.

Telling a co-parent that you plan to marry need not be negatively anticipated. If you have been truly co-parenting, the fact that a co-parent is getting married should be no surprise. Following Bonus Family Etiquette, your co-parent would have already met your new partner when you decided to be exclusive, and as tough as it may be, all three of you (possibly four of you if both co-parents have new partners) would be doing your best to work together for the sake of the children in your collective care long before anyone announces their plan to marry.

Telling Your Children

Younger children follow your lead. Therefore, if you have laid the proper groundwork as a bonus couple, it will not come as a surprise to your kids that you are discussing committing to one another. The response will be different, however, if you move too quickly and they are not yet open to a new person in their lives. Add to that the fact that they may be concerned that their other parent will be lonely or feel left out, and that's when the reception will be less than favorable.

To prevent resentment, guard against surprises. Explain everything thoroughly and use age-appropriate language that they will understand. Don't be surprised if you must repeat yourself or explain what is happening in another way.

Age-Appropriate Language

What children are really concerned with when hearing big news, like "We are getting married," is what that news means for them. Parents often take it for granted that their children understand what they are talking about and use words or concepts that confuse them. When you talk about big changes, like getting married, make sure you listen to your children's concerns and answer all their questions using language that they will understand.

I often tell the story of a little girl who saw a Napa Valley wine-tasting/hot air balloon-themed wedding on TV. The couple got married as they sailed over the top of beautiful vineyards in the middle of Napa Valley. When the officiant said, "You may kiss the bride," the hot air balloon pilot hit the fire propelling the balloon and it frightened the little girl. Her idea from that day forward was that people got married in hot air balloons with fire. That's why, when her mother announced that she and her bonus dad were getting married, her reaction was less than favorable.

I worked with another child about the same age as the child above who did not understand what a honeymoon was. It was explained to him that it was a time when his daddy and his bonus mom would go away without him. He was to stay with his bonus mom's parents while they were away. He had no idea how long the honeymoon would be, and based on that, did not want his father to get married. It took a while to figure out the reason for his strong reaction. Just saying, "We are going on a honeymoon after the wedding and you will be staying with Madeline's parents," was not enough explanation for a 4-year-old.

WHEN THE COUPLE HAS ADULT CHILDREN

The steps to forming a bonus family are not just for parents with younger children. Parents with older children may divorce or their spouse pass away and meeting someone new when you are older is quite the challenge. Thinking that adult children will understand the ways of the heart and the desire for a life partner, many parents don't take the time and care to integrate new people into bonus family life. Ironically, it is sometimes harder to get adult children on board than young children. They may not be as open to change as their younger counterparts and see their parent's new love interests as intruders.

I was married for 30 years and have two children [who are] now well into adulthood. I've recently begun seeing a wonderful man who lost his wife of 32 years to cancer 7 years ago. We really enjoy each other's company and plan to marry soon. His children, however, who are even older than mine and have children of their own, are not accepting of someone new in their dad's life. They have been very nasty to him, ignoring me when I am around and saying things like, "How can you do this to Mom?" This makes him feel very guilty, and he thinks they will not even come to our wedding!

Emphasis is usually put on how difficult it is for younger children to accept a parent's new partner, but adult children have just as much trouble accepting change. Adult children had more time with their deceased or divorced parent and have formed long-term intense allegiances. If divorced or widowed parents go too fast, like the adult children in this example, they may see their parent's acceptance of someone new as a betrayal of their other parent and this can certainly slow down the bonding process with their parent's new partner.

In the case above, even though it's been 7 years since their parent passed, if Dad and his new partner met and moved quickly, the length of time since the passing doesn't make as much difference to the adult children as the length of time it took the new partners to meet and talk marriage. The kids will say, "You are going too fast; it's been less than a year!" The adults marrying will say, "What do you mean? *It's been 7 years!*"

To reinforce this different point of view, as you age, time seems to pass more quickly. Because of this, older surviving spouses may feel as if they don't need the luxury of a long courtship before committing to a new partner. Seniors have volunteered that long engagements seem like a waste of precious time, but their adult children may still be in mourning and resent their surviving parent's ability to move on so quickly.

Parents of adult children who wish to move on must make it clear that someone new is not a replacement for the deceased parent. The new person is the chosen companion for this time in their life. Of course they would not have written the story as it turned out, but isn't it wonderful that they found someone they like so much? Surviving parents might also consider suggesting their children not devalue their deceased parent's memory by comparing them to someone else. These are two completely different people, and they are two completely different relationships. Comparing does a disservice to the deceased parent's memory and to the new partner and will make it even more difficult for all the parties to move on.

BONUS FAMILY PRENUPTIAL AGREEMENTS

A prenuptial agreement is a contract between two people that spells out how assets will be divided if there should be a divorce or death of one of the partners.

There are two schools of thought concerning prenuptial agreements. Some feel that signing a prenuptial agreement undermines trust in the marriage. It assumes there will be a divorce and assigns the division of assets beforehand. Others believe that it offers partners a safety net if both own property, if there is a large difference in assets between partners, or if one or both were affected by what they feel was an unbalanced division of property in a past breakup.

Whether you should enter into a prenuptial agreement depends on your life circumstances. Prenups are common practice if

- there is a great discrepancy between personal wealth when the parties decide to marry or form a domestic partnership;
- both own property prior to the marriage and wish to keep all assets separate throughout the marriage;
- you own a business or are involved in a family company;

- you have children from a previous relationship and want their inheritance protected or want the distribution of wealth to consider any additions to the family;
- you are concerned about your future spouse's significant debt; and/or
- you have other concerns and want to protect your personal assets.

Some find it uncomfortable to discuss each other's assets and debts. It is not uncommon to believe that the question of a prenup is a sign that one or both parties cannot be trusted, or there is a question if their affection is sincere. The truth is, if you find it difficult to discuss this prior to marriage, it will still be difficult to discuss while married and even more difficult if there is a divorce. Being honest with each other now sets the stage for an open and honest relationship in the future.

Custom Tailoring Your Event: It's Up to You

Although my mom and bonus mom get along quite well, I'm afraid they might step on each other's toes when planning my wedding. My bonus mom is very hands-on and will want to be included in all the planning. My mom will not like it. She's told me all my life how she's looking forward to planning my wedding.

Bonus parents have to remind themselves their responsibility is that of support, not as a decision maker. The bonus parent can be the official backup for anything from running errands to overseeing the guest book. In my case, my bonus daughter asked me to be part of her wedding procession, but with a twist. She was very close to her paternal grandfather who was quite ill when she married. She wanted him to be part of the procession as she walked down the aisle but knew he would need help. She also wanted her father to "give her away." So, prior to her and her father walking, she asked me to walk with her grandfather. I held his arm as we walked, and we both sat on the aisle in the second row. Her mother had already entered and was sitting in the front row. Then the bride and her father entered.

My mom and bonus dad have just moved into a new home with a huge yard that backs up to a private lake. My fiancé and I have a very limited budget—it's the second wedding for both of us and we each have two children. I would love to have our wedding in my mom's backyard, and she said she would love it, too, but I'm afraid my dad and my bonus mom will not come. They will view it as picking my mom over them, and that's not it at all.

Over the years, children learn to pilot this kind of turbulence, but there has always been one factor that made it a little easier to fly—their parents were rarely in the same place at the same time. Not so at their child's wedding when both parents will hopefully take an active role. The fact that their parents will now be forced to appear together in public after a long relationship hiatus could test even the most confident first-time marriage partner. This is another reason to strive for cooperation when co-parenting your youngsters. It is practice for when years down the road you must appear cordial in public for the sake of your children.

If parents find themselves giving their children the impression that they must choose, check yourself immediately. Even though you may think you are being honest and letting your adult child know how you feel, your comments and actions may ask your child to choose between you and their other parent.

It is important to note: If children continue to anticipate their parents' hurt feelings and run defense for battling parents, things will never improve. This would be the time for personal boundaries to be stated and the parties making the commitment to politely inform their parents *and* their new partners *and* extended family of *their* wishes for *their* wedding.

Choosing a Bonus Family Officiant

Your choice of officiant to preside over your bonus family ceremony is an important one. The officiant directs the ceremony and does their best to tie each stage of the ceremony together. If religious, your officiant can be a priest or clergyperson, or if you are not religious, a friend or acquaintance you respect.

It is important to note that some faiths or officiants may not approve of divorce or having children outside of marriage. They may frown on various rituals that integrate children from previous relationships or even the couples' own children born prior to marriage participating in the ceremony. For example, having your children from a previous relationship light a unity candle during the ceremony or having counterpartners unite in walking the bride down the aisle. Some religions prevent the officiant from performing the ceremony if the bride or groom has been married before. Make sure the clergyperson you choose is comfortable with your lifestyle and plans for the ceremony.

Discuss your plans for your ceremony with your prospective officiant, the vows you wish to say, whether conventional or your own. Are you comfortable with language like "Who gives this bride?" or would you like to use a different expression in your vows that is not gender specific or possibly includes specific bonus family members and/or your children? Let the officiant know if you want friends, extended family, or your children to participate in the ceremony by participating in the readings, singing, or even lighting candles. Many couples who already have children modify the "Who gives this woman in marriage?" to a more appropriate, "Who will support this bonus family with their love and prayers?" Everyone attending may then respond with a hearty, "We do!"

I am Jewish, and my fiancé was brought up Methodist. For our sake and the sake of our children, we would like both of our faiths honored at our ceremony. How common is it to have a representative of two faiths co-officiate?

Incorporating aspects of both faiths into the ceremony, especially if there are children involved, is an excellent way to demonstrate tolerance and acceptance for each individual family member's beliefs, plus it sets the stage for the family's future together.

Although it sounds nice to have "co-officiants," one for each faith, sometimes religious officiants refuse to perform the ceremony in conjunction with another religion's representative. Plus, in some states only one officiant can sign legal paperwork after performing the ceremony. Check to see what the laws are in the state in which the ceremony is performed. Even if co-officiants cannot both sign the paperwork, if asked they sometimes agree to perform the ceremony together, yet only one will sign and record the legal paperwork.

Vows

Your vows are the cornerstone of the ceremony. It is when the couple publicly pledges their acceptance and devotion to one another. If this is a bonus family ceremony, with each family member participating in some way, each one may be invited to say words or read something meaningful to them. Most look for something poignant and significant, a heartfelt expression of how they feel about their new partner and forming this bonus family.

One way to ensure that the ceremonial vows are truly special is to write them yourself. You may want to do it privately or possibly sit down with your partner or your bonus family members and plan together. If you all participate, make a list of what you would like to say to each other, your extended family, and friends about what you pledge to one another and what you envision your life/lives will be like from this day forward. Take note that there may be some terminology that must legally be included. Your officiant can give you that information. If you are having a religious ceremony, check with the clergyperson you chose to see if there are any standardized words of faith you might want to include.

If you have writer's block, there are many books and websites that can serve as helpful guides. Feel free to borrow different portions of various vows to personalize the words you say. When getting married or participating in a commitment ceremony, adult children usually pay special attention to their feelings about commitment, trust, and family, while couples who have been married or already have children look for vows that specifically mention their children and what they envision collectively for their life together in the future.

Suggestions for Possible Bonus Family Vows

I, _____, choose you, _____, and our children [If only one partner has children, then this would be changed to "your children" or "my children"] to be my family. I promise to honor and respect all of you and to make our home a sanctuary where trust, love, and laughter abound. I make these promises with all my heart and soul and vow to honor each of you all the days of my life.

Each family member can repeat a variation of the above, either separately or together, or the person performing the ceremony might also ask the children the following questions as vows:

Officiant: And now, [children's names], do you promise to care for _____as your bonus parent?

Children: We do.

Officiant: To treat them with respect as a member of your bonus family and know that they sincerely care for you?

Children: We do.

Officiant: Do you promise to be an active member of this bonus family with the understanding that your mother, father, and [name of new bonus parent] understand the importance of both your families and do not wish you to choose one over the other, but to love and be loved by both?

Children: We do.

Parents may also want to personalize their vows by adding more romantic references or possibly humor. Something like, "I promise not to mess with the thermostat when you have set it to 74. I will look for a sweater." Or "You can be right on Mondays, Wednesdays, and Fridays."

Choosing Bonus Family Wedding Attendants

Choosing your wedding party is a major sticking point that plagues any wedding. If your parents have remarried or have a long-time significant other, you have siblings and bonus siblings you may want to include, not to mention good friends. Bonus siblings are often born years before the child shared by the bonus couple, so there may be a huge age difference between them. This presents its own set of problems. Will they seem out of place if asked to attend? And, if the partners marrying have adult children, should their children be asked to be attendants?

What this chapter is trying to communicate is that a bonus family wedding can be anything the couple wants. It can be as conventional or unconventional as the people making the commitment. Love is the tie that binds *all* families.

My fiancé and I have both been married before and we just want a small wedding. I have four brothers and a bonus sister. He has a bonus brother and sister. Must we have attendants?

You do not need attendants if you want to keep the ceremony small, but you will need someone to witness the marriage certificate if you are choosing to formally marry. If you elope, the justice of the peace will have someone in attendance who can act as witness.

Children Participating in the Ceremony

My fiancé and I want to do something a little unconventional. I would like to have my fiancé's 8-year-old daughter as my maid of honor, and he would like my 6-year-old son as his best man.

It's not that unconventional but does need some forethought if you are serious about asking. Asking your partner's children to be part of the ceremony is a great way to include them and promote family unity. However, if you are having an elaborate ceremony, this may not be the time to ask them to be your primary attendants. These two attendants have specific duties, and asking a young child to serve in that capacity may just double your workload. You will have to fill in when the little ones can't. You may then have to ask another attendant for help, and they may get a little miffed that they are asked but don't garnish the big title. Perhaps "Junior Maid of Honor" is a better title.

Also, it's rare that children, even teenagers, understand the compliment you are offering by asking them to be your maid of honor or best man. If it's a smaller, more intimate ceremony with no bridal showers or big get-aways prior to the ceremony, then including the children in this way is a lovely gesture.

My fiancé and I are about to marry after living together for a year. His children's mother passed on 3 years ago when his son was 2 and his daughter was 6. I get along great with his son but his daughter shies away from me. I do not have children yet. This is my family, and I would like both of the kids to be in our wedding. His daughter refuses.

The writer's bonus son was very young when his mother passed away. She is probably the only mother he remembers at this point. If she is good to him, as it sounds like she is, he is probably crazy about her and wants her to marry Daddy as soon as possible. Her bonus daughter, on the other hand, is another story.

She was 6 when her mother passed. She is now 9. She remembers her mother and probably misses her very much. And it would not be uncommon that the nicer the partner is to the child, the more the child resents her. She is secretly comparing Mom to Bonus Mom and is worried that she is betraying her mother by allowing her bonus mom in. That's why she keeps Bonus Mom at arm's length. The child must learn to trust this new person—and at this point, she may not allow herself to do that.

Years ago, I worked with a family who also faced this exact problem. We had many discussions about comparing and not making it an either/or choice between a deceased mother and a new mother figure. One night, after a very heated argument which culminated in the dreaded "You're not my mother!" the bonus mom decided a heart-to-heart with her bonus daughter was the best course of action. She could tell the child was hurting more than she was resentful and approached the disagreement using CARE.

First, she acknowledged that she understood that the child would always have a special place in her heart for her mother. She then asked if she thought her mother would want her to be lonely and not feel safe. Of course, the child replied no, her mother would never want her to feel that way. The bonus mom then asked the child if she could look at it as if she was helping her mother to take care of her. She presented herself as the child's deceased mother's partner in raising the child, working alongside her memory, never taking her mother's place, but being a parent figure who now cared for the child because her mother could no longer do it herself. That is when the child began to accept her bonus mom. When the child realized that she didn't have to choose between her mother and bonus mother, she let down her guard and began to trust.

Many forget that the child's allegiance to the deceased parent does not stop because the parent is deceased. Love remains in the child's heart, and it may feel as if accepting a new person betrays their biological parent. The bonus parent presenting the relationship as a partnership with the deceased parent, not as a replacement, makes it easier for the child to accept a new person into their life.

My fiancé has two children. I don't want kids at the wedding.

That's a red flag! The children should not only attend the wedding but should participate in the ceremony in some way. They should be included in the preparations and consulted as the ceremony comes together. The amount of involvement depends on their age, but even little ones can be flower girls and ring bearers.

Let's backtrack a little. Yes, this commitment you are making is between two people; however, the approach when a partner has children and shares custody is not the same as the approach to a first-time marriage. If you approach a marriage to someone with children as "This is *our* marriage and those are *their* children," you are starting your life together reinforcing that the children are an afterthought when, in fact, they are an integral part of your bonus family. And there is nothing that will undermine a marriage quicker than excluding your partner's children. When one or both partners has children, it is not only the couple making the commitment; it's the whole family. All must feel as if they are part of something. If those marrying cannot approach their union with this in mind, they should not marry. Their partner's children are a very real part of their family from this day forward. The more inclusive and accepting you can be, the more endearing you will become to your partner.

The Guest List
Inviting Your Co-Parent to Your Wedding

My co-parent takes a very active role in co-parenting our children and he and my fiancé have built quite a friendship. We are getting

married soon and we have both agreed to invite my children's dad.
Is this acceptable or are we being silly?

When couples stay in contact and work together in the name of their children after a breakup, it's not surprising when animosity is left behind and a true friendship emerges. I can tell you from personal experience that is exactly how my bonus children's mother and I forged a friendship, and she attends every milestone my family faces.

With that in mind, inviting your children's other parent, if your fiancé approves, is perfectly predictable. However, the basic criterion for making decision of this sort is, "How will this decision affect our children?" If their father's presence will embarrass or confuse the children in any way, it would be best to forgo the invitation and invite him to a private family get-together at some other time.

My second husband, Constantine, and I are divorced, and I am
getting married again. Although we never had kids together, he is
the only father figure my son from my first marriage has known, and
he is also good friends with my fiancé. My son and my fiancé would
both like Constantine to attend the wedding. I'm ok with it, but my
mother will never forgive that he cheated and she has threatened to
make a scene if he attends.

The bride dictates the final guest list. Although it seems unconventional to invite an ex, in this case, the bride's son and her fiancé want to invite this man who continues to act as a father figure to the child. That's quite a statement.

The bride's mother loves her daughter and saw the hurt as she navigated through the pain of divorce. Because she has not forgiven the pain Constantine caused her daughter, she is holding a grudge in her name.

That is a noble response, but that energy could be put to better use. Holding a grudge doesn't make us feel better, heal our hurt, or affect the other person at all. A grudge is a private anger only you feel. In fact, at the end of the day, all we end up with when we hold a grudge is the all-consuming negativity the grudge holds over us. We all know the negative impact stress can have on our body and mental state. A grudge is that stress pointed inward.

Some things both Mom and Grandma must consider before going forward:

First, Grandma must know that it could be to the child's detriment if she interferes in a well-established relationship between the bride's ex and her child. When a bonus parent and child become close and have learned to depend on each other, denying contact could impact the child's emotional and psychological adjustment. Unfortunately, the bride's mother may not take the relationship seriously and does not understand the importance of father figure and child remaining close. Just because this man is not the child's biological father, doesn't mean the child doesn't feel he is. The writer even acknowledged, "Constantine is the only father my son has ever known." If the bride's fiancé feels comfortable with Constantine attending, his presence will only add to the child's feelings of security at the wedding. He now has two male role models to look up to.

Finally, the bride must set her own boundaries, reminding her mother that what she really needs right now is her support, not a public reprimand of her ex. Her mother is stuck in the hurt, but the bride is not and has moved on. If the bride's mother really wants to be there for her daughter, she will enthusiastically embrace her effort to start a new life. The sweetest revenge is to successfully move on—and that is what the bride has done. With a hug, the bride can invite her to do the same.

Inviting Former Relatives

I was married for 10 years to a wonderful man. Sadly, he was killed in a plane crash 5 years ago, I am currently in a great relationship, and we plan to marry next year. I am still very close to his parents, my former in-laws, even closer to them than my own parents and I know they will share in my joy of finding someone with whom I want to share my future. Is it appropriate to add them to the guest list? I would love them to be there.

Normally, former in-laws are not invited for obvious reasons; however, in this case, it would be completely appropriate for them to attend the wedding, particularly if the former couple had children. This might be difficult for the new partner to understand until he considers the fact that these in-laws are his bonus kids' grandparents, and it is the bonus parent's responsibility to support existing relationships between bonus children and their extended family.

If the in-laws are not invited, it would be a kind gesture to call them personally, offer a gesture of continued affection, and explain the awkwardness of the situation. They will most likely understand and not be offended. Additionally, another kind gesture might be to suggest a private dinner after things have settled down, where you can all meet, comfortably talk, and relax.

THE CEREMONY

The ceremony, whether it is a wedding ceremony or a commitment ceremony, is the ultimate public expression of a couple's true desire to come together and create a family. This expression of unity can be especially meaningful if the parents of the couple making the commitment have previously broken up or if the couple has children, either together or from previous relationships.

The ceremony marking the coming together of two people whose parents are divorced or separated is handled just as any first wedding would be, with a few special considerations. Seating becomes a problem if relationships are strained. Things get even more convoluted when both sides' parents are divorced. Hopefully, those attending will follow the bonus couple's lead for love and acceptance and no one attending thinks a wedding is the place to air their private differences.

Seating

When the couple tying the knot is having a conventional wedding, the bride's relatives sit on the left as you face the wedding site. The groom's relatives sit on the right, unless it is an Orthodox Jewish wedding, in which case, the sides are reversed. The parents of the bride and groom sit in the first row on the corresponding side. As the guests enter, the ushers ask on whose side they would like to be seated. If ushers are not used, guests seat themselves. Easy, right? Then parents divorce, remarry, perhaps divorce again, or live with their soul mate, and seating arrangements can get really complicated.

Children of divorce can have lots of people on their guest list to consider. First, their parents and biological extended family. Then bonus parents and bonus extended family. Then there are a ton of kids, related biologically or bonus. Just remember to keep the first three or four rows clear for family and honored guests. Then you can get creative with the seating, hopefully not offending anyone who used to be with someone else.

Standard practice dictates that when parents have broken up, the mother of each of the participants making the commitment and her significant other sits in the front row on their side. The father sits in the second row unless the parents are cordial and have worked this all out before the ceremony.

The mother of the bride or groom always seems to be seated in the front row at the ceremony. My fiancé was raised by his father. Although his mother was in his life, his dad was the one who raised him. After all that, it doesn't seem right that his father and bonus mom should be relegated to the second or third row.

I included this question to reinforce that everyone's circumstances are different and because of this there are always exceptions to the rules. The bonus concept is based on the exception to the rules! It would be logical in this case that father sits in the front row with his partner and mother sits in the second row with her partner—unless they have worked it out and have decided together that they will approach this differently.

Over the years I have become quite close to my bonus grandparents who live nearby. They are so great to me and have always treated me like part of their family. I would like them to sit closer to the front during the ceremony because they don't hear well, but my grandparents have always been a little jealous of our relationship. How do I handle this tastefully?

It is not uncommon to have lots of honored guests when relatives break up and change partners. And the last thing the new couple wants to worry about as they prepare for their nuptials is if they are offending someone they love with their seating assignment.

I have found that a great way to solve the seating dilemma is to enlist the help of the ushers—or the people you have assigned to help seat elderly guests. This might be the father of the groom or even a bonus parent. (Bonus parents are always looking for something to do at their bonus child's wedding.) Bring pictures of the special guests of concern and explain to the ushers where you would like them to sit. This need not be discussed with the people being seated; the ushers can simply direct them to their chosen seat of importance.

If there are no ushers and seating is open, you may just have to reserve, possibly rope off, the first five rows for family and honored guests.

Who Walks the Bride Down the Aisle?

How many of us have seen the heartwarming video shorts of the dad and bonus dad sharing the honor of walking their daughter down the aisle? More and more dads are doing this, and from the child's point of view, it really takes the pressure off.

Traditionally, the walk down the aisle is reserved for the father of the bride, but breakups and new starts have changed tradition, and many adjust protocol to exactly what works for them. Same-sex couples also don't necessarily follow the traditional walk down the aisle, setting the stage for approaching the couple's entrance exactly how the couple envisions it. It's lovely when parents and bonus parents can put their issues aside to support the children they have raised together—especially at a huge milestone like their child's wedding. Bonus is truly a state of mind—and heart.

I have seen walking down the aisle handled a few different ways. First, the father and bonus father stand on either side of the bride. They walk together, guiding her down the aisle. If the bride would like to add an added gesture to her father, she takes his arm while her bonus dad walks beside her. Once they get to the front, the bonus dad sits next to the bride's mother and the father stands next to the bride.

Second, the bonus dad walks the bride down to the seat where the father sits, he stops, hands off the bride to her father, and her father walks her the rest of the way down the aisle. A reverse of this order is also possible.

A third possibility is the father walks the bride down the aisle, she stops at her bonus dad's seat and either offers him a hug or a flower from her bouquet and continues down the aisle to be presented by her father.

Fourth, both parents walk the bride down the aisle. This is a common tradition for Jewish families and may be a lovely approach for same-sex parents.

Fifth, when the bride was raised by a single mother, the mother walks the bride down the aisle and answers the officiant.

Finally, to avoid family drama, the bride walks alone, or the couple walks together without their parents. If they would like to acknowledge their parents or someone special, they stop at where that person is sitting and offer the gesture decided by the couple—a flower, a hug, a high five, a handshake . . .

Anything is acceptable if it is done with love and does not openly insult anyone.

Honoring a Bonus Parent During the Ceremony

> *I was raised by my dad and bonus mom. They were divorced last year, and he is now dating someone else, but my bonus mom remains my bonus mom and is certainly invited to my wedding. I would like to offer her some sort of special gesture at some point during the ceremony, but I'm not sure how or when. I'd like to do something that won't cause too much of a fuss or anger my dad, but by the same token, this woman raised me, and I love her.*

Some adult children hold a special place in their hearts for their bonus parents and wish to honor them at their wedding in some way. Truth is, biological parents usually take precedence at their child's wedding ceremonies, and bonus parents certainly appreciate acknowledgment.

Here's a lovely way to acknowledge a bonus parent. Hold a seat at the aisle open in the second or third row with their name prominently displayed so no one else will sit there. After the ceremony, and as you and your partner walk back up the aisle, stop at their seat, pull a flower from your bouquet, and hand it to them as you exit. A hug might also be a nice gesture. This says, "I love you," without too much fuss. This is also a lovely gesture to offer a bonus parent during the ceremony, as well.

Couples who wish to include their parents in their ceremony may also want to include bonus parents, particularly if there is no bad blood between the biological parent and bonus parent (counterpartner). Like a parent, a bonus parent may be asked to read a poem, light a candle, or possibly oversee the guest book. They may be mentioned in the invitation along with their partner and be escorted down the aisle if the couple sees fit. They may also be offered a bouquet or boutonniere. A bonus parent can help with anything assigned to them, but it must be remembered that a bonus parent is not the parent and should not step on toes. Stay graciously in the background unless the couple asks otherwise.

Demonstrating Bonus Family Unity

More than a ceremony in which two people unite, bonus family weddings and commitment ceremonies combine two families through the union of two parents. Some think that combining two families is a modern concept, but many ancient cultures understood the importance of family acceptance and integrated extended family into the ceremony.

There are pages and pages of examples of family unity rituals for weddings and commitment ceremonies on the internet. Get creative! Invent your own!

Some of my favorites are listed here.

Datar Ceremony

The *Datar*, or salt ritual, is a lovely tradition sometimes initially observed by Hindu couples immediately after they marry. Here, it has been adjusted with bonus family flare. In this example, the bride starts, but either member of a couple can start the ritual.

The bride picks up a handful of salt and places it in the hands of her partner. They pass it back and forth three times without spilling any salt. Then the bride passes the salt to a family member (possibly a child standing with the couple), who passes it to the next family member, and so on until it is returned to the bride.

This ceremony symbolizes that as salt enhances the flavors of food when it is added, the addition of family members enhances the strength of a bonus family and will allow each other to flourish both individually and altogether. In a bonus family, it is not only the couple who must adjust to living with one another. All family members must accept their new role as part of the bonus family, vow to contribute, accept one another, be kind to one another, and support each other. With a little adjustment, the salt ritual is a perfect way to symbolize bonus family unity.

The Unity Candle

A standard at weddings and commitment ceremonies, the unity candle is one of the most common ways used to symbolize the combining of two families in Western culture. The candle display is most often situated at the front of the wedding site, near where the officiant will stand to perform the ceremony. It consists of two taper candles on either side of a larger candle. After the processional for a first-time marriage, the mothers of the bride and groom both light a taper candle in honor of the children. They return to their seat and the taper remains lit for the remainder of the ceremony. After the vows and rings have been exchanged, the officiant explains the meaning of the unity candle. The officiant then asks the couple to take each taper candle and light the main candle together, symbolizing combining their lives together.

This tradition can easily be modified as a ritual for bonus families, adding additional taper candles for each child and asking the children to participate in the lighting.

Incorporating Children Into the Ceremony

There are many age-appropriate ways that kids can participate in the ceremony—and it is imperative that they do. Very young children can be flower girls or ring bearers. Older children can be junior ushers or junior bridesmaids. My own bonus son was 4 at the time of our marriage, and he was delighted to be invited to be best man—even though he had no idea what that meant. All he knew was he got to wear a tux. The smallest tux I had ever seen, but he was enthralled with the look. He matched his dad.

His sister and my daughter, his bonus sister, were my attendants. That was the wedding party. There was no procession, no one giving the bride away. It was both of our second weddings. We got married at our home with our parents and closest friends in attendance. The kids, my husband, and I all stood together while the officiant married our family. We all exchanged rings. There were toasts and proclamations of love and affection, and that was our wedding. It was on New Year's Eve, a symbol of our new beginning.

The Bonus Family Bouquet

Each family member taking part in the ceremony holds a flower (each a different color or different variety of flower to symbolize their individuality) and says something personal as they place a flower in a vase to create a family bouquet. The bouquet symbolizes family unity while celebrating each individual flower's (family member's) uniqueness.

Here are some other ways to incorporate your children into the proceedings:

- Have them sit in the front row and reference them by name during the ceremony.
- Allow older children to join the unity candle ceremonial lighting.
- Offer each child a flower from the bride's bouquet at some time during the ceremony.
- Allow them to read a favorite verse, say anything they like, or sing a song.

- You may also consider asking older children to oversee the guest book.

Incorporating Adult Children Into the Ceremony

Many parents of adult children assume that because their children no longer live at home, they can combine families with few problems. In reality, the opposite is often true. Adult children have had years to build an allegiance with their parents. When a parent dies or a there is a breakup later in life, some adult children have a very difficult time accepting their parent's choice of new partner. Therefore, asking an adult child to participate in your ceremony by being involved in one of the rituals described here is an excellent way to demonstrate your respect for them and your desire for bonus family unity. But you may have to do a little more homework than you do with younger children. Older children can be skeptical about a parent's re-coupling and look to acts and deeds more than lip service. If you act like you are devoted to their parent or attend *their* children's extracurricular activities, these are the things that signal you are invested—and that will pave the way for them to comfortably participate in a ceremony.

WHERE TO POSITION BONUS FAMILY MEMBERS FOR PICTURES AND VIDEOS

A few years ago, I was asked to attend a bonus family wedding. I had been working with the family prior to their moving in together and deciding to marry was a huge victory for everyone. The children ranged from 4 to 12 and all were very excited about the ceremony. After the event, I overheard a guest approach the family who were standing together at the front of the room. "OK, who belongs to who?" the guest asked, inquiring about the children's biological parentage. This was truly a bonus family with "yours, mine, and ours" kids. One child was even adopted from another country and their exact parentage could not be traced. That's when one of the children piped up, "We belong together." I can still hear the child's voice . . .

For those who already have children prior to the ceremony, place the bonus couple near the middle and their biological children on their side of the picture. If the couple has children together, as well, those children are placed in front or between the bonus couple.

The Reception
Bonus Family Toasts

I've asked my son to be my best man at my upcoming wedding, but he is only 14 and has no idea how to make a toast at a reception. Is there someone else who can start the toasts out right?

This is one of the negatives associated with asking a child to be the best man. Along with the best man distinction comes some important responsibilities, and if a child is too young to take on those responsibilities, then you will have to ask someone else to help.

If your son is too shy or he needs help, suggest that he lean on your father, your brother, brother-in-law, or best friend to guide him—any one of which would have probably been your alternative best man choice. Another option might be to ask his grandfather (your dad) to make the best man toast with your son standing next to him as they both lift their glasses.

The toast might be something like, "And along with Justin (grandson/son of the groom), Michael's son (Michael is the groom), I would like to congratulate . . . " Then allow Justin to finish the toast with, "So let us lift our glasses to my dad and my bonus mom, Michelle!"

First Dances
Dance Formalities
If it is a smaller more intimate ceremony and reception, the first dance is for the couple tying the knot, but a nice bonus family

touch is the children join their parents on the dance floor toward the end of the dance. Then as the bonus family dance continues, the couple can motion to extended family and friends to join them all on the dance floor. Of course, first dances with only the couple are perfectly acceptable; just remember that when someone marries for the second or subsequent time, there are usually children included, which means more than two people coming together—there are two families coming together. First dances at a bonus family wedding or commitment ceremony take on a special meaning. Right from the beginning, your dance card is full.

Father-Daughter Dance

Here's where past wedding and reception protocol shifts a little. The whole concept of "bonus" is to offer respect and acceptance to the family created after a breakup. So, rules from the past may no longer apply. This is *your* bonus family's day.

That said, many look forward to the father-daughter dance, although it originated long ago when most marriages were arranged rather than based on love. Then unions were centered on social standing, political affiliation, and monetary alliances. The father-daughter dance served as a sort of final statement by the bride's father before their husband became the most important man in their life. After this dance, the bride would be able to dance with their new spouse, whom she had likely just met prior to the ceremony.

In contemporary American culture the father-daughter dance no longer carries the same weight as days gone by, and it is seldom the first dance of the reception. Most often it comes after the first dance of the couple marrying, but even so, the order of all the dances is often changed to match the desires of the couple.

Add a little bonus family flare and old-school protocol goes right out the window.

My dad was in the service and gone most of my childhood. I believe this is what contributed to my parents' divorce. My mom married my bonus dad when I was 6. He was the one who raised me. I am not angry with my father, I respect his serving our country, but my bonus dad was the one I grew to depend on and that's the one with whom I would like to dance the father/daughter dance.

The question this bride is asking is how do I honor my bonus dad without insulting my father? And, using the father-daughter dance as the criterion for the conversation, there are a few ways to do it other than just having two dances, but first a little discussion.

It's not uncommon for various people to cut in while the new couple is dancing. This can be symbolic, and it reduces the time guests must wait as the families dance together. The father of the bride might cut in or even the grandfather of the bride might cut in as the bride and groom dance their first dance. It's a lovely gesture that signifies love, family, and support for the new union. However, if a bonus parent cuts in on a biological parent during a dance, which may be interpreted as stepping on the bioparent's toes—and since the bonus family concept is all about acceptance—if cutting in is done, the order in which it is done is important.

In the case above, the bride is looking for a way to honor both Dad and Bonus Dad without snubbing her biological father. Using a little planned choreography often lightens the mood, so consider something like a brief dance with the bride's father, another family member (brother, Grandpa, cousin) cuts in and continues the dance, then her bonus dad cuts in as the final partner to dance the rest of the dance with the bride. This example would be symbolic of how the bride's life progressed and would honor all the men in her life. I have also seen the groom approach his dance with family members in the same manner, and most recently, at a same sex marriage, both people marrying danced with all the people they honored in their lives, including the children, before they asked their guests to join them on the dance floor. Quite frankly, many of the bonus family weddings I have attended recently forgo the formal dancing and everyone just dances together—if there even is dancing at the reception.

I would like special dances with my dad, my bonus dad, and my new father-in-law, and my husband would like special dances with his mother, his bonus mom and my mom.

Although a beautiful sentiment, that's six special dances, and you have guests waiting. If you don't want family members to cut in while dancing, sprinkle these dances throughout the reception.

Holidays, Celebrations, and More Bonus Milestones

MOST HOLIDAYS SERVE AS A REASON TO COME TOGETHER, COUNT our blessings, and acknowledge family and friendship. But, if you have faced a breakup, holidays will feel different for a while. Then you meet someone new, and their family traditions impact your family traditions. As you re-examine your new bonus family identity, an important thing to remember is that as time moves forward and your family transitions into a more cohesive unit, adjustments can be made to better match your bonus family's needs. Nothing is written in stone. Flexibility takes on new meaning.

This chapter will look at how creating your own bonus family traditions at holiday times can create a more positive and loving experience for bonus family members and their extended families. The good news is you do not have to abandon beloved family traditions because there was a breakup—adjustments can be made to honor the past while celebrating the future.

HAVE REASONABLE EXPECTATIONS FOR HOLIDAY CELEBRATIONS

Let's be honest, very few of us look forward to our first big holiday after a breakup. The second or third is no walk in the park either. Although co-parents try to put on a smiling face when the kids are around, it's tough to muster up that *ho-ho-ho* spirit when one year the kids are with you and the next they are with your co-parent. Don't set yourself up for disappointment by expecting things to be perfect or even the way they used to be—that only leads to frustration and disappointment. Look for ways to make it new by integrating cherished family memories with new bonus family traditions.

HOLIDAY TRADITIONS AND RITUALS

Decorating the tree was a big deal at our home before the divorce. Everyone had a specific duty assigned to them. My husband and the kids chopped down the tree while I sorted the lights and ornaments. Each of the kids had their favorite snacks and they were ready for them to eat as they decorated the tree. We even had colored ornaments assigned to each child. Graham decorated with red ones, Marcus decorated with gold ones, and Lucy had green. My husband always hung the tree topper because he was the tallest and didn't need a chair to stand on. Now that we have moved in with Samuel and his daughter, Quinn, things are so different. This is our first Christmas together. The kids always looked so forward to this and I'm afraid of disaster.

– MICHELLE, MOTHER AND BONUS MOM

Adjusting Family Traditions

Family traditions and rituals evolve over generations. That's why after a divorce or separation, conflict arises when traditions from the past interfere with celebrating in the present. You get used to doing something one way, there's a breakup, and everything changes. The key is to adjust family traditions, not abandon them. Tradition is what makes holiday celebrations special.

What is the difference between family tradition and family ritual?

Tradition is what families do—for example, decorate the Christmas tree. Ritual is how they do it; for example, one parent strings the lights while the other arranges the ornaments. The lighting of the menorah during the 8 days of Chanukah is a family tradition in Jewish households. If the family does it in a special manner—say a parent lights a Hanukkah candle, then passes it to a different child each night to light the menorah—that's the family ritual.

Part of what is special about family rituals is who participates in the ritual ceremony. If the players change—say, the parents break up—and one is no longer there to participate, the tradition feels broken. That's when you may hear the words "It just feels like something is missing." And those who once looked forward to a particular time of year stop wanting to celebrate.

The truth is something *is* missing, and denying it can be counterproductive—breakups change everything, and acknowledging that there is a change is the beginning of healing. That's why bonus family members must try as best they can to maintain past family rituals around the holidays. But if that becomes too painful for the children or the parents and prevents the parents from setting a positive example, the family should not be afraid to adjust or modify the tradition or ritual.

Look for ways to integrate the preferences of all bonus family members without completely abandoning past traditions. A well-adjusted bonus family respects all traditions brought to the table. They cherish the similarities and respect the differences in each family member's holiday experience. And, if need be, they start from scratch and establish new traditions of their own.

Spending the Holidays With Your Co-Parent

The kids are scheduled to be with me. I don't want to spend the holiday with my co-parent.

Ask children about the holidays after a breakup and many will tell you they do not have happy memories. Holidays, from birthdays to Christmas, are often vivid reminders that their dad and mom stopped living together. And if the parents add to that stress by squabbling over whose time it is with the kids, why so-and-so was late, why he/she brought *him/her* to the celebration, etc., it just puts more pressure on the kids. If parents can change *that* trend for their kids' sakes, they might consider celebrating together. However, parents should NEVER attempt to spend time together before they are ready—and they may never be. It must be a natural progression after successfully working together in the name of their children.

Helping Your Child Transition from House to House During the Holidays

There are some changes co-parents can easily make that will help ease their children's transition from house to house during the holidays. Notice I didn't say "suggestions for parents to cope with the holidays." Ultimately, your goal is to create an environment where your children can thrive; therefore, *parents make the changes.* Your family's ability to cope is a result of the positive changes *you* make.

Begin by making the transition from house to house as stress-free as you can by coordinating efforts with your co-parent well in advance. Knowing exactly what time your child will leave (or when you will pick them up) and planning for it—bags packed at the door rather than scrambling around at the last minute—will help. Avoid saying things like "This holiday just won't be the same without you here" or "I'm going to miss you so much" as the children prepare to leave. Even if you do feel that, saying so just makes the transition more difficult for the child. They may worry they are leaving you alone and feel guilty for leaving. Give them a hug and tell them you love them, and then send them on their way.

Agree on a time you will check in and stick to it. Do not call the child every 5 minutes to check up or to remind them that they are the most important thing in your life. This is quite disruptive for the other home and causes the child more anxiety than comfort. If your child is truly the most important thing in your life, allow them to settle in at their other parent's home so that they can enjoy their time together. A constant reminder that you miss them is not putting your child first—it's putting your child in the middle. Both parents should agree that they will be supportive of contact with the other parent when the child initiates it. "May I call Daddy and wish him a Merry Christmas?" should always be met with, "Sure!" If you are out and about, it may be helpful to give the child a time limit, "We will be home in an hour and we will call him then."

Gift Giving
Presents for the Kids

> *I should have gotten Jacob the bike. Why did I consent to letting his father get it for him? I know he will like it better than clothes and it was my idea.*

This was a quote from a co-parent with whom I was working during the holidays last season. She and the child's father were in a constant battle to gain the child's attention in the hopes the child would want to live with one of them and not the other. When I asked them *why* in a session, neither could give me an answer. They were both so embroiled in their battle for the child's attention that they couldn't tell me why they had forgotten the other's importance in their child's life.

Always look at your motivation when having negative based emotions like envy, jealousy, anger, or a desire to one up your co-parent. Do your best to coordinate efforts. If the presents are too expensive for one parent to afford, consider splitting the cost. Always look for the compromise. Then let everything go. Don't stew over the agreement you just made in the best interest of the children you both love.

I am very close to my 12-year-old daughter, but the truth is, she has a more conventional home with her mother and stepfather, or as you say, her bonus dad, and when he was transferred for business 6 months ago, I decided not to protest thinking it was really best for her not to be in the middle of a custody battle. Thing is, now that she lives 5 hours away, I rarely see her. Nothing like the two or three times a week and every other weekend that we used to share. Now the holidays are coming around and I feel like I just don't know her anymore. I miss her terribly and I have no idea what to get her for Christmas—or any time, for that matter. What do I do?

– Terry, father to Julianna, age 12

Knowing that parents want to surprise their child when offering a present eliminates the most obvious approach—simply asking the child what they would like. The second possible approach also seems obvious but is often the last thing co-parents think of, particularly if they are estranged—coordinating efforts with your co-parent.

When children live a distance away from one of their parents, it's especially important that parents cultivate a working relationship. If one parent spends more time with the child because of extenuating circumstances, long distance as in this case, that parent probably has insight into what the child is currently into. Ask for ideas—and remember to thank them for their suggestions.

There are quite a few presents parents can give their kids that will help promote better communication. The clearest choice—a cell phone. Although I occasionally run into parents who believe adolescents shouldn't carry cell phones, as a child gets older a cell phone can be a useful tool to stay in touch.

Phones also offer a video conferencing component that allows for real-time, face-to-face interaction between long-distance parent and child. Now they no longer have to boot up a computer to video chat because everything is at their fingertips.

This becomes a problem when co-parents are not on the same page for their children's phone use. Some feel that FaceTime or

Zoom calls are an invasion of privacy. "You can see my house and I don't want you near me!" is something I have heard on more than one occasion. If parents are so estranged that they do not feel comfortable with Zoom or FaceTime calls between their child and their co-parent, it's time to examine what BOTH co-parents are doing to perpetuate such an attitude.

Of all parenting plans, long-distance parenting requires the most cooperation between parents. Since it is well recognized that children need both parents in their lives, it's a co-parent's job to help facilitate a positive relationship between their child and their other parent—not interfere with it. If a court must eventually decide on primary placement of a child, the criteria on which that decision is based is "the parent who is most likely to facilitate a relationship between the child and the child's other parent."

Presents for Co-Parents and Counterpartners

Should we buy a present for my partner's co-parent?

When people break up and meet someone new, gift giving at holidays gets really complex. You may now find yourself buying presents for people you never would have dreamed you'd be buying them for.

> *"If someone had told me I would someday be buying a present for my ex-wife's husband," one divorced father confided, "I would have laughed in their face. But there I was last year buying him a box of golf balls for Hannukah."*
> — Paul, father to Caleb, 9 and Luke, age 15

Interacting with an ex's new partner in such a casual manner would have been unthinkable in the past, but today, because the children go back and forth between homes, co-parents and their new partners often become friendly over the years, and exchanging gifts under those circumstances is not surprising. Gifts can also be symbolic in nature. A gift given to or from a co-parent can serve as a peace offering, a gesture of goodwill, or even as an example for the children. Take special care when choosing a gift for a co-parent or counterpartner, however. Never choose a gift that may be misconstrued as a show of criticism or disapproval or a reminder of a painful or past relationship. It would be inappropriate, for example, to give your co-parent a gift certificate to the restaurant you both used to love on Saturday nights or a CD that included "your song" just as a reminder. Presents that are generic in nature are best for this occasion. Flowers, a fruit basket, candy, or candles are all good choices. They provide the gesture without any possibility of offense.

Presents From the Kids

> *Today my husband called from work and asked me to buy a present for his ex from the kids. Is that my responsibility?*

Supporting the relationship between your bonus children and their parent (your counterpartner) will strengthen your relationship with everyone concerned. It promotes trust, which is the basis of any good relationship, and proves to your bonus children that they can depend on you.

I remember the first time I took the kids out to buy a Christmas present for their mother. Their dad had left it to the last minute. I thought he was crazy to ask me to do it and told him so. He didn't care, he just needed my help; so reluctantly, I loaded the kids in the car, and we headed for the mall.

When you buy a present for someone, you must consider what they like. I didn't know their mom's favorite color or that she was allergic to wool at the time, so I had to consult the kids. I watched as they lit up talking about their mom—and that was my "Ah ha moment." It wasn't me against her—it was all of us for the kids we all loved. We had just wasted a lot of time acting foolish.

As the kids and I considered this or that for their mother's present, my then 9-year-old bonus daughter squealed "This is so fun!" I can still hear her voice—and there was the shift. Rather than feel jealousy or anger, the act that I had been dreading instantly became a privilege. Buying a present for her mother made a child I loved happy. From then on, I took the kids out every year to buy a present for their mother. Sometimes their dad went, sometimes he didn't, but the act of openly considering what their mother might like brought us closer. Although we never discussed it, it brought their mom and me closer, too. She knew who was buying the presents and it changed her attitude toward me, as well.

You know the saying, "Out of the mouths of babes"? My kids taught me the meaning behind any holiday, no matter your faith, is love. We were their role models, and if we loved them, we had to set the example.

Keeping Everything Fair

Something bonus family parents rarely address around the holidays is that a child they have created together may not understand why kids who they have been told are their siblings get extra presents from other parents.

To confront the extra-presents dilemma, have a conversation with the other children's parent to make sure the presents they gave their child really must go back to your house. It's understandable if a child wants to take them back and forth; however, if there are other children in the home, bonus or half-siblings, it may cause problems.

Once a divorced parent gets involved with someone with children, *all* the children's best interests must be at the forefront.

When I explained this to a divorced parent who shared custody of his children with a co-parent, their comment was, "I understand the need to cooperate, but I'm certainly not going to take her children with her new husband into consideration when I make decisions for my own children." This attitude is understandable, but there will be times that your decisions for your children will affect your co-parent's children with a new partner—and vice versa. The bonus family primary directive, "Put the children first," does not include a reference as to whose children they are. That's because it really doesn't matter.

In my family's case, working out of my home office allowed me to spend lots of time with my bonus kids while their mother juggled work to find extra moments with them. Sometimes all she could do was run to the mall for pizza with her kids and then rush them back to our home for the evening. Meanwhile my youngest daughter (the "ours" child) would sit patiently waiting for her siblings to return. In they would walk with a special lollipop or a little stuffed animal, and my daughter would begin to cry. She was being raised understanding that these kids were her siblings. If that was so, why did her siblings get a present when she didn't?

My bonus kids' mom had no idea that buying her children a little gift would prompt such sadness in another child. This went on for a month, and it did give us the opportunity to discuss "bragging" and "flaunting" with the children, but those conversations did little to appease my 4-year-old.

Although I dreaded the conversation, I called the kids' mom and explained the situation. I asked her to please consider whether the presents had to return to our house after her visit with the children. If they did, then of course I understood, but if they didn't, keeping the presents at her house would give the children something special when they were there and eliminate hurt feelings at my house. In true bonus family spirit, the next time the children returned to our house with a special lollipop, they also had one for my daughter. I was not expecting that approach, but that was the kind of person my bonus kid's mom is. No matter what the situation, she really tried to put the kids first—*all* the kids—and that was proof.

Gift Giving and Extended Family

Some grandparents or other extended family balk at the idea of giving presents to children to whom they are not biologically related. Even my own mother, in the midst of all my bonus talk, used to sneak my daughter, her oldest biological grandchild, an extra $50 when no one was looking. Being a kid, of course my daughter let everyone know. Although I intellectually understood my mother's blood-relation preference and attributed it to her subscribing to an old-school attitude about breakups and step-children, I did not approve of her actions. Young children wonder what they did to make Grandma not like them. Older children may understand better but still feel rejected when an adult obviously prefers another member of their family.

If becoming a bonus family makes your family huge and gift-giving grows troublesome, try picking numbers or names of family members, buying presents for only the kids, or agreeing on a price ceiling for each present. White elephant parties are fun, too. The goal is for everyone to feel included. Even though some extended family members may at first be unwilling to participate as part of a bonus family, over time they will observe the example of kindness and acceptance and hopefully begin to understand and accept their responsibility to help all the children cope.

I am very close to my former in-laws, and each Christmas prior to the breakup we exchanged presents while I was married to their daughter. Do I continue to offer presents now that we are divorced?

Family ties are not easily severed, and that is the reason why these sorts of questions are asked. Many former in-laws have told me, "We didn't divorce her (or him), our child did." Therefore, much to the dismay of their child, they choose to continue to have a relationship with their child's former spouse even after the breakup. Their child may be disappointed by their decision, expecting allegiance. Here lies the problem—their child's ex is the mother or father of their grandchild. So, requesting allegiance puts the grandchild right in the middle of the most important people in their life—Mom, Dad, Grandma, and Grandpa, not to mention aunts, uncles, and cousins.

The answer here really depends on the kind of relationship you wish to perpetuate after the breakup. If all wish to interact and no one sees ongoing contact as betrayal, then the answer is simple, you continue to spend the holidays together (if all are comfortable) and offering presents would be the natural order of things.

What if parents opt to spend the holidays separately? Let's say they aren't necessarily at odds, just don't agree on spending holidays together. Should former in-laws continue to exchange presents?

A good alternative is for whatever presents are offered are exchanged "from the children" or "for the children." This way allegiance is not questioned, and important familiar relationships are honored.

HALLOWEEN

We left Halloween off the parenting plan, so how do we decide from which home the kids trick-or-treat?

The premise for making the right decision is always "in the best interest of the children." Therefore, both put your self-interests aside, and you know the answer. Where will the kids have the most fun?

Halloween is a night your children trick-or-treat with friends—and their parents, of course—but the real fun is hanging with friends late into the evening on a school night and eating way too much sugar. So, if most of their friends live near your co-parent, making them trick-or-treat in another neighborhood they aren't used to just because it's your designated holiday seems selfish to say the least. If you all can't go together, pick the neighborhood you know the children would prefer and let them have their Halloween with the parent who lives in that neighborhood overseeing the festivities. Since you are not ready to trick-or-treat together, that means one parent might have a little more time with the child this week. This could be an incentive to look at the effectiveness of your co-parenting and adjust the parenting plan to reflect how you know the children would prefer to celebrate.

Halloween is coming up and the person I am seeing has three children about the same age as mine. I was thinking all of us going trick or treating together might be a good first date for the kids to meet.

It's best to stay away from holidays for first introductions. Most families have family rituals they like to stick to around a holiday, and introducing new potential family members puts those family rituals in competition with each other.

"We bob for apples on Halloween, and we give my dad all the Sweet Tarts after trick or treating!"

"I don't want to give your dad my Sweet Tarts!"

Can you see where this is going? Pressure to give up Sweet Tarts can complicate a first meeting and impact how quickly these children bond with the bonus parent and with each other. Don't use holidays infused with family rituals for first introductions just because you think the kids are all the same age. They are not in the same place on the acceptance timeline and each child's individuality must be respected if you want an easy transition into bonus family life.

THANKSGIVING

My parents have been divorced for 10 years. They get along but live in different states. I thought when I got older, I wouldn't have to

*deal with where I would spend Thanksgiving, but I do. My mom
takes it very personally if I am not there and although he doesn't say
anything, I know my dad feels bad when I am not with him, as well.
Now, I'm getting married, and not only do I have my two parents'
homes to cope with, I have my fiancé's custody arrangement where
he celebrates with his kids and their mother. Plus, I have married
siblings who want me to visit them. It's overwhelming. No one is
happy, especially me.*

Truth be told, divorce and breakups affect us all at some point.
If it's not our parents' divorce, it's our sister's or brother's, grandparents', child's, best friend's, even our own partner's breakup.
Breakups seem to set the stage—how you handle them is key to
ensuring bonus family get-togethers run smoothly.

That's why I try to remind everyone that "the holidays" are
not necessarily just one day but *an entire holiday season.* Between
mid-November and January 1, there are quite a few days to celebrate with loved ones. It doesn't necessarily have to be on THE
designated day. You're looking for the family feeling of celebrating
together. Who said that the only day everyone can create that
feeling is on the fourth Thursday in November?

The key to having successful holiday get-togethers after a
breakup is to be flexible. Modifying, rather than abandoning,
old traditions will certainly help. In my case, our Thanksgiving
tradition has evolved over the years. For years we all celebrated
together potluck style at my bonus kids' mom's home, but as the
kids got older and had kids of their own, the oldest child (my
bonus daughter) began to host Thanksgiving. That got to be too
much, as well. Everyone had too many places to be on Thanksgiving Day. We took a poll and decided that the week between
Christmas and New Year's is a "down week" and that is now our
time to celebrate. Kids are out of school and work schedules are
usually not as strict, and since we now approach the holidays as
a season and not specific days, that's when we have our bonus
family holiday—and I usually fly to visit them. On Thanksgiving

everyone goes where they need to go, but we still have a day set aside where we are all together. Communicating how much you care for each other is what is important. To alleviate some of the guilt of not being together on a specific day, try a Bonus Family Holiday Zoom Call. Send the link to everyone with an assigned time, and thanks to the wonders of technology, you're together!

HANNUKAH

Hannukah is the celebration of the triumph of the Maccabees (Jews) over Greek persecution in 165 BC. Once victorious, the Jewish army rededicated the temple (the word "Hannukah" means "dedication"), but they were unable to find enough oil to light the menorah, or candle holder, to be used in the service. The Maccabees found only one bottle of oil, enough for one night, but miraculously the oil lasted for 8 days. That is why the holiday is celebrated over an 8-day period. Each night a candle is lit, and prayers are said to commemorate the miracle. Small gifts may be offered to family and friends.

Because the holiday spans 8 days, divorced or separated Jewish parents often split the days equally, dividing the children's time between Mom and Dad. Or like any other holiday, the parents may opt to alternate days, or even the entire block of time.

What is important is that all parents look for the compromise that will create the most loving holiday memories possible. How that is done will be different for each family, depending on where they are in the bonus family timeline. Remember, do not abandon family traditions when there is a breakup, adjust them to your current circumstances.

CHRISTMAS

We've been engaged for 6 months and have dated for over a year. We are having Christmas at our house this year. My daughters are in college and his daughter is 8. We have his daughter every weekend and we have a really good bond with her. Last night, my fiancé got a call from his daughter's mother saying that she didn't think their daughter wants to be at our house for Christmas. We were under the assumption she did. She's been talking about it since Halloween.

Whenever I hear one parent tell me that a child has told them something completely different than they have told the other parent, that is a big red flag that the parents do not talk to each other. The child is either using the fact that their parents don't talk to manipulate the situation or they are running defense for their parents.

Here's a common scenario: When a parent is going to be alone this Christmas, they could have said something like, "Oh honey, this year you are going to be spending Christmas with your mom/dad. It just won't be the same." The response from the child might be, "Will you be lonely?" And the parent's response could easily be something like, "I'm always lonely when you aren't around, sweetie." And now you have an 8-year-old feeling bad that she's leaving a parent alone not only on Christmas but always. Did the parent mean to put all this on their child? Probably not. The response given was most likely offered to reinforce the parent's love for the child, but you can see how this kind of response can unintentionally put the child right in the middle. Eight-year-olds don't have the emotional makeup to rationalize that the agreed-upon parenting plan splits the holidays equally and next year, she will be spending Christmas with the other parent. All she knows is this year my mommy or daddy will be lonely without me.

At some point most children say they don't want to go to the other parent's home for their scheduled time. I see two responses used quite a bit—either the parent tells the child, "Tell your mom/dad you don't want to go," or they tell the parent that the child has told them they do not want to go, and the other parent doesn't believe them. Neither approach will produce the desired results.

So, what's a better response? Not, "I know you don't want to go, but you'll be home soon." That implies the other home and child/parent relationship is not as valid and is less important. To the first example where the parent asked the child to directly communicate how they felt—that puts the child right in the middle of their parents. Try saying something like, "It's your time with your dad (or mom) and he (she) really looks forward to spending time with you," plus adding some calming language making sure the child understands that you will be fine.

Addressing the next scenario where the parent has told their co-parent that the child does not want to go—there are all sorts of reasons why a child might balk about visiting the other parent, from not wanting to witness parental arguments at an exchange to simply being more comfortable in their bed at that residence. Some sort of abuse is also a possibility. If you hear this from a child, particularly around a holiday, that should prompt some investigation. However, the most successful approach is to let the child know that you will discuss whatever the concern is with their other parent, and once you come to an agreement, then explain, "Your mother/father and I have discussed this, and we have decided that . . . " Now the child knows that you and their other parent speak and are on the same page with their best interest in mind.

A Different Kind of "Secret Santa"

My fiancé and I moved in together about 9 months ago and this is our first Christmas together. Together we have four kids, ages 14, 13, 6, and 4. Mine are the younger ones who can't wait for Santa to visit on Christmas morning. I'm so afraid that the older ones will say something, and I don't know how to handle it.

    – RACHAEL, MOTHER AND BONUS MOM TO FOUR CHILDREN

It all depends on the vibe at your house. If it's a yours-against-mine sort of feel in the household, the older ones may do exactly what you fear. But if that's what you're facing, working on acceptance and integrating family members are things that bonus families should work on all year round so that everyone feels included well in advance of the season.

Rather than just coming right out and telling middle schoolers not to tell—because that can be a cue for them to spill everything, ask them for their help in keeping Christmas magical for the little ones. That will make them feel valuable and an integral part of the bonus family tradition. You may also want to brainstorm with them for creative ways to surprise the little ones. This will keep the Santa tradition going and include them in helping to perpetuate a holiday ritual.

EID

There are two Eid festivals observed by the Muslim faith: Eid al-Fitr and Eid al-Adha. The Islamic calendar follows the 12-month lunar calendar, which means the dates of both Eids change each year, but Eid al-Adha is always a little over 2 months after Eid al-Fitr.

Eid al-Fitr marks the end of the holy month of Ramadan. This is when Muslims from all around the world are getting ready to finish their month of fasting and religious observance. It is common for Muslims to take a day off from school, work, and their day-to-day activities. It is a day full of family affairs for those who observe, and it is understandable if each parent wants the children with them. Like any other holiday, separated Muslim parents are faced with deciding which parent will have the children with them on that special day.

Muslim clients often ask Eid to be included in their children's parenting plan. Most common is to alternate the festival holidays, unless one parent is more observant than the other and then a special arrangement is made between the parents.

HOLIDAY REMINISCING

I just saw a perfect Valentine's Day card for my co-parent, but he has a new girlfriend and I'm wondering if I should even bother.

When co-parents are friendly, boundaries may become blurry, and that's when reminiscing and "remember whens" pop up unexpectedly. Most will say it's all innocent, but every year around Valentine's Day, I get, "Should I send a Valentine to my ex?" questions. The reasons given are always the same.

"It's just for old times' sake" or "maybe we . . ." or "it's really not from me, it's from the kids."

The truth is, a Valentine is your proclamation of love. So, think twice before you send one to your co-parent. Ask yourself, "What am I really saying when I send this card? 'I still love you'? 'I want you back'?" You can say that on 364 other days. "Boy, did we have some good times?" Again, say that on another day, and your co-parent won't be scratching their head wondering what's behind the card. "It's really from the kids"? In that case, make sure it looks like a Valentine from the kids—enlist their help to make the card so it can't be misconstrued as a way to keep those ex-embers burning—especially if your co-parent has a new partner or is now married. If they have made a serious commitment to someone else, it's really in poor taste to go after them—especially if they have kids with their new partner.

We all understand bittersweet memories of a time together, but that doesn't give someone the right to disrespect their co-parent's relationship with another person. A good way to figure out if you have ulterior motives is to consider if you would feel comfortable giving the card to your co-parent in front of their new partner. If it's one of those little secret things you might do with a wink when the new partner is not around, then you're lying to yourself if you think "it's from the kids." Now that you are divorced, your responsibility to each other is as parents—not former lovers.

By the same token, if you both find yourselves single around Valentine's Day and you would like to offer a card or present, that's fine, but be prepared for the consequences—not just between the two of you, but if you have children together. Let that Valentine be seen by kids old enough to understand what it means, and it could open a whole can of worms. Don't play fast and loose with your children's emotions. Unless you are both openly trying to reconcile, don't display the Valentine from Mommy or Daddy on the refrigerator—until you are ready to buy groceries together again. If that's not in the cards, don't send one.

Mother's Day and Father's Day

Mother's Day or Father's Day may be the most emotional days on the calendar for divorced parents. Ironically, Mother's Day, the first of the two holidays to come into being, began as a day of peace. In 1872, overcome by the suffering of war, Julia Ward Howe wrote a proclamation—later known as "Mother's Day Proclamation"—suggesting that mothers come together to stop the bloodshed. This eventually turned into what we now know as Mother's Day. Father's Day soon followed.

When Mrs. Howe wrote her original proclamation, she had no idea her proposed day of peace would someday actually initiate conflict. But parents who are already at odds with their child's bonus parent know that on this special day that conflict can become even more obvious. Many parents are as possessive of the day as they are of their children, and each time Mother's Day or Father's Day rolls around it opens a wound. These parents fear that their children will prefer another and resent having to share their children's affections. Sharing the day does not come naturally.

Sometimes anger and jealousy cloud our reason, and our kids have to watch our struggle to rise above. That's not necessarily bad if you use your struggle as a teachable moment. If you realize it's time to change your behavior, what better lesson than to change it right in front of your kids?

Logic tells us that kids should be with their mother on Mother's Day and their father on Father's Day. Efforts should be coordinated among adults so that the child can spend that day with the appropriate parent. Of course, if the parent does not wish to spend the day with the child, no issue should be made. I mention this rule specifically for parents who demand that visitation schedules are adhered to strictly, without weighing the true impact of their decision. An example would be when the parenting plan states that a parent should spend every other weekend with a child without considering that the designated weekend may be Mother's Day or Father's Day and the child is scheduled to be with the other parent. Most court-ordered parenting plans take this into consideration, but there are times I have seen that parents simply forget to designate the day to one parent or the other. This also becomes a problem in the LGBTQIA+ community when there may be same-sex parents who both want to spend time with their children on that day. In these cases, just like any holiday, the day can be shared or alternated, whatever works for your family. All parents must consider leaving their own personal considerations behind and make the appropriate changes in the best interests of the children in their care—and as a courtesy to the other parent.

RELIGIOUS TRAINING, EDUCATION, AND FAMILY MILESTONES

I am Jewish by heritage, but not particularly religious. My co-parent isn't religious, either, but if you have to pick a religious orientation, I'd say she is Christian. The subject never really came up when we were together. We broke up when our son was 3. As time went on I felt it was important to offer some sort of religious training to our child, so I began to attend temple and took him to Sunday school. My co-parent was very upset with my decision and does not want our son to attend Sunday school with me.

When couples have children and do not practice the same religion, they often agree on how their children will be raised before the child is born. If this agreement is sincere, a breakup should not change the decision.

Regrettably, this isn't always the case. As in this example, there was no discussion while the parents were together, so after the breakup the parent felt he was deciding in the child's best interest. However, there was still no discussion with the child's other parent before a decision was made—and that is an important oversight. It is both parents' right to weigh in and both should be consulted.

If one of the parents re-couples with someone from another faith, whether the parent converts to the new faith or not, it is still that parent's responsibility to uphold the original agreement.

What if you disagree? How do you decide what religion your child should practice?

Unfortunately, there is no right or wrong answer. But the proper response lies in having respect for your co-parent and their personal beliefs. The United States of America is based on the freedom to worship any way you like—and this includes within families. It has been my experience that if this subject is brought to court, the court will not formally pick one parent's religion over another but will allow the child to accompany each parent to their choice of worship.

The challenge then becomes how to speak to your child about a religion that you may not believe in but is followed by their other parent. Respectfully, this is a very difficult task since how one believes in God goes to the very essence of that person. Do your best to respect your co-parent's choices and never put down the other parent's religious beliefs in front of the children. Answer all questions honestly about your faith and suggest the child discuss your co-parent's faith directly with them. It may come down to, "Daddy and Mommy believe differently," and do your best not to present one religion as right and one as wrong. It puts too much pressure on children to choose. You will see, it won't end up being about religion but a choice between Mom or Dad.

COMING-OF-AGE CELEBRATIONS

Depending on the culture or religion, coming-of-age ceremonies note some sort of achievement or milestone for a child. Coming-of-age ceremonies are occasions where families meet and celebrate together, and if the parents or other extended family are divorced or estranged, it can be a very uncomfortable time—especially for the child. In some cultures, the planning of coming-of-age ceremonies is as elaborate as wedding preparations and can be quite expensive. Take the emotional toll of a breakup and add the financial burden associated with the ceremony and you have what is known as a perfect storm—an extremely bad situation where lots of bad things happen all at the same time.

To unravel this perfect storm, parents must remember to use their children's welfare as the criteria for their decisions, and then, rather than facing yet another conflict, decisions easily fall into place. Nothing that has ever happened is important enough to take precedence over your child's ability to comfortably celebrate an important achievement or milestone. This is the time to put aside vendettas and celebrate your child.

CHRISTENINGS AND BAPTISMS

My husband had two children when I married him. We have worked hard to include the mother of his children in all decisions, and we really do have quite a cordial relationship. However, I am expecting our first child very soon, and his children's mother expects to attend the christening! As much as I want to keep the relationship comfortable, I don't want to invite my husband's co-parent to my baby's christening.

We walk a fine line when we become friendly with our partner's co-parent. Parents must set boundaries from the beginning or else they will find themselves constantly juggling what's appropriate and what's not.

When co-parents and their partners become friendly, they may come to think of each other as extended family—but this connection can be very tricky. Their relationship has become intertwined because of the shared children in their care, but there is more here to consider. Once a person re-couples after a breakup, they become the primary relationship or bonus couple in their family. They are the center decision-makers, and the family branches out from there. The bonus concept teaches us to integrate past with present, but present must also be allowed to exist on its own. Baptisms and christenings are exclusive to the new family; they are not focused on the shared children. Therefore, the befriended ex becomes a potential invited guest—just like everyone else.

For most people, it would be inappropriate if the co-parent of one of the parents attended a new child's christening, and it would certainly be understandable if the new spouse did not want them in attendance. However, I have run into counterpartners who have so overcome their animosity for each other that they have asked their spouse's co-parent to be the godparent to their newborn. Based on that, I certainly do not want to discourage positive relationships between counterpartners, but I must reiterate the appropriateness of waiting for an invitation before discussing attendance at such an event.

First Communion and Confirmation
Many Catholics are baptized as infants, receive first Communion as children, and receive Confirmation as adolescents. Confirmation is the final step to becoming a full member of the Catholic Church. It is marked by a special church service in which the person confirms the promises that were made when they were baptized. If they were baptized at a christening when they were a

child, their parents and godparents made these promises on their behalf.

Godparents are usually chosen from very good friends or relatives of one or both parents. If there has been a breakup and parents go their separate ways, good friends or relatives often take sides. This is just one more reason why the choice of godparents is very important. It is a godparent's responsibility to serve as a mentor to the child and guide the child emotionally and spiritually. Hopefully, the godparent can put their parental allegiances aside and remain dedicated to the child amidst parental drama.

Prior to Confirmation, a child must take Catechism classes in preparation. These classes take years and are taught on a regular basis. That means both parents must be invested in supporting their child's religious training for them to successfully reach Confirmation.

Parenting plans rarely take Catechism classes into consideration, and this is where I have seen a parental breakup affect a child's religious training. If both parents are not supportive of the classes, the child does not advance toward Confirmation as predicted, and this puts unwarranted pressure on the child, causing added conflict between co-parents. If the agreement is the child starts Catechism, it is the responsibility of both parents to make the child available for their Catechism classes when the child is scheduled to be with them.

My twin daughters will receive their first Communion in a couple of weeks. My co-parent recently presented me with a schedule for the ceremony that includes us walking up the aisle of the church together and then sitting next to one another in the front row. My new partner is uncomfortable with this display, noting that we are no longer married and that she should be sitting next to me. I feel like I am walking a tightrope between my co-parent and my partner—with my twin daughters right in the middle. How do I stay involved without angering everyone? Should I ask my partner not to attend? If she does attend, should she sit with me? I can't seem to produce a strategy that will make everyone, especially my daughters, comfortable.

The Catholic Church does not recognize divorce, so there is no formal precedent for the scenario described here. But, if you think about it, there's not much difference in this scenario than any other situation where there has been a breakup, and a parent has a new partner. The new partner feels they are the partner now and that statement should be made publicly by the seating arrangement. The mother of the child is following the precedent set by the Church since divorce is technically not recognized.

Since the first Communion is a ceremony performed in church, civil interaction is expected between divorced parents and their family members out of respect for the surroundings. Special care must be taken to seat battling parents and former family a safe distance apart, possibly separated by friends or relatives. If there is a party following the first Communion, all who attend must remember to have respect for the host, the host's home, and the children present. If they do not feel they can be civil, they should not attend the after-party.

Whether a new partner should attend this sort of religious ceremony depends on how long she has been a new partner. If this is a recent pairing and she does not have a relationship with the children, a first Communion—or any coming of age or milestone, for that matter—is not the appropriate place to make first introductions. If she has been a part of the children's life and supports the co-parenting efforts, then her presence would most likely be missed if she did not attend.

Protocol can get sticky in situations like this, but this is the reason bonus families must consider innovative approaches. Whether co-parents walk together really depends on their current relationship and how well they co-parent together. The statement the father's new partner wants him to make about their relationship has nothing to do with his position as co-parent, but his position as her partner. Therefore, if her attitude about the co-parents walking together is reframed to two parents walking to support their children rather than two former lovers, she may more readily accept the mother's proposal. With that in mind, she might be seated at the front waiting for the mother and father to present the children, then have the father sit with her with the mother nearby.

Parents must remember to have a prior conversation and come to agreement for how they would like to handle things. Forget about protocol and design an approach that works for your family. If the parents decide to walk down the aisle together as suggested, placing the twins between them as they walk seems the most logical. If there is a reception afterward, that is when the father can make the social statement with his partner at his side.

BAR MITZVAHS AND BAT MITZVAHS

In the Jewish faith, a bar/bat mitzvah is the time when the young person is *held accountable* for the commands of the Torah and is considered an adult member of the Jewish community. The celebration marks a time at which point they begin to be held accountable for their own actions.

Bar mitzvahs and bat mitzvahs are the most important occasions for Jewish children aside from their wedding. Elaborate bar mitzvah and bat mitzvah ceremonies and receptions are common today and are quite lavish celebrations. If the parents of the child are no longer together, the planning and financing of the bar mitzvah can be just as complicated as planning a wedding and reception.

If the parents split up before the child comes of age, they should make decisions about the cost of the upcoming bar mitzvah or bat mitzvah at the time of the breakup and include that information in the divorce decree. If they don't do this, it's best to agree to each financial responsibility prior to the ceremony.

Seating

Unlike a wedding where the parents of those getting married are assigned sides of the room and rows for seating, there is no formal seating guide at bar mitzvah or bat mitzvah ceremonies. The parents usually sit closer to the front of the temple to watch their child read from the Torah.

If parents have remarried or have a significant other, they are seated with the significant other. Like a wedding, both parents, regardless of their relationship status, should attend. Estranged co-parents should always put their differences aside for the day to create a pleasant memory for their child.

The ceremony may also be the first time the recipient receives their first tallith, or prayer shawl. The tallith has great family significance. It is usually offered as a special gift between father and son, teacher and student, or later in life between father-in-law and son-in-law and worn during religious services. The tradition is certainly complicated if there is a breakup, particularly if the tallith was offered between father-in-law to son-in-law prior to a severed relationship. If the couple had a child, the tallith offering tradition would remain intact and should be passed on to the child. If there were no children born, it would be in good taste to return the tallith to the family who offered it.

QUINCEAÑERA

When a girl reaches her 15th birthday in the Latin American community, a common practice is to celebrate her quinceañera, an important coming-of-age ceremony marking her entrance into womanhood. Often a large, extravagant celebration, mothers and fathers and extended family play an important part in the preparation that may take years to plan. The family priest performs the ceremony in a church, and the young woman's baptismal godparents oversee the spiritual aspects of the celebration. Add a parental breakup, and the planning responsibilities become very complicated.

Here's something else to consider: Most in the Latin American community are of the Roman Catholic faith and continue to follow their faith when they move to another country. Divorce and remarriage are not recognized within the Roman Catholic church, so parents and other family members who are estranged from one another may not live together but may not be formally divorced, either. They may have new partners and bonus siblings, plus added responsibilities, and juggling all this puts a huge strain on everyone. Even so, estranged parents must still co-parent their children, and if planning a quinceañera, this is just another hurdle divorced or separated parents must face.

Today's quinceañera often resembles a lavish cotillion or debutante celebration with elaborate dresses, food, and festivities. Modern quinceañeras feature a court of 15 people, which usually includes family and friends. There are flowers, decorations, and music to consider, plus a reception is held at which guests are served lunch or dinner.

One of the most memorable moments during the quinceañera is when the father dances with his daughter. This usually opens the reception. A meaningful song is chosen, often with Spanish lyrics and the two dance together, symbolizing this new milestone in her life. The father/daughter dance is always a sentimental time, but it is even more poignant when her parents are separated and if there is also a bonus parent included in the planning of the dance.

The cost of a quinceañera is handled in a similar fashion to a wedding. The father usually finances, or there may be another arrangement between the parents.

GRADUATIONS

Every year around June I am bombarded with questions about the proper etiquette for estranged parents attending their child's graduation. Divorced parents tend to find all sorts of reasons why they should not attend if their ex is planning to attend with someone that does not suit them. These parents must remember that they are not graduating. Their child is, and their child deserves to have both of their parents—and anyone else who loves them—cheer them on.

In recent years, to have room in a celebratory venue for all the students to have someone support them, tickets are often distributed with only a few allotted to each student. This forces a child to choose who will attend the ceremony. If the child's parents are no longer together and now have new partners, it may be difficult to decide who should attend. Add siblings, bonus siblings, and extended family and now there's really a problem. Who stays and who goes?

Of course, this dilemma is limited to specific schools that employ this practice, but you can see how it might add to the stress of graduation if a limited number of tickets are available. Although parents who now have new partners will most likely want their new partners to attend, if there is a question, the child's parents are the first to be chosen.

Following the graduation ceremony, parents often host a reception where those who could not attend the ceremony may congratulate the graduate.

Graduations and other child-centered celebrations are not times to introduce new dates to the family. If the parent has a long-time partner that has cultivated a relationship with the child, then of course, they should attend along with their partner.

My son is graduating this weekend and his mother and I don't agree who should host the party afterwards. I want everyone to come to my home for a casual BBQ. I remarried and have two little ones and it would just be easier to stay here. She wants to host a dinner at our son's favorite Mexican restaurant. Our son told me in confidence that he would prefer the BBQ but understands why his mother might be uncomfortable at my home now that I have remarried.

This is a perfect example of how children in bonus families learn to go with the flow so to speak, but this one has a twist. This young man has become quite the diplomat and has learned to juggle his parents' personalities like a pro. He has told his father that he would prefer to do what he wants but understands why his mother might be uncomfortable coming to his home. This implies that the best alternative is to do what Mom wants—but the graduate is not picking sides. He's allowing his father to be the bigger person and make the choice. Quite clever. Now, if Dad makes the concession, it's of his own free will, which will hopefully eliminate any animosity he might feel about not getting what he wanted. This young person has been in the middle of his parents for a very long time.

When it is difficult for parents to celebrate at either of their homes, it's best to search for neutral territory to hold the celebration. Our home is our private domain, and it's not surprising if your co-parent feels uncomfortable attending a get-together at your house, particularly when you have remarried and have two little ones underfoot. You might feel uncomfortable, as well. Having an ex at your home can be disconcerting, even if that ex is the mother or father of your child. That said, *it always starts with a conversation.*

Let's look at a way for all to get what they want. Say the child truly prefers a casual BBQ; a good alternative might be to hold the BBQ celebration at a park where those attending can grill their favorite dishes, bring potluck sides, but celebrate together on neutral ground. So Mom doesn't feel completely left out, she can plan the menu and oversee the invitations, but Dad gets his causal BBQ and Mom gets her neutral place, albeit not a Mexican restaurant. The child is surrounded by family and friends. It's a win-win. Is it everything that everyone wants? It's a compromise—a bonus solution.

CHAPTER 8

CHILDREN'S BIRTHDAY PARTIES
I don't want my co-parent's partner at my kid's birthday party.

Children's birthday parties can get very complicated when the parents of the birthday child no longer live together and have a new partner. Biological parents often face feelings of insecurity and jealousy once their co-parent moves on, but all must eventually accept that both you and your former partner will re-couple at some point and that new partner will be a very real part of your child's family.

Who Will Host the Party?
Estranged parents usually opt for the two-party solution, but that may not be the best idea. Does a child really need two of everything, including parties? If a child's parents were not divorced, a child that got two of everything would be regarded as spoiled. But, it appears, a child of divorce who has two of everything is not spoiled, a very strange double standard.

If the parents do not feel comfortable hosting the party together, the best solution might be to switch hosting the party each year, say one parent in even years, the other in odd years.

Who Will Attend?
This brings the guest list into question. Ideally, start with the child's friends, followed by both co-parents' extended family if they wish to attend. If anyone feels uncomfortable attending, it should be that person's option to decline the invitation. Some family members may feel inclined to inquire who is invited to the party. For example, this may happen when a former in-law holds a grudge against a former son or daughter-in-law because of the breakup. The knowledge that they are attending the party may then prompt comments along the lines of "If he's coming, I'm not!"

Guests must remember it's not the adult's party with all their breakup drama. They are attending to support the guest of honor, and if the guest of honor is 6 years old, it would be advisable not to act the same age.

Where Will the Party Be Held?

If divorced parents and new spouses are to attend together and if interacting with each other is a new experience, it should be on neutral territory—a park, a pizza parlor, a bowling alley, or an arcade, for example—rather than the home of the parent hosting the party.

If parents and bonus parents simply cannot put their feelings aside and remain civil in the presence of a former relative, then for the sake of the children in attendance, they should not attend parties together. Experts agree that it is better for the child of divorced parents to keep things separate after the split than to attempt to spend time together and fight in front of the child. Ongoing arguing affects a child's emotional and psychological development and well-being.

A Parent's Insensitivity

> *Today is my 8-year-old son Bishop's birthday, and he seemed somewhat grumpy. Suddenly, he ran into his bedroom and locked the door. He knows he's not supposed to do that, so I knew something was really bothering him. When he finally did let me in, he fell into my arms sobbing. Through his tears, he explained that his mother had forgotten his birthday. What should have been my response?*

Birthdays are always important to children, particularly little ones. It's the one day they are singled out to be the star, and if Mom or Dad forgets their day, it can be devastating for the kids, but also for the parent or bonus parent who has to watch the child be hurt. At times like this it is important to remain a stabilizing force for the child. It would be easy to take offense in their name and bad-mouth the offending parent. For the sake of the child and the future of your relationship with them, don't do it. Hugs are the best support of all.

Let's use the CARE model to address this problem.

C is for Communication: Create an environment where your child will not shut down or feel that certain emotions are off the table for discussion. Although you may be tempted in the name of comforting your child, don't squelch strong emotions. Talk them out.

A is for Acceptance: Make sure the child knows that it is normal to feel like he is, and he can share these feelings with you without judgment. As you lead him through his ability to cope with everyday feelings, he will become better equipped to maneuver the bigger emotions as he gets older.

R is for Respect: Teach the child respect for himself and not to blame himself for his parent's insensitivity. An appropriate response might be, "Just because we are your parents and all grown up doesn't mean we don't have things to learn."

E is for Empathy: Take care not to let your feelings of compassion for your child's position prompt you to retaliate against the mother. Bad-mouthing Mom for her misdeed will not increase this child's sense of security or help his self-esteem. Your responsibility is to comfort the child and help him cope with this disappointment. Right now, he is afraid his mother doesn't love him. Reinforce that forgetting doesn't mean he isn't lovable. That's the important issue to address, that he feels loved despite his mother's poor choices.

FUNERALS

What is my responsibility when my children's mother dies and there is a viewing and formal funeral? Ours was a long-term 20-year marriage that ended in a brutal divorce due to her infidelity and remarriage. We had three children, now all adults, to whom I am very close. Will there be any adverse effects for my children if I choose not to attend the services?

Funeral services are designed to offer respect to the deceased but more importantly to support those who are left behind. In this case, the writer's children are most definitely grieving the loss of their mother, and although I'm sure he didn't support his ex-wife's actions, he will certainly want to support his children as they mourn her loss. That would be the reason he would attend the viewing and the funeral—not to maintain the grudge he holds, but for his children.

My own mother passed unexpectedly, and one of the loveliest acknowledgments I received after her death was a note from my daughter's father. Although we were cordial because of co-parenting our daughter, the conversation did not always flow easily. In his note he expressed his deep sorrow and his affection for my mother and offered his assistance in any way. It was a lovely sentiment and greatly appreciated not only by me but by the rest of my extended family, as well. As my family met with the minister before my mother's memorial service, he timidly entered the room and was warmly embraced by all family members, including my husband. All were there to support each other in an intense time of sorrow. I would hope it would be the same for the writer and his children.

Don't discount the fact that the death of a loved one can break down long-time barriers and put many past issues into their proper perspective. Although I had remarried, and my daughter had formed a loving bond with her bonus father, there was nothing like having her daddy next to her in her time of grief after her grandmother's passing. Her dad's kind words and loving presence at my mother's funeral allowed everyone to interact more easily in the future. Putting the children first is always the best barometer when the propriety of a co-parent's attendance is in question.

My mother passed away unexpectedly earlier this week while our children, ages 10 and 12, were in their father's care. The kids were very close to her. I made him aware of her passing when I asked him to swap time with me so that the kids and I could attend her funeral out of state. He declined and expected me to allow the children to stay with him [for] 3 extra days while I attended her funeral alone. My family went to great expense to rearrange the schedule so that the children could be at the funeral. He doesn't think he has done anything inappropriate.

The concept behind bonus family unity is working together to make a difficult situation easier on the children, particularly at times when they are vulnerable and need the support of both of their parents and bonus parents. The fact that this mother and their father are no longer together should mean nothing in a time of crisis. Their mutual goal should be to put the children first, and a grandparent's passing is a perfect time for them to do just that.

Granted, sometimes people have difficulty coping with unexpected changes, and this father may be one of them. Normally, I would suggest giving a parent time to digest a proposed change so that negotiation can move more smoothly. However, flexibility is an important component of good co-parenting, particularly in times of crisis. If these parents were truly co-parenting, Mom would call the children's father to explain what had happened and he would make them available so she could gently inform them. This might even include dropping them off at Mom's home a day early if necessary. A supportive co-parent would also check if it would be appropriate for them to stay to help comfort the children when the news has been passed on.

This approach might mean that some of Dad's assigned parenting time was lost that week, but with cooperation, he could easily be compensated with further negotiation. More time could be added here or there or even during an upcoming school break. Or co-parents could resign themselves to "it's no big deal" and simply help each other out. I often ask co-parents arguing about time if "in 10 years do they think their child will realize that 10 years ago I spent 3 days more with Mom than Dad one month? Doubtful. But they may remember how kind Dad was to Mom when Grandma passed.

ANNIVERSARIES
Anniversaries are not only dates that mark a marriage or proposal. The remembrance of any occasion can be regarded as an anniversary. The 4th of July is the anniversary of the United States' independence. When discussing the passing of a loved one, the day is often explained as "the anniversary of their death." The yearly reminder of overcoming a past diagnosis, a divorce, a particular success or failure, or even a "sober date" when one stopped using alcohol and/or drugs and entered recovery, are all regarded as important life markers—and days that are personally acknowledged or celebrated with the help of friends and family.

How bonus families celebrate the days they regard as special is up to them. They may integrate an already established holiday, like Mother's Day or Father's Day, with their own bonus family twist or it could be a day to mark a family milestone, like the day they first moved in together.

A successful bonus family is only as great as the sum of its parts. It's important that each family member develops as an individual and thereby contributes to the success of the whole. I encourage all bonus families to think outside of the box and search for unique ways to celebrate their own bonus family milestones.

PART IV

CO-PARENTING AND BONUS FAMILY PITFALLS

CHAPTER 9

Bonus Blunders, Backslides, and Course Corrections

YOU MIGHT HAVE READ THIS QUOTE BY ALBERT EINSTEIN before: "Problems cannot be solved using the same thinking that created them."[1] It's even more likely you have read another version of the quote: "The definition of insanity is doing the same thing over and over again, expecting a different result."[2] That is also attributed to Albert Einstein, but after extensive online research it appears what he really said was, "A new type of thinking is essential if mankind is to survive and move to higher levels."[3] When analyzed, all the quotes could mean the same thing—or do they? Somehow, the true wording has been lost in translation and the revised edition has been assumed to be true.

This happens all the time in bonus families. As the kids go between their parents' homes and build allegiances with different people, bio and bonus, the transfer of information can easily get convoluted. A child will hear something, pass on information, and the information passed is taken as gospel. Everyone assumes they know what someone feels or what they said. Accusations abound and tempers fly.

This chapter will address some of the most common problems faced by co-parents and their bonus families. We have touched on some of these "blunders" in previous chapters, but here we will examine them more closely using real-life scenarios, starting with a major obstacle to achieving successful co-parenting and reaching bonus status.

Accusations and Assumptions

Kelly's dad, Robert, explained, "Last week when Kelly came back from her mother Flora's home, I could see something was wrong. We share custody and Kelly is 8 years old. When I asked what she did at Mom's, she broke out crying. 'I never want to go back there again! Mommy said I'm going to kill brother.' She was difficult to console. 'I don't want to kill Walker!'"

My wife, Julie, and I have a little boy who is about 9 months old. Kelly adores him but after the last couple of exchanges she has been very distant. I couldn't understand it and tried to ignore it. I figured she was 8 and just being a kid. Kelly's mother and I have been going to co-parenting classes, and I knew that I should tell her mother what was said—so I did. I called her up and said, "Kelly doesn't want to go back to your house. She said you told her that she is going to kill her brother and now she is hysterical. How could you say that to a little girl?"

My wife walked in and scooped Kelly into her arms, trying to comfort her. Kelly clung to her, 'Don't make me go back, Sweet Pea. I want to stay with you and Walker.'"

"Sweet Pea" was Kelly and Julie's mutual pet name for each other. Julie also had children and did not think calling her "Mommy" was appropriate, so she and Kelly decided to call each other the same name that she called Kelly—Sweet Pea. It was an interesting approach, and it worked well for their bonus family.

According to both parents, the conversation got out of hand. Julie continued to rock Kelly on the sofa as Robert continued to chastise Flora. Kelly grew more inconsolable. Julie continued to rock her while the two parents argued.

Reading this you may think this example is far-fetched, but it is a true-life example. The names have been changed, of course, but it is indicative of the type of stories reported as children go back and forth between their parents' homes. We all must remember, it's not only the parents' homes. These three parents have additional children besides Kelly and Walker. Kelly's mother has another child from a previous relationship, and Julie has two children who live with her and Robert. It's a bonus family and Kelly is not the only one who goes back and forth. Julie shares custody with her children's father and her kids live in two homes, as well.

Plus, the situation could be reversed. Julie could have said something to Kelly. She could have then gone back to her mother's home and Flora be the one calling Robert. "What did your wife say to Kelly?! She's hysterical!"

The assumption is that a parent *actually said* exactly what the child reported and then aggressively accused the other parent of saying something inappropriate to the child. It's predictable that a parent accused would then defend themselves. That's when communication spins out of control. No one trusts each other.

What is the correct course to take?

Course Correction

When co-parents hear something questionable about each other from their child, it is always advisable to check with their co-parent for clarification. Don't assign blame or fault prior to the conversation. The mindset should now be, "I'm concerned about the information passed on by our child. Perhaps my co-parent can shed some insight."

Unfortunately, co-parents who want to avoid confrontation often feel safer texting, particularly those who do not trust each other. But texting is best used for notification, not clarification. If true communication is the goal, using a direct method— voice or face-to-face—is better suited to help the parties gain understanding.

A better approach would be, "I need clarification, Flora. Kelly is very upset. She's telling me you told her that she is going to kill her brother. Fill me in. I'm sure something got lost in the translation." Stop there and listen. Don't editorialize with a further explanation of why you are right and your co-parent is wrong. You are trying to find out the truth. This approach offers your co-parent the benefit of the doubt and they will be more willing to be honest rather than argue or become defensive.

During your exploration, if you add something like, "How could you say that to a little girl?" that is *accusatory* and *assumes* what was reported is exactly what happened. Kelly is 8. Eight-year-olds process language differently than adults. What Flora said and what Kelly thought her mother meant may easily be two different things. There needs to be some exploration, not accusations, if these two parents want to create an environment where their child feels safe in both homes. And don't forget, how Robert and Flora handle this will affect the other children's comfort. They see Kelly hysterical and want to know what's wrong. They see Julie rocking Kelly, hear Robert and Flora fighting over the phone, and now their life is turned upside down even though this problem has nothing to do with them.

Let's take it one step further . . . Julie's kids also go back and forth between their parents' homes. So, Julie's kids go back to their father's home with a story that Kelly is going to kill her brother. Then Julie gets a text. "What the heck is going on at your house?" her co-parent writes. "There's domestic violence over there! That kid is crazy. I'm calling CPS and filing for custody!"

Do you think I've taken this too far? Believe me, I did not. When parents don't work together and consult each other when faced with something questionable, information can easily be misconstrued.

Would you like to know what was really said to Kelly? After a very long session, we figured it out, and both parents realized the importance of giving each other the benefit of the doubt. This was during the Covid pandemic and Kelly did not like wearing a mask. Her mother tried to explain that she must wear a mask or else she could get her little brother very sick. Kelly then saw the news that night that talked about the death toll of those with Covid and why masks were important. In her little 8-year-old head, she took all that she was told by her mother and what she heard on the news and deduced that her little brother might die because she previously refused to wear a mask. She didn't want to return to her mother's because she was afraid she might get sick there and then give Covid to her little brother. That came out as, "Mommy said I'm going to kill Walker. I don't want to go back to Mommy's."

There was more to complicate this interaction. Flora was convinced that Robert or Julie had bad-mouthed her in some way, and that was why Kelly did not want to return. She was on a completely different page when the clarifying conversation began, and this made it very difficult for her to slow down and listen to what Robert was really saying.

There were some other behaviors that could have been improved. It was wonderful that Kelly sought comfort from Julie, but Julie should have removed herself and Kelly from the room, not allowed her to hear her parents fight over the phone, nor allow the other children in the home to witness the chaos. Either Robert or Julie should have removed themselves from the room; someone should have taken the initiative to protect Kelly and the other children from seeing so much negativity. Both Robert and Julie said they were so caught up in the argument that they overlooked their part in it. That was not okay, and they understood they must be more proactive if this ever happens again.

There was a positive aspect that should be noted—the fact that Julie and Kelly had picked a nickname other than Mommy for Julie. Most parents with whom I have worked do not like their children to call anyone else "Mom" or "Dad." Julie and Kelly picked a special name just for them and even took it one step further—they both called each other the same sweet name. Julie, understanding how easily children can be aware of favoritism, had nicknames for all her children so that they did not feel left out when she shared a name with Kelly.

THE RIPPLE EFFECT

As you can see from this scenario, one family's problem is not only their problem. When families share children, struggles produce a ripple effect. Although unintentional, Kelly's misunderstanding affected Julie's children and prompted her co-parent to react. Then Julie became resentful because she felt Flora's comments impacted her custody agreement. "If Flora wasn't so stupid! She knew better than to say those things to Kelly . . ."

First Robert and Flora were at odds, but now, Julie and Flora weren't talking either. Julie's co-parent wanted to change the custody agreement because he *assumed* there was domestic violence at Julie's house—and the truth was that none of what was supposed to have been said to Kelly was ever said. This is the reason I advocate a cooperative approach because when we share custody, our actions do not only affect those living within our four walls. The aftermath ripples from house to house and there must be a forum to nip all this in the bud. Without a change in approach parents who share custody will just continue the cycle of trauma and pass it down over generations.

Intergenerational Trauma

According to the Coalition Against Domestic Violence, 1 in 3 women and 1 in 4 men have experienced some form of physical violence by an intimate partner. This includes a range of behaviors including slapping, shoving, or pushing, and when polled, many do not feel those types of behaviors are considered "domestic violence." But if your kids are watching it or experiencing it, whatever it is called, it's traumatic. The same source goes on to quote that 1 in 7 women and 1 in 25 men have been injured by an intimate partner.

While working at a superior court as a child custody mediator, when I was faced with parents who had a history of domestic violence, I often asked the perpetrator if they had witnessed one of their parents interacting with the other in that manner. Almost all said yes. I then asked them how it made them feel at the time—and that question usually hit home. Until that second, they did not realize they were doing exactly what they hated about their own upbringing—not only the domestic violence aspect but contributing to their children's emotional abuse, as well, from their children having to watch it.

Clients have often vowed not to re-create the co-parenting atmosphere created by their parents. They described it as cruel and retaliatory, only to act exactly as they described their parents had acted. As a result, they are unintentionally inflicting the same pain on their children as their parents inflicted on them. That's intergenerational trauma, or a trauma cycle, when someone experiences trauma and then creates a similar experience for children in their care.

Does that mean that parents who experienced trauma as children are destined to perpetuate the same behaviors as their parents? Not necessarily, if parents stop the cycle. But many who have faced trauma as children become avoidant as adults and, in their effort to not replicate traumatic interactions, manifest other negative coping behaviors such as communicating passive-aggressively or abusing drugs or alcohol to cope with their anxiety. Their children then model those behaviors and the cycle continues.

My father had a very bad temper as I grew up. He acted out by yelling and acting aggressively. As a child I saw how his behavior controlled the rest of the family and I remember as young as 6 thinking if I get angry and stomp up to a sibling while yelling at them, they will back down. It worked, which reinforced that behavior and I continued to do it until early adulthood when my partner announced he was leaving because of my ranting. I had to change my behavior. Once I had children, when I was calm, I used parenting techniques

*I learned from parenting books and attending therapy, but when I
was under stress and had to discipline, I found myself automatically
disciplining as I had been disciplined as a child and had to work
hard not to recreate that behavior and what I had felt as a child.*
— TROY, FATHER TO MICHAEL, AGE 10, AND KRISTEN, AGE 12

Course Correction

Healing starts by learning how to identify, acknowledge, and
accept your trauma. Practicing mindfulness and meditation is
helpful, as well as learning to set boundaries or, better said, being
honest with yourself and others about what you have experienced
and what makes you uncomfortable. *Don't be afraid to seek counseling.* The cycle of trauma is too big for many of us to face on our
own. Openly communicating and finding support from others,
possibly attending group therapy guided by a counselor who spe-
cializes in coping with trauma, will help to set you on the road to
healing.

The next step is to incorporate your newfound coping skills
into your parenting and co-parenting. Again, you may need the
help of a professional. Overcoming trauma is a process and takes
time—meanwhile your children are getting older. That is why
it is so important to be proactive in your efforts to change your
approach.

WHEN A CHILD IN YOUR BONUS FAMILY HAS SPECIAL NEEDS

*Two years ago, my daughter, Hannah, was diagnosed "on the
Autistic Spectrum." I pushed for the evaluation. She was having
trouble assimilating into mainstream education and she did not
easily make friends. When things were difficult for her to grasp,
she would throw a tantrum. That's understandable in a toddler,
but Hannah is almost 9. Her father would not admit she had a
problem. The diagnosis confirmed my suspicions, and she was also
diagnosed with obsessive-compulsive disorder, but her father will do
nothing to learn about her issues. He believes she is just angry with*

me because I remarried last year. Although we rarely speak, he has made it clear that he thinks a change in the parenting plan is all that is needed. "Hannah just needs more time with me," he continually says, implying less time with me and my family would be better for our child. Now he is taking me back to court. He is suggesting that she live with him for 2 days, then us for 2 days, then alternate the weekends. She currently sees him on alternating weekends with a Wednesday night dinner to break up the time he does not see her. Hannah's behavior is getting worse. She often tells me she does not want to go to the Wednesday night dinner and throws a tantrum each time I say, "It's Wednesday . . . " It is affecting the other children in my home—her bonus siblings—and I am afraid the other kids will not want to live with her.

– Sylvia, mother to Hannah, age 9

In family therapy, there is a concept called the "identified patient." It's the person in the family that everyone points to, believing they are behind the family's inner conflict when, in fact, there are other issues at play. Currently, all eyes are on Hannah. Dad believes her diagnosis is not serious and can be addressed by a change in custody. Mom believes Hannah's acting out is what is preventing her bonus family from jelling as she expected. Meanwhile, as the mother states, Hannah's behavior is getting worse.

The described discord is quite familiar when a child has been diagnosed with special needs. The parents believe the diagnosis and associated behavior is the catalyst behind the chaos, but there are quite a few red flags alerting us to problems in this family. The largest one is that these co-parents do not speak. It doesn't matter what happened in the past, a child diagnosed with special needs will face challenges. Studies show that OCD symptoms increase in response to stress or stressful events. Parental arguments are stressful events for children. It may not be Hannah's diagnosis that is causing the problems at both homes, but her parents' inability to work together.

Course Correction

In most cases, when there is a problem of this sort, the last thing co-parents who are at odds think to do is reach out to one another for help. However, I'm sure both will acknowledge they love their child very much. Both are upset by their child's inability to assimilate into mainstream education and how her peers might tease her "different" behaviors. Both parents celebrate her success and are saddened by her failures. These parents are not alone in raising Hannah, and if their co-parenting relationship were more positive, this would be obvious to them.

That said, something often overlooked when laying out a parenting plan for a child with autism spectrum disorder (ASD) is how much these children struggle with disorganization. Those with ASD have trouble navigating their emotions. They have trouble reading other's facial cues, so they may not understand when someone is happy or angry with them. They can be irritated by loud or different sounds—and now a new baby has been added to one of their homes. With all that seems like chaos, is it any wonder a child struggling like this might manifest a soothing mechanism (like OCD) or ritual to cope?

"It's Wednesday; time to go to Dad's."

Further, it is difficult for children with this diagnosis to adjust to change, so it may not be in Hannah's best interest to switch homes every couple of days. Many children with this disorder also face anxiety, panic attacks, and/or emotional meltdowns when they are unable to easily process the surrounding stimuli produced by a change in their environment. Much to Dad's dismay, a change in the parenting plan with more back and forth may do exactly the opposite of what he sees as the answer.

At this point, the best course of action when co-parents have a child with special needs is to coordinate efforts with the professionals treating the child to zero in on proven strategies that work for their child's diagnosis.

This segues into another issue expressed by the mother in this scenario—the fear that her bonus children may not want to live with *her* because her child has special needs. As a result, her husband will become angry that his children do not want to spend time in their home and he will reject *her,* as well.

Whether a parent will outwardly admit this fear or not, many in this position have confided it is a real concern. The remedy is twofold:

1. Pay special attention to the Before Bonus Exercise where it asks the bonus parent how they will cultivate a relationship with their partner's child. This will help the bonus parent be prepared for the challenges ahead.

2. Approach the concern with CARE.

This means improving your **C**ommunication by confiding your worries to your partner and working together to address them.

Educate family members about the limitations and struggles a person with a diagnosis might face so that they can better address the challenges and maintain a mindset of **A**cceptance.

Respect *all* family members' differences.

Each family member has a take on this situation. Put yourself in their shoes to **E**mpathize with how they might be feeling in order to best address their concerns.

WHEN A CO-PARENT HAS BEEN DIAGNOSED WITH A MENTAL ILLNESS

My ex has been diagnosed with bipolar disorder. It makes it very difficult to co-parent. I'm thinking about going back to court to ask for full custody . . .

Lots of people struggle with mental illness. If there is a question of primary custody between parents, it's the parent's behavior that determines with whom the child will live, not the diagnosis.

For example, if your co-parent has cancer, that diagnosis is certainly not a reason to adjust custody. But if the parent is so sick that they can't take care of the child, that's when a decision might be made to adjust the child's time with the parent—not because the parent is sick, but because the parent is so sick, the child may not be safe.

Let's take this a little further. Does that mean a sick parent might be penalized because he or she is ill? This is where good co-parenting comes in. It has been my experience that judges greatly respect a parent who will step in to help a sick co-parent—who will fill in when their co-parent can't pick up or drop off, who will or let a child visit more often during the day because it's easier to maneuver a day visit than an overnight.

As the ill parent improves, the co-parent is trusted to return to the original parenting plan. Things get sketchy when a co-parent steps in to help and then refuses to return to the original plan. They use their co-parent's illness to "get more time" instead of realizing that their child needs time with both parents and celebrating when an ill parent has recovered. Bonus parents can be a great support to sick parents as well. If bonus parents develop a "We are all in this together" attitude, they can help to keep a child's life consistent when they are worried about their ill parent.

Finally, bipolar disorder is a difficult diagnosis for all concerned; however, it is a disorder that can be managed with therapy and medication. It is not necessarily a reason for a custody change. Pinpointing the correct meds and dosage can be frustrating and like most illnesses, stress exacerbates the symptoms. The severity of symptoms can be different for everyone.

***

My co-parent is a lost cause. They are a narcissist! I looked it up on the internet and they check all the boxes. They think they are perfect, always right, and try to manipulate me and the kids to get their own way. They act like they care, but they obviously don't. I'm trying to get a court order to keep the kids away from them!

"My co-parent is a narcissist!" seems to be this year's co-parenting battle cry. In past years it has been, "My ex has bi-polar disorder!" or schizophrenic—co-parents grasping at any straw to explain their former partner's manipulative, grandiose, conceited behavior. But just about everyone's ex is difficult at the time of the break-up. Your ex probably feels the same way about you.

Before I go on, let's identify what narcissism in a co-parent really looks like. A narcissistic co-parent may act in many ways that can make co-parenting seem almost impossible. For example, they may not take your requests or observations seriously and openly disregard your opinion. Your boundaries mean nothing to a narcissistic co-parent, especially if they are inconvenient or get in the way of their preferences. A narcissistic co-parent lacks empathy. They cannot see your point of view and if they do, they don't value it as much as theirs. They have a tendency to be inflexible if you ask for help or want to make some sort of trade. They can be negative and belittling, and they can have a very difficult time with criticism. They may openly bad-mouth you in front of the children or extended family and friends and try to make you believe that something did or didn't happen in the story to fit their narrative (gaslighting). They may attempt to wear you down when they want something, one-up you with the children, discredit your ideas, and/or schedule things on your allotted time with the kids. A narcissistic parent is the kind of co-parent that undermines your parenting. They might accuse you of being a "bad" parent, believing they are superior in every way. A common ploy of a narcissistic co-parent is to deliberately change an appointment for the child to their parenting time and then not notify their co-parent. Obviously, this type of behavior does not jive with the bonus family concept of co-parenting, but it is something very real that some must deal with and thus merits discussion.

That said, because you find a former partner unpredictable, angry, manipulative, and only seeing their point of view is not enough to pin a narcissistic diagnosis on them. Truth be told, according to recent studies only 1 or 2% of the US population actually falls into that category.[4] That's 1 or 2 people out of 100. It's more likely that they are manifesting narcissistic tendencies—and unfortunately quite a few of our exes seem to fall into that category. When people are frustrated, angry, or concerned that someone doesn't respect their opinion, they often become unreasonable. Unfortunately, if that's someone with whom you must co-parent, it's a problem.

However, it's important to note that it is rare for the courts to stop someone's time with their children simply because of a mental health diagnosis. People who struggle with their mental health still have a right to see their children, and their children still have the right to see their parents. I have seen the court step in when the parent could not take care of themselves or the children for a multitude of reasons, such as a history of addiction and neglect to intimate partner violence. Of course, there may have been a diagnosis present, but the basis on which the decision was made was the children's safety.

If your children's other parent is truly a narcissist, you may have to adopt what is called parallel parenting. Parallel parenting is where each parent has their own parenting approach and responsibilities when their children are with them. The children have two homes, two existences, and they travel between their parents following a parenting plan that does not require the parents to consult each other when decisions are made. There are usually exceptions made for times of emergency, like a medical decision. Battling parents must talk to each other and agree if their child is to undergo an operation, for example.

You can imagine how difficult this is on children. Although parallel parenting is adopted to prevent the children from witnessing ongoing conflict, they still know what's going on and it weighs heavily on their shoulders. I have never worked with a child who liked this parenting approach. Unfortunately, many ended up being "the messenger" for their battling parents and were asked to pass on information because their parents refused to talk to each other. That is breaking every co-parenting commandment there is. When children become messengers for their parents, it actually perpetuates the trauma they experienced when their parents' split. They feel as if they must pick a side and often run defense for the parent they perceive to be the underdog. They don't pass on information or don't pass it on correctly believing it will prevent their parents from arguing. The list of ways children attempt to intercede between battling parents is long—and nothing good ever comes of it.

Ultimately, what is best for your children is to put your own issues aside and come together in their name. Understandably, this is a tall order when a co-parent displays narcissistic tendencies. Once again, approaching your narcissistic co-parent with CARE may be the answer:

Communication:

Be clear about your parenting expectations. A narcissist will attempt to push the limits you set.

Avoid emotional arguments. Limit communication to only what is necessary.

Don't let conversations spiral. You will never "prove your point" with a narcissist. Don't try.

Document everything. It may be helpful to use a co-parenting app that records conversations and allows professionals to oversee your communication.

Acceptance:

Accept that your co-parent was not born a narcissist. It is behavior adopted in response to their upbringing. You must accept them for who they are, acknowledging their history and background that provoked the narcissistic behavior. You cannot change your co-parent, whether they are a narcissist or not. Most narcissists have no idea they are a narcissist. They think it's you with the problem.

Respect:

It is difficult to respect someone you feel is disrespecting you. However, respect in this sense may not be for the other person. Respect yourself enough to not buy into narcissistic manipulation. Learn to identify "gaslighting" and do not question your personal truth when someone tries to convince you of something other than you know is true.

Empathy:

Although a true narcissist is unable to feel empathy, that doesn't mean you can't. You can put yourself in their shoes prior to a co-parenting negotiation and make your decisions accordingly. You can be the bigger person and set the example for your children.

Course Correction

What can you do as a supportive co-parent if your co-parent is mentally or physically ill?

1. Be available to fill in so that disruption for your child is kept to a minimum.

2. Urge your co-parent to stay med-compliant and attend therapy sessions.

3. Don't use your co-parent's vulnerabilities against them. Your child loves both of you and needs both of you in their life.

4. Intercede if your child is unsafe, but monitor your co-parent's progress, if possible, in order to return to the past parenting plan if and when it is safe for your children.

5. Never bad-mouth your co-parent in front of your children, no matter how unpredictable or ill your co-parent seems. The children will not feel safe in their ill parent's presence,

and when the parent improves and parent and child reunite, you may have some backtracking to do. Help, don't hinder.

More Bonus Blunders
Parental Alienation

It is unfortunate that I must include this subject in *The Bonus Family Handbook* since parental alienation is so contrary to the bonus mindset. However, it remains a problem for co-parents and their bonus families, so let's take a look at how easy it is to get caught up in it. If you see yourself in this scenario, stop!

To backtrack a second, it is important to note that the jury is still out on whether parental alienation is a "syndrome," per se, or a contributing factor to another diagnosis. Parental alienation is not formally currently listed as a diagnosis in the *Diagnostic and Statistical Manual of Mental Disorders* (DSM-5) but ask any psychologist or marriage and family therapist and they will tell you the behavior (and its aftermath) is very real.

This is how it might start . . .

Because of my job, I used to live 4 hours from my boys, and so they lived predominantly with their mother, Georgia. She remarried and had two more boys. I couldn't stand it anymore and quit my job 2 years ago so I could move closer to my children. It really didn't matter. By then they were so used to living with their mother, I felt like a stranger.

And so Benjamin decided to win over the boys. He would take them to the beach for a fun weekend. The boys returned to Mom's house and told her what a wonderful time they had with Dad. They said that Ben was really cool and let them stay up all hours when they spent the night. Georgia was secretly jealous, worried that the boys would now prefer life with Benjamin. Their siblings were also jealous—they wanted to go to the beach and have no bedtime, as well. The contrast between homes became more obvious with each visit, and Georgia slowly became resentful that Benjamin had moved closer.

The next opportunity, Georgia took all the kids to the beach for a week. They returned to tell Ben all about their fabulous time at the beach, and he started to worry that the boys wouldn't want to come see him. "They have more fun with their mom."

Time passed, and Georgia knew the kids would love to go to the AAA baseball game in the nearby town. Ben heard about it from the kids and bought season tickets for their favorite National League team but bought tickets only for himself and his two biological children. Their siblings, who live full-time with Georgia, were left out. Because they all live together, the younger boys are now swept up in the co-parenting antics (the Ripple Effect). The siblings are just innocent bystanders.

The situation came to a head when I met with these parents in my office for help with co-parenting. "I am convinced he's just doing this out of spite. He just one-ups me to lure the kids away from me," Georgia explained. Her frustration was obvious. "I'm so afraid the boys won't want to stay with me. They will think my house is no fun and want to stay with their dad."

Ben admitted he worried about the same thing. As a result, both parents backed off on discipline and both overcompensated by buying gifts and taking trips to ensure the kids liked their home best. An either/or philosophy was adopted—either Mom OR Dad. Not Mom AND Dad. "I was just gone for so long," Benjamin admitted. "I had no other ammunition."

Ammunition. This was war.

Neither parent realized they were perpetuating a malicious game of one-upmanship—the prize being their kids. Their need to win the boys over was brought on by their own insecurity and fear of losing the boys' devotion. They had put their boys right in the middle, something both parents admitted neither of them wanted. Not to mention, their poor behavior now involved the boys' younger siblings. They felt left out and overlooked, the attention always being on Ben and Georgia's children.

"I didn't realize I was trying to alienate our boys from their father," Georgia confessed. "I just felt powerless when their dad returned and felt I had to do something when the boys seemed so excited. I didn't want them to forget their bonus dad, either. Before their dad returned to town, we were this one big happy family. He comes back and everything is different. I thought I was fighting fire with fire."

"When I bought those season tickets," Ben admitted. "I knew I had won. I just didn't realize how all this was hurting our boys and Georgia's boys, as well. That was never my intention."

I was surprised that he had used the words won and ammunition in his explanation. Both parents felt it was a war. Neither admitted it until now.

Course Correction: Ending the War

We all know how judgment can become questionable when parents are angry and vengeful and who struggle with past resentments. Add possibly dealing with mental illness or drug or alcohol abuse, which can alter judgment if left untreated, and it's a perfect storm, of sorts. The potential for attempted alienation is real.

In Georgia and Ben's case, it was caught early and, therefore, did not reach the level of true parental alienation. If that had been the case, their attempts to sway the children would have become extreme, and the children would have gravitated to only one parent, refusing to see the other. True parental alienation begins with a pervasive campaign of degradation that systematically undermines the other parent. The children become almost brainwashed by the ongoing attempts to undermine the targeted parent. Sometimes, those scars cannot be healed and the parent/child relationship is affected forever.

To Benjamin and Georgia's credit, when they realized what they were doing, they both became equally invested in correcting the behaviors. THEY did the work, improving their Communication slowly by first attending co-parenting behavior counseling and using the Bonus Family Problem Solving Model and I messages to more effectively speak and listen to each other. Then they progressed to Accepting each other's importance in their children's lives, Respecting each other's place as equally crucial to their children's well-being, and finally, possibly the most profound healing agent in the CARE model to improve their ability to work together, used their Empathetic abilities and put themselves in their children's shoes. They felt their children's confusion, their growing distrust of both their parents, and their fear and insecurity because their parents were so out of control.

Georgia and Ben are a success story. They took control of their own actions and made an about-face in the way they related to each other because they inherently saw what their behaviors were doing to their children.

Taking it one step further, Ben also saw the impact his behavior had on Georgia's bonus children, something to which those who live in bonus families can certainly relate. That had a huge impact on Georgia's ability to let down her guard and begin to trust Ben.

In my work with struggling co-parents, I have found some consistent behaviors that can be labeled "alienating," but when nipped in the bud, as with Georgia and Ben, the amount of damage to the parent/child relationship is minimized. Be on the lookout. If you see yourself in the following behaviors, acknowledge it, stop, and put the wheels in motion to correct it.

Bad-mouthing

I don't believe the mother in the following story realized she was bad-mouthing the child's father. She did not expect to get the reaction she got.

Years ago, while standing in line at the supermarket, the woman in front of me caught my eye. She had a little one in a car seat perched in the front of her shopping cart and a child of about 4 standing at her side.

"I probably shouldn't be saying this to you," I said, "But you look exhausted."

"Oh," she said with a sigh. "It's my ex. He drives me crazy, and I wish he would just move on."

"Move on?" cried the little 4-year-old. "Move on? You want my daddy to move on?"

It was difficult to console her, and that's when both children started to cry. I held the baby while mom tried to calm her 4-year-old.

Let's analyze what happened here so you understand why I included this story as an example.

First, Mom didn't grasp how her throwaway comment would cause such an uproar. She was exhausted and just talking, but that's how allusive bad-mouthing can be. It can be as simple as "I hate waiting for your mother! She's never on time!" A child will personalize anything, even a little derogatory, about their other parent. That's their DNA you are talking about.

Most co-parents tell me they regard bad-mouthing as something that is planned with intent. Swearing, calling their co-parent a name, or openly disapproving of something their co-parent did—all knowingly and on purpose right in front of the children. But bad-mouthing can be anything with a derogatory edge. From an exasperated comment like what this mother said to more obvious name-calling and commenting on their co-parent's character. You may think your children don't pick up on it, but children are intuitive creatures. To your child, that's their daddy or mommy you are talking about.

Course Correction

"I didn't realize saying my co-parent makes bad food choices was bad-mouthing." Even something as innocuous as commenting about a parent's food choices can negatively impact your child if not presented positively. Watch the motivation behind those throwaway comments in front of your children. *Everything* you say about their other parent affects them.

Kids in the Middle

> *My ex asked my son to be available today to help him finish painting a house that he's trying to flip. We have had plans for months for this day—my son's bonus dad and I plus our other three kids were trying to surprise my son with hockey tickets. His birthday is next week, and this is as close to his day as we could get. It's a day he's scheduled to be with us. As a result, his dad knew nothing about the outing. My son had to call his father—he's almost 15—and tell him he couldn't help him because he was attending the hockey game. He told me not to worry about it, that he would just "let Dad know." I didn't ask my son to call his dad, but I don't think he wanted to put his father and I in contact with each other. This is where I'm stuck: My son's dad enjoys obligating our son to different things when he is with me without discussing it directly with me first. I feel this puts our son in the middle and I'm afraid our son is looking for ways to keep us from talking so we don't fight.*

Many parents don't understand what "put the child in the middle" means. They have heard the phrase and proclaim to never do it, but they do it all the same. It means creating an environment where your child must choose between their parents, and that's exactly what is happening in the above scenario.

Obligating a child to anything on a day he's designated to be with the other parent—without talking to the other parent first—puts the child right in the middle. It asks the child to choose which parent they would rather spend time with. It's no longer about spending quality time with the kids or sharing the children's time, it's about who can one-up the other parent to lure the kids to their camp.

Course Correction

When either parent has special plans for their child, let the other parent know well in advance. If it's a surprise, swear the parent to secrecy—but let them in on the surprise so they can reinforce your efforts. When either parent wants time with their child that is not a designated visitation day, the parent requests it from the parent—not the child. They may choose to trade days or weekends, or trading may not be necessary at all, but let each other in on the planning, then present the change to the child as a united front.

"*Your mom/dad and I talked about this, and we have decided____ (fill in the blank).*"

Older teens may want to be consulted about their social calendar before decisions are made, but parents still must remain steadfastly on the same page even when deciding for teenagers.

There's another BIG Bonus Blunder here that needs additional discussion. It is allowing your child to bad-mouth their other parent.

There's more to the above story that I did not include in the original scenario.

Remember that the child offered to call Dad? Mom felt it was because the child didn't want her to talk to Dad to prevent a possible argument. There is that aspect to consider, but the mother explained that she overheard her son complaining about her to Dad during the phone call. She heard only one side of the conversation but felt father and son were commiserating about how awful it was to "be stuck here at this house." This is an important observation and a common practice of children placed in the middle of their estranged parents. The child has learned that if he puts down Mom, as in this example, Dad seems to be more understanding and doesn't get as upset. Therefore, he buffered the message he was passing on with complaints and irritation about life with Mom. Dad then became more amicable to the fact that the child couldn't spend the day with him.

When a child bad-mouths a parent, it goes without saying that he may be angry or disappointed, but it may also be done for parental approval. The child knows that his parent dislikes the other parent, and to get on that parent's good side, he jumps on the Bash Mom or Dad Bandwagon. If you allow your child to bash their other parent, you are teaching them that disrespect can be a useful tool to gain acceptance. Don't be surprised when this backfires. A child reasons, "If it's okay to disrespect one parent—and it gets me what I want—it will be okay to disrespect the other." For this reason, it is imperative both parents reinforce each other's parental importance.

It is also important for co-parents to realize that while many of these alienating behaviors *do* distance the child from their other parent, undermining a parent also undermines the child's self-esteem and feelings of security.

Most parents who practice alienating behavior have let the disagreement become a personal vendetta, assigning a winner and a loser. They can combat this attitude by improving the following:

Communication between homes by consulting one another prior to making plans when the child is scheduled to be with the other parent.

Accepting the child's dual citizenship. They live with both parents, and their allegiance is to both parents.

Respecting the child's time with their other parent. Neither home is more important than the other, and the child needs both parents for proper emotional and psychological adjustment.

Becoming **E**mpathetic by putting themselves in the child's shoes and never making their child choose between the two people they love the most.

Using Your Children as Messengers

"Tell your mom (dad) to _____ *(fill in the blank)."*

Let's say a child lives predominantly with one parent, and it's the child's scheduled weekend to see their other parent. That parent has been anticipating the visit all week. The custodial parent runs late and asks the child to call their other parent and tell them they will be late. The parent waiting for the child answers the phone, hears that the child will be late, and gets angry, telling the child how irresponsible it is to be late, ending the conversation with an angry, "And you just tell your mother (or father) that I said so!"

How do you think this child might feel as a result of this exchange? Most likely, he'll feel like he's in trouble because his angry parent yelled at him. After all, the child was the bearer of the bad news that made that parent angry. The child may also become afraid to talk to either parent, learning to shrink from confrontation or hide things from others to prevent an angry interaction. Parents who are angry with each other in front of the children also force a child to consider their allegiance to either parent. "Whose side am I on?" or "Should I tell them what Mom/Dad told me to say?" The child may feel as if they must lie to protect the underdog parent, and if the message is not conveyed correctly, blame themself for the parents' arguing. So, what does the child do? They say, "I don't want to go," not because he doesn't want to see his parent, but because he can't take the arguing or being in the middle. He feels that staying right where he is is the answer to his problem.

Here's where this then takes on a life of its own—and it can be either parent that then takes it in this direction.

When the custodial parent hears that the child does not want to go, he or she immediately goes into protective parent mode: "My baby prefers it here. He likes me best. I'm not going to make him do something he doesn't want to do." So that parent reinforces that the child does not have to go to the other parent's home. Now, it's a custody battle. The arguments ensue, and both parents blame the other.

Neither parent has any idea that they have both contributed to this problem. Nor do they realize the stress from this kind of scenario bleeds into every aspect of their child's life. Preschoolers may act out, become clingy, and/or regress in their development skills. Elementary school children may become depressed, may be unable to concentrate, or may mimic ADHD symptoms. The teen years are already a vulnerable time for high-risk behaviors, and family disruption can contribute to depression, withdrawal from friends and family, and even drug or alcohol abuse. And it all started with, "Tell your mother (or father) . . ."

Course Correction

Do not ask your child to pass on information. It asks them to weigh their allegiance to their parents and choose which one is right and which one is wrong. No child, no matter their age, wants to choose one parent over the other. It's like asking them, "Where would you rather go? Disneyland with Dad or Hawaii with Mom?" and then making them tell their parent their choice. Don't make them do it.

Resentment After a Breakup

I was married for 6 years and had three children. My husband passed in an accident. I was devastated and so were the children, but after 5 years, I met someone who seemed to love my children as much as I did. We married and we were over-the-top happy. We referred to ourselves as a bonus family and adopted all the principles as our way of life. My youngest daughter, in particular, accepted my husband as her dad. He was close to all the kids, but they shared a special bond.

Four years ago, he abruptly ended the marriage, but he has stayed connected with the children, especially my youngest daughter, the mother of my only grandchildren. She has made it clear that she would like my ex-husband to be their "grandpa." He has been living with someone else for the last 3 years and has avoided any contact with me. I trusted him with my children, and he hurt us all by divorcing me. I think I'm over all the hurt until I see her name on the tags for presents for my grandkids, and I resent any interaction my ex or she has with my children.

– SAMANTHA, MOTHER OF THREE AND
FORMER PARTNER TO JESS

While in a relationship, parents promote an exclusive connection between bonus parent and child. They rejoice when a bond has been built between the two. Then there is a breakup, and the parent may disregard the established bond. Suddenly, that connection is not respected. "These are my children. I shared them with you once, but you chose to leave . . . so leave me and my children alone."

But that attitude is from the parent's perspective, not the child's. How the child wants to navigate that relationship after a breakup really depends on the relationship *they* have built with their bonus parent. In the above scenario, the child is doing exactly what the parent hoped she would do when she remarried and formed a bonus family. She built a loving relationship with her bonus parent. Sounds like Bonus Dad did the same thing and is merely following his bonus daughter's lead.

To complicate the issue, Mom has not found someone new, so her ex (Bonus Dad) is the most logical candidate to fulfill grandpa duties—and he is even approaching *that* properly. He's looking for alternative times and places to spend time with his bonus daughter and family. He offers presents when appropriate and attends family get-togethers only when formally invited. Everyone is happy except Mom. And if someone took her aside and said, "Do you want all this to stop?" she would probably say, "Of course not." But it doesn't stop how badly she feels.

Unfortunately, this situation is quite common. More couples break up than stay together, and as a result, parents must be aware of the pressure each relationship they enter puts on their children. In the past, attitudes like, "A stepparent has no obligation to their stepchild after a divorce," were expected, even reinforced once the adults went their separate ways. However, now, we expect our partners to care for our children, be involved, and think of them as their own—when they do, and we break up, no one knows exactly how to navigate it.

Course Correction

As difficult as it might be for a parent to accept that their child wishes to continue their relationship with their bonus parent after a breakup, that child is the one to decide to maintain or terminate that relationship. The parent is obliged to follow their lead unless the child is too young to be aware that interaction might be detrimental to their safety or well-being. In those cases, a parent should consider the guidance of a professional to help the child with the transition.

When Parents and Bonus Parents Don't Do Their Homework

My husband was married and had a son, age 6. His wife died 5 years ago, and we were married a year ago. I have a daughter, Ahana, age 9. My daughter's father lives in another country and has not seen her since the day she was born. My husband and his family dote on his son and completely forget about my daughter. Just last week, we spent the night at my husband's parents' home. The next morning, my mother-in-law cooked a special hot breakfast for my husband's son, but my daughter was told to have cold cereal. However, that isn't our biggest problem—the kids have a vacation coming up and I would like to take my daughter to Disneyland. She has never been to Disneyland, but my husband's son has been there quite a few times with his grandmother.

My husband's son is scheduled to spend the time at his grandmother's house when we are scheduled to go to Disneyland, but my husband refuses to go without his son. Does that mean we can't take my daughter? We have never taken her anywhere special. If we can't go to Disneyland over this vacation, I'm thinking I'll just take her myself.

I'm just so angry and resentful and I'm starting to lash out at my husband and his son. I'm so frustrated I'm ready to leave. I feel like nothing I do is good enough. Over the past 5 years this dead woman has become a saint in everyone's eyes and my daughter and I are just nothing. I don't want to get a divorce, but I feel so alone, and I ache inside each time I see how my daughter is overlooked.

— AAYUSHI, MOTHER TO AHANA, AGE 9

I wish I could say that the feelings expressed by this mother are unique, but they are not, particularly when parents do not do their homework prior to combining their lives. This is the reason I designed the Before Bonus Exercise featured in Chapter 3. The exercise sets the stage for success, removes victimhood, and asks for honest participation from each member of the family, beginning with the parents, who are the role models and set the example for the other family members to follow.

Course Correction

Rather than incorporate the Before Bonus Exercise here in its entirety, I will summarize what needs to be done if this family wants to reach bonus status, using the Before Bonus Exercise for reference. I must also note there are some serious special circumstances with this case, namely the death of a spouse and mother on the father's side and abandonment of a mother and child on the mother's side. These are significant concerns with deep psychological implications that must be taken seriously when combining families. This family may not be able to address all these things properly by themselves and may need professional help from a therapist. But, to begin, some of the things they can do by themselves are:

Check Your Mindset: The writer continually refers to "his son" and "my daughter" all the way through the question. Although these labels are accurate, referring to the children in that manner is not indicative of an inclusive mindset. Moreover, it demonstrates a desire to retain separate ownership of each child. Bonus endorses an inclusive mindset, not a separate one. The key is for each family member to be seen as an individual. Of course, the boy is the father's son, and the daughter is the mother's daughter, but they *also* must be accepted as an integral part of the family unit. That is not happening here. There are two separate factions to this family.

We all know that automatically feeling close to our partner's children is rare. It takes time and a sincere effort. The family members must be given time to get to know each other, but most of all, parents must examine and ultimately take responsibility for what they will do to cultivate a loving relationship with their partner's children. The parents referring to the children as "my bonus son" or "my bonus daughter," is a step in the right direction. It respects their origin but does not split the family into factions based on the children's biology while offering the children parental acceptance and security.

Abbreviated Version of the Before Bonus Exercise

Having a mutual goal gives a couple something to work toward—together. Since they are the leaders of the family, having a mutual goal lays the groundwork for success. Even if this couple did not do the Before Bonus Exercise in its entirety prior to making the commitment to each other, there is one part of the exercise that will help them be successful—decide upon their mutual goal for the future. They must take the time to come to an agreement on the questions listed below in an abbreviated version of the Before Bonus Exercise:

- *How do we envision our life together as a couple? As a family?*
- *What is our role with each other's children?*
- *How will we integrate our extended families?*

Each question holds its own weight and sets the stage for their future life together. If these parents are not on the same page, from how they will discipline the children to the boundaries they put in place when interacting with extended family, they will not jell as a bonus family.

How will they make this life unique from what we have both experienced in the past?

Really important question! Aside from the problems of adjustment we have already discussed, it's quite common for new partners who marry someone after the death of their spouse to feel as if they are competing with a ghost. All their flaws are forgotten, and they glow in the memory of their loved ones. The new partner feels as if they will never reach equal status.

In truth, both women, one in memory and one in reality, must be accepted as two separate and unique individuals, never compared. To explore and reconcile one's feelings about this subject is important to the couple's commitment to their future. Individual therapy may be helpful. It is not something that can be swept under the rug.

Plus, the writer's bonus son may still be dealing with the issues concerning the death of his mother and be afraid to accept the writer as a mother figure for fear he is betraying his mother's memory. This may also be a concern of the child's father, even though he has chosen to marry after the death of his first wife. We haven't even begun to discuss what the father must do to help his bonus daughter feel accepted and secure. He is the first father figure she has had—that is a huge responsibility he must take seriously.

At face value, this family found each other after each of the
family members faced incredible loss. Many would feel relieved
that they can help each other through life—but there are a lot
of moving parts, combining families and homes, and moving in
together before addressing their previous emotional turmoil has
slowed down this bonus family's progress. When there is no plan
for how to come together, bonus families break into factions and
separate down familiar lines.

Addressing Vacation Plans

It is important to note that bonus families are not like first-time
families, therefore the family created by the union will not model
a first-time family. After a breakup, it is understood that parents
will take separate vacations with their children, and parents often
feel guilty when their children cannot attend fun events because
they are scheduled to be with the other parent. In response, they
may not schedule special events until all can attend. However, in
this case, the son often goes on trips with his grandparents without his bonus sister accompanying him. Mom can't understand
why the same policy does not apply to her daughter.

This father and mother simply do not have the same idea
of what constitutes "family." Both have accepted that the family
has split into factions as a way of life. Once they realize that
their bonus family starts with them, the bonus couple and their
combined children, then branches out to extended family, their
concept of "family" will be the same and they won't make separate
arrangements for the children that interfere with family priorities.

This concept will not prevent a child from spending alone
time with a parent or grandparent. Grandparents are extremely
important to extended bonus family life, particularly in this case
when Grandma may have stepped in when the child's mother
passed. It just sets a precedent, reiterating an inclusive, rather than
exclusive point of view.

Jealousy

We've touched on jealous behavior in previous chapters, but here is a real-life issue that many bonus families face . . .

> *I know my co-parent's new partner cannot stand me. I can tell. I spend the holidays at my former in-laws' home, with them, my co-parent, our son, and my bonus kids. On Easter, I walked into the kitchen with my potluck offering and my co-parent's new partner took one look at me and walked out the back door. The holidays used to be so fun; even though we were divorced, we still kept it cordial for the kids. Now, everything is a problem.*

It is certainly possible that your co-parent's partner feels some sort of animosity toward you and, believe it or not, your co-parent could be behind their attitude. You have no idea how your co-parent presented you to their new partner. You could have been presented as the terrible person from hell or the one that got away. Both explanations could make a new partner feel uneasy. However, feeling uneasy is not an adequate reason for an adult to act out and display rude, disrespectful behavior. They must have more control than that to set a cooperative example, particularly while children are watching.

Course Correction

This is yet another reason why it is so important for co-parents and their new partners to take the Before Bonus Exercise seriously. The exercise will allow this bonus couple to discuss their expectations and establish reasonable boundaries for each relationship created by their union. The exercise specifically asks the new partner what they will do to cultivate a positive relationship with their partner's co-parent and allows the co-parent to weigh in with boundaries that will aid that interaction.

Counterproductive Phone Calls

I was divorced from my children's mother 5 years ago. We had a daughter, Lucy, who is now 7. We share Lucy's time equally, but it has always been difficult for her mother, Sara, to let go. Because of that, Sara likes to call Lucy a lot when she is with me. I remarried last year and have two bonus kids, Michael, age 5, and Annie, age 8. Annie shares a bedroom with Lucy. My wife, Lindsay, is pregnant with our first child. Lindsay and Lucy are quite close, and Lucy is looking forward to the baby joining us in a few months.

The phone calls have always been disruptive, but for the last year, Sara calls Lucy at bedtime. Sara tells Lucy how much she misses her and how difficult it is to sleep when she is not with her. (They sleep in the same bed.) Lucy is sometimes difficult to console while she tells me she feels bad that her mommy is lonely without her. This makes it difficult for Annie to sleep because they share a room.

I have asked Sara if it is really necessary to call every day and she becomes incensed, telling me that I am trying to take her daughter away from me and that it is cruel to prevent her from talking to her. I don't prevent her from talking to her! It's the timing and what she says! These phone calls are making life unbearable.

Phone calls can be a great way to stay in touch when you cannot be with your child, but they can be counterproductive when not handled correctly. It is not helpful when a parent calls and sorrowfully proclaims how much the child is missed or the parent attempts to entice the child back to their home with purchases they know the child would like. "We just bought a puppy," or "We just bought a Ping-Pong table," and all will be available "when you get home."

This masterful manipulation of the child's feelings is done to ensure the child will prefer one home over the other. Ironically, the phone calls before bed began about the time the father remarried, and because Lucy likes Lindsay, Mom's insecurity may have increased, so the phone calls were stepped up. Basically, the phone calls are saying, "I know you like Lindsay, but don't forget about me, your mommy who loves you."

To get on the other side of this, parents must *honestly* consider their motivation and how they want their children to feel after speaking to them. Do you want your child to feel comforted? Happy? Connected? Or anxious and guilt-ridden? If the answer is comforted, some phone call boundaries can easily be put into place. If the honest answer is guilt-ridden to control the child's preferences, some serious soul-searching must be done. That is the beginning of parental alienation.

Phone Call Boundaries

Phone calls are often assigned as part of a parenting plan with the intention of parent and child staying connected. When calling your child at the other home, the timing of the phone calls is crucial. Calling right before bed, when handled properly, can calmly whisk the child off to sleep, but if handled improperly, as it appears to be in this example, it can make a child anxious, interfere with their sleep patterns, and distance them from their other parent. Not to mention the impact this has on Annie, Dad's bonus daughter, who shares a room with Lucy. (Remember the Ripple Effect.)

Some suggestions for other times to connect when the child is not with you are in the morning upon waking. The call should not take too long so as to interfere with the morning routine, but be long enough to say, "Good morning, Sunshine! Have a wonderful day." Another suggestion, a call after school could be to check in how school went that day or to help with homework via Zoom. An after-dinner call, again, might be a wind-down call at the end of the day to discuss the best part of their day. At no time should there be mention of the sadness and pain of not being together and an inability to sleep without the child in their bed.

Ultimately, parents who share their children's time must also consider whether a daily phone call is even necessary. If it is disruptive or causing the child anxiety, it is not doing what it is designed to do. Brainstorm with your co-parent how changes can be made—with your child's best interest as the deciding factor.

Course Correction

In reality, it is not Dad's sole responsibility to decide how to approach the soccer game dilemma. The Bonus Couple must take a cooperative approach, decide what they want for their family and set that approach in motion.

Dad also has some personal work to do. To address his guilt, he must accept that his relationship with his son's mother is over, but he can still be an active loving father and a supportive co-parent. He cannot make things better by not requiring James to be an active member of the bonus family. The basis behind the bonus concept is acceptance and support for each family member's differences, but not at the expense of the whole. Demonstrating allegiance to one's bonus sibling, in this case, by watching their soccer game, is at the core of bonus family bonding.

It's Another Breakup

> *I am a senior in high school, planning to graduate in 5 months. Both of my parents have been married twice. After they divorced each other, they remarried and then divorced again. I was quite close to my stepparents and my stepsiblings, but they are no longer my stepparents or my stepsiblings. So, who are they to me? Is there such a thing as ex-stepparents? Or ex-stepsiblings? And, if my parents remarry again, will I then have multiple stepparents and stepsiblings? Are we even still related?*
>
> – MALLORY, AGE 17

Legally, a divorce severs all ties, but we all know emotionally, that's just not true. The terminology described is quite convoluted, but the truth is, legally, a stepparent is only a stepparent while they are married to the child's parent. This is yet another reason why "bonus" is a good word choice. Unlike the word "step," "bonus" is a term of endearment that is not dependent on current marital status.

Breakups Are Not Easier for Adult Children

I have heard from many adult children that dealing with their parents' divorce did not get easier as they got older. Over time, issues popped up that they thought they had dealt with years ago. "Nothing changed, really," one adult child told me. "The situations just changed." Her parents, after many years, could not be in the same room. She explained that it was a different kind of mourning—intellectually, she understood that the divorce was years ago, but in her heart, whenever there was a milestone for her own children, she longed for a holiday where all could be together.

> My grandparents' home was the center of our world. They lived around the corner from my dad. They were the consistent ones, and I always knew they would be together and available. It was comforting to walk into their house and see it decorated for Christmas and how excited they got when I came to hang out. I want that for my children, but my parents can't even be in the same room. You'd think a decade of anger and resentment would be enough. Evidently, it's not. My mom spends Christmas Eve with us every year and my dad spends Christmas Day. I'm used to it now, but what really bothers me is that they both can't be at my children's birthdays. They alternate them, like a parenting plan for children. One year the children are with Dad for their birthday, the next year Mom. It's not what I'd prefer. Not even a little bit."
> – SHERRY L., MOTHER TO CAMERON, AGE 9, AND ELISA, AGE 8

Backsliding

"I just feel like we were doing so well. I don't know what happened, but now we can barely talk to each other, and I feel like we are all going backwards."

When this was said to me during a co-parenting session, I asked, "Who is 'all'"?

Tomi, one-half of the co-parenting couple in for a review, asked, "What do you mean, 'Who is all?'"

"Well," I said, "You said, 'We all are going backwards.' Who is 'all?'"

"Oh," she said. "All of us. My husband, his ex, her husband, me, all the kids—everyone. It's crazy."

"Really?" I said. "You just named every member of your bonus family, complete with co-parents and new partners. You aren't backsliding as much as you think."

"What do you mean?" Tomi asked.

"Bonus is a state of mind—inclusive, loving, and accepting. You verified that you are there when you automatically referred to 'all of us.' You didn't think about it for a second, even though you were talking about going backwards. You inherently knew you are all in it together."

"Huh," Tomi smirked, and her co-parent, Sam, snickered. "Maybe we aren't that far off after all."

"Maybe you aren't," I said.

Our actions as our children grow set the stage for their own relationships when they get older. They watch every move we make, and if we make mistakes, they watch how we maneuver a course correction. Backsliding is part of the process. It's how you come out on the other side that sets the example and offers the lesson. That's what is important to pass on to our children and every member of our bonus family—that a correction was made, and things have improved as a result. Don't be concerned about your mistakes. Be concerned about not correcting them.

CONCLUSION

Bonus . . . It's a Step in the Right Direction

As you read this book, I hope you realized that co-parenting and bonus family life has a beginning, but there is no end point in sight. As a matter of fact, life events are likely to intensify the need to work together, to co-parent, and to continue to build your bonus family.

No one knows what lies ahead. Of course, we can all hope that our bonus family will stay intact, but they say the odds are against us. Statistics can be reframed, however. If 50% of all marriages fail, that means 50% don't. They say second or subsequent marriages have an even lesser chance of success. Any time someone says something can't be done, that has always given me an added incentive to prove that it can.

Truth be told, I don't look at the end of a coupling as being a failure. Relationships can end, but families don't have to. They can continue to flourish after a breakup. Parents can continue to support each other and their children. That is not dependent on a marriage license or the fact that parents no longer live together. It's based on the mutual love of their children.

To close, I'd like to share one of my favorite success stories. I worked with this family a year ago and was impressed by their dedication and determination to change in order to offer their children a happy life after their breakup. There were definite growing pains on the way to reaching bonus status, as this dad explains in the following story of encouragement.

When my children's mother and I decided to part ways, one of the things I was really conscious of was who I introduced them to once we all settled in after the divorce. Their mother felt the same way so I never worried that the kids would be exposed to something that was too much for them. I have to admit, however, when their mother started to see Don, I was surprised how uncomfortable I felt with the idea of her dating and someone else being around the kids. I worried that he might hurt them. Actually, I worried that anyone might hurt them and that made me skeptical of any attention he offered. Sherry, the kids' mother, knows me and knew that I would be hard-pressed to accept anyone in their lives. It really bugged me when he started to show up to my eldest's soccer game.

Each time my son missed a goal or made a sketchy play, Don would yell, "Felix!" and it was really pissing me off. I guess I was being pretty obnoxious, and Sherry, their mom, had had enough. I could see her out of the corner of my eye get up from where she was sitting in the stands and as she walked past me, she whispered, "Can I talk to you for a second?" I was so mad at that point, I'm sure I said something I shouldn't have, but I followed her around the back of the stands. She stood there looking at the ground.

"What?" I growled. "What do you want?"

"It's a code word."

"What's a code word?"

"Felix. It's a code word to remind him to focus."

My son, Jack, was diagnosed with ADHD a year ago and was really struggling with staying focused. But he hated it when someone called it to his attention. It really embarrassed him. Evidently, Don and Jack had worked out a code word to remind him to keep his attention on the game. They thought any word would be better than "Focus!" Felix was their dog.

I guess Don was standing behind me just far enough away to overhear the conversation. He walked up to me, put his hand out, and just waited for me to take it. He stood there for a while like that, and then he said, "Felix!"

I got what he meant. Focus. Focus on what is important. I shook his hand and things slowly started to improve. Not immediately, but we eventually learned to work together. Now we focus on what is important: Jack. And if you ask me, I'd call us a bonus family. It took time, that is for sure, but I changed my attitude for my son. I don't look at Don as a replacement for me anymore; I look at him as an asset. Someone else who loves my kid and puts him first.

Bonus . . . it's a step in the right direction.

Notes

Chapter 1

1. Du Rocher Schudlich, T. D., White, C. R., Fleischhauer, E. A., & Fitzgerald, K. A. (2011). Observed infant reactions during live interparental conflict. *Journal of Marriage and Family, 73*(1), 221–35. https://doi.org/10.1111/j.1741-3737.2010.00800.x.

2. Lorber, M. F., Del Vecchio, T., & Slep, A. M. S. (2018). The development of individual physically aggressive behaviors from infancy to toddlerhood. *Developmental Psychology, 54*(4), 601–12. https://doi.org/10.1037/dev0000450.

3. Paul, M. (2012, September 19). Your memory is like the Telephone Game. https://news.northwestern.edu/stories/2012/09/your-memory-is-like-the-telephone-game/.

Chapter 5

1. Tyson, P., Davies, S., Scorey, S., & Greville, W. J. (2022). Fear of clowns: An investigation into the prevalence of coulrophobia in an international sample. *International Journal of Mental Health, 52*(1), 84–99. https://doi.org/10.1080/00207411.2022.2046925.

Chapter 9

1. *Albert Einstein—The Decision Lab.* (n.d.). The Decision Lab. https://thedecisionlab.com/thinkers/philosophy/albert-einstein.

2. Who really said these 5 famous phrases? (n.d.). *Google Arts & Culture.* https://artsandculture.google.com/story/who-really-said-these-5-famous-phrases/JAXh1xsiCEHOqw?hl=en.

3. *Albert Einstein Quote.* (n.d.). Lib Quotes. https://libquotes.com/albert-einstein/quote/lbr4l4l.

4. The percentage of the worldwide population speculated to truly have a narcissistic personality disorder diagnosis is about 1% to 2% of the US population.

See: Weinberg, I., & Ronningstam, E. (2022). Narcissistic personality disorder: Progress in understanding and treatment. *Focus, 20*(4), 368–77. https://doi.org/10.1176/appi.focus.20220052.

Index

abandonment: feelings of in/ for children, 100, 182; feelings of in/for former partners, 100, 313; of traditions, 245–47, 258, 259

abuse: domestic violence and, 290–92; intergenerational trauma and, 290–92; trauma and, 46, 290–92

acceptance: bonus family and, 150–54; in bonus team, 125, 128–29; in CARE method, 21–22, 37, 44–45, 86, 150–54; for children, 44–45, 86; in counterpartner relationship, 128–29; after death of loved one, 198–99; disagreement and, 22; unaccepting bonus relatives and, 203–4. *See also* CARE method

accusations: anger and, 285; assumptions and, 286–90; communication and, 30–32

active listening, 16–17

adoption, 176–77

adult children. *See* children, adult children

affairs and infidelity: anger about, 136–37, 230–31; bonus team and, 133–39; child custody and, 136; children and communication about, 134–36; child's anger about, 135–36; counterpartner relationship and, 133–39; emotions and, 134–38; forgiveness and, 136–38; narratives and, 137–39

age: chores and, 101–2; coming-of-age celebrations and, 267, 271–73; communication and, 134, 217–18, 286–88; sleeping arrangements and, 96–98

alcohol, 145, 281; dating and, 56–57; intergenerational trauma and, 291

alienation: outsider feelings of bonus parent, 157–58; parental, 301–4

bedroom
  sharing: communication
  and, 98–100; sleeping
  arrangements and, 94–100
Before Bonus Exercise,
  177–78; abbreviated version
  of, 311–12; bonus family
  and relationship list and,
  79–80; Bonus Family
  Workshop and, 78–84; for
  extended bonus family,
  185–90; importance of
  taking seriously, 313–14; for
  moving in together, 78–84;
  special needs and, 295
behavior: past and future,
  9–10; preconceived notions
  and, 10–11, 82, 126;
  thoughts become actions
  and, 11–12. *See also* avoidant
  behavior
betrayal, 152–53
biological parent: bonus parent
  vs., 123–26, 156–57; death
  of, 49, 176–77, 203–4,
  218–20, 227–29, 278–80,
  307, 313, 315. *See also*
  specific topics
biology and sleeping
  arrangements, 96–98
bipolar disorder, 296
birthdays: CARE method
  and, 277–78; deciding host
  for birthday party, 276;

deciding place for birthday
  party, 277; forgotten,
  277–78; guest list for, 276;
  parent's insensitivity about,
  277–78; planning birthday
  parties, 275–78
blame: anger and, 162–64;
  conflict resolution without,
  110–11; fault and, 12–13,
  36, 139, 164, 287; guilt and,
  36; victim mentality and,
  12–13
breakup, 13, 35–36, 38–39,
  41–42, 44–49, 54–55, 60,
  62, 63–73
bonus attitude, 119–20
bonus family: acceptance and,
  150–54; adoption and,
  176–77; autonomy, 154–56;
  babies and, 171–74; bonus
  dating and integrating
  someone new, 41–73;
  Before Bonus Exercise
  and planning for, 78–84,
  177–78, 185–90, 295,
  311–14; bonus family and
  relationship list, 79–80;
  bouquet, 239; CARE
  method and preparing
  for, 85–87; concept of,
  3–4; confusion about
  bonus family breakups
  and ex-relationships,
  316–18; coordinating efforts

breaking up: in another breakup, 316–18; co-parenting and life after, 39; divorce and, 3–5, 320–21; guilt about, 42; resentment after, 321
business approach to problem solving, 24–27, 71

CARE method: acceptance in, 21–22, 37, 44–45, 86, 150–54; birthdays and, 277–78; bonus family preparation and, 85–87; for bonus team, 125–32; for children, 37, 43–47, 85–87; communication in, 15–21, 37, 43–44, 86; co-parenting and, 14–24; for counterpartner relationship, 127–33; dating and, 43–47, 66–67; empathy in, 23–24, 37, 45–47, 86–87; fear and, 154; for house rules, 92; individuality and, 154; for kids in the "middle," 304–5; moving in together and, 85–87; overview of, 14–15; for parental alienation, 300–301; for privacy, 98; problem solving and, 24, 27–30, 127–32, 183–84; respect in, 22, 37, 44–45, 86; for sleeping arrangements,

98–100; special needs and, 295
Catechism, 269
celebrations. *See* holidays; holidays and celebrations; weddings
cell phones, 20, 250–51; and children, 20, 250–51
change: babies and, 173–74; children and, 5, 54–56, 85–86, 173–74; mental health and, 294–95
"checks and balances," 83–84
child custody, 118; affairs and, 136; laws, 4; schedules, 180–84
child custody mediation: active listening in, 16–17; domestic violence and, 291
child-free weddings, 229
children: acceptance for, 44–45, 86; adoption and, 176–77; adult children, 218–20, 240; affairs and anger of, 135–36; affairs and communication with, 134–36; age and communication with, 134, 217–18, 286–88; arguing in front of, 288–90; birthday parties and celebrations, 275–78; bonus family preparation for, 84–87; bonus parent, love, and, 123–24, 162–66;

for bonus parent/bonus
child rapport, 163–64;
business approach to,
24–27, 71; CARE method
and, 24, 27–30, 127–32,
183–84; for child custody
schedules, 180–84; conflict
resolution and, 109–14;
for co-parents, 24–39; for
counterproductive phone
calls, 316; dating and,
63–66; disagreement and,
13–14, 24–25, 109–14;
Einstein on, 285; for
intergenerational trauma,
292; for jealousy, 317;
mistakes and, 285–86;
negotiation and, 26–27, 66;
with new partners, 81; for
parental alienation, 301–4;
for placing kids in the
"middle," 306–8; quotes on,
285; real-life example of
using all tools for, 180–84;
for resentment, 310–12; for
special needs, 294–95; with
unconventional solutions,
160; for using kids as
"messenger," 309–10; victim
mentality and, 12–13
PTSD. *See* post-traumatic
stress disorder
puberty, 164–66; bonus parents
and, 166–67

quality time: bonus parent/
bonus child, 164–66; one-
on-one time for partners,
159–60; one-on-one time
with children, 159, 174
quinceañera, 272–73

rapport, 19; building bonus
parent/bonus child rapport,
161–66
receptions, wedding, 241–44
reconciliation hopes, 38–39, 68
red flags: bonus parent/bonus
child rapport and, 161–62;
dating, 51–58; new partner,
52–53, 57–58
relationships: bonus family
and relationship list, 79–80;
building, with your partner's
co-parent or co-parent's
partner, 127–33; building
bonus parent/bonus
child rapport, 161–66;
counterpartner, 118–19,
127–39, 145–46; cultivating
individual, 188–90;
expectations and, 185–90;
ex-relationships, 7–14,
37–39, 146–47, 190–93,
310–11, 319–21; fostering
positive relationship
with new partners,
81–84; friendships and,
201–2; maintaining loving

relationship with bonus child, 164–66; moving in together and, 79; multiple partner dilemma and, 197; perspective and, 192–93; triad, 119

religion: Christian and Catholic celebrations and, 246, 255–56, 259–62, 267–73; disagreement about, 265–66; divorce and, 272–73; family traditions and, 246–47, 265–66; godparents and, 204–5, 269; Hindus and, 237–38; Jewish celebrations and, 246–47, 259, 271–72; Muslims and, 262; religious training and celebrations, 265–73; weddings and, 223–24, 237–38

re-marriage: anger about, 119–21; boundaries and, 132–33; communication about, 210, 216–22; former in-laws and, 231–32; inviting co-parent to wedding, 229–31; inviting former relatives to wedding, 231–32; multiple partner dilemma and, 197; prenuptial agreements and, 220–21; weddings and, 119–21, 209–44

reminiscing, 263–64

resentment, 23–24; after breaking up, 310–12; comparisons and, 156–57; grudges and, 13, 109, 230–31, 276–79; problem solving for, 308; problem with, 310; retaliation and, 109

resilience, 5

respect: in bonus team, 125–26, 129–31; in CARE method, 22, 37, 44–45, 86; for children, 44–45, 84–86; in counterpartner relationship, 129–31; dating and, 62–63, 71–72; how to cultivate, 129–30. *See also* CARE method

retaliation, 109

ripple effect, 290–92

rules. *See* house rules

safety: intimacies and, 168, 171; sleeping arrangements and, 95–97

salt ritual, 237–38

same sex marriage, 212, 235

Santa Claus, 261–62

scary movies, 151

schedule coordination: child custody, 180–84; during holidays, 248–49, 257–59, 264–65; for phone calls, 314–16; planning and,

About the Author

Jann Blackstone, PsyD, coined the term "bonus" in lieu of "step" over 30 years ago in an effort to reframe the negative associations with being a stepmother. Until that time most subscribed to the wicked step associations, and parents who were attempting to combine families were clamoring for a new positive blended family identity. Dr. Blackstone has been spreading the word ever since, offering a new and improved model of the combined family based in love, empathy, and respect for each family member's individuality and history.

Dr. Jann, as she is often called, has appeared on television shows like the *Today Show* and the *Oprah Winfrey Show*, and has written numerous books chronicling her life experience as a co-parent, including *Ex-Etiquette for Parents, Ex-Etiquette for Holidays and Special Occasions*, and *Co-Parenting Through Separation and Divorce* (coauthored with Dr. David Hill). Currently in private practice as a child custody mediator and co-parenting counselor, Dr. Blackstone also continues as the founder and director of Bonus Families, the nonprofit organization she founded that is dedicated to supporting co-parents and their efforts to combined families. She also writes a weekly column, *Ex-etiquette: Good Behavior After Divorce or Separation*, syndicated by Tribune Content since 2004. Today, it runs in hundreds of newspapers and websites all over the world. Dr. Blackstone invites you to write her with your questions and concerns via the Bonus Families website at jann@bonusfamilies.com.